JS 7385 .T63 A73 1995
Neighborhood and nation in
Hastings, Sally A

210363

DATE DUE

MAR 1 9 1999	

Pitt Series in
POLICY AND INSTITUTIONAL STUDIES

Neighborhood and Nation in Tokyo, 1905–1937

Sally Ann Hastings

University of Pittsburgh Press
Pittsburgh and London

Published by the University of Pittsburgh Press, Pittsburgh, Pa.,
15260
Copyright © 1995, University of Pittsburgh Press
All rights reserved
Manufactured in the United States of America
Printed on acid-free paper

Designed by Jane Tenenbaum

Library of Congress Cataloging-in-Publication Data
Hastings, Sally A.
    Neighborhood and nation in Tokyo, 1905–1937 / Sally Ann Hastings.
        p.   cm. — (Pitt series in policy and institutional studies)
    Includes bibliographical references (p.   ) and index.
    ISBN 0-8229-3884-7 (cloth : acid-free paper)
    1. Tokyo (Japan)—Politics and government.   2. Tokyo (Japan)—
Social policy.   3. Political participation—Japan—Tokyo—
History—20th century.   4. Working class—Japan—Tokyo—Political
activity—History—20th century.   5. Neighborhood—Japan—Tokyo
—History—20th century.   I. Title.   II. Series.
JS7385.T63A73   1995
320.952'135'09041—dc20   95-14319
                                                                            CIP

A CIP catalogue record for this book is available from the
British Library.
Eurospan, London

To my parents,
Florence Mary Ames Hastings
and
Dana Bowers Hastings

Contents

Acknowledgments

In writing this book, I have incurred a great many debts to institutions and individuals. The University of Chicago supported two years of dissertation research in Japan, where I was affiliated with Waseda University. Northeastern Illinois University, where I was a member of the faculty from 1979 to 1990, provided support for the summer of 1982 and an eight-month, half-pay sabbatical in 1988–1989. The dissertation would never have become a book were it not for a postdoctoral fellowship from the Japan Institute of Harvard University in 1983–1984, when Albert Craig was acting director. I am deeply indebted to him and to Harvard for that year of research and reflection on the process of writing. I received a summer fellowship from the Purdue Research Foundation in 1991.

Tetsuo Najita was in every sense my major professor at the University of Chicago, and he has provided encouragement and support at several crucial junctures since I finished the dissertation under his direction. The other members of the committee, Harry Harootunian and Bernard Silberman, offered ready encouragement and perceptive insights. Harriet Hutchison kept copies of every draft of the dissertation, and Linda Darling edited it.

Among the scholars who have read and made valuable comments on various drafts of the book manuscript are Gail Bernstein, Sidney Brown, Sheldon Garon, Andrew Gordon, Gregory Kasza, Susan Pharr, Richard Smethurst, Bob Wakabayashi, Susan Weiner, and George Wilson. The publication review process provided a number of useful suggestions, and I remain indebted to several anonymous readers. I take responsibility for any problems that remain.

To sustain our work, we need to feel that we have some kind of home. Among those in Japan who opened their homes to me were Kyoto Matsuko, Kimura Kan and his wife Chieko, Iwasaki Shigeo and his wife Yoko, Take Rinko, and Chuck and Sally Bonson. Of my colleagues at Northeastern, I am particularly grateful for the friendship of Duke and Edris Frederick, Carl Hammond, Zachary Schiffman, and

Craig Smith. Several colleagues at Purdue offered advice and encouragement: Berenice Carroll, John Contreni, Nancy Gabin, Leonard Gordon, William Gorman, and Lois Magner. In a wider academic world, the Midwest Japan Seminar has for a long time been a stimulating intellectual home. A special group of friends has provided sustained support in the academic life, through many years and across considerable distances: Linda Darling, Jill Rierdan, Lois Fusek, Anne Walthall, the late Sharon Nolte, Edith Couturier, Alice Karl, and Rachel Bell.

For assistance in word processing, I am indebted to Ellen Fiedler who taught me to use her computer and to my parents, who gave me one of my own. Purdue University provided a computer and a printer in my office and Thomas Kesler transferred the book manuscript from one word processing system to another.

I am grateful to Lilya Lorrin, Acquisitions Editor for the University of Pittsburgh Press, for facilitating the review process. Pippa Letsky edited the manuscript with admirable care, and Jane Flanders ably guided it through the editorial and production process.

My husband, Reid Nolte, while engaged in meaningful and gainful employment of his own, has provided me with a home far better than any I could ever make for myself.

Neighborhood
and Nation
in Tokyo,
1905–1937

Introduction

Japanese democracy has been so stable over the past four and a half decades that political scientists almost invariably classify Japan with the advanced industrial democracies of the West. The political system has all the essential characteristics of democracy: competition for all effective positions of government, widely inclusive political participation, and a high level of civil and political liberties.[1]

The constitutional foundations of this democracy are a legacy from the American Occupation, which followed defeat in the Pacific War. We must remember, however, that Americans brought "unconditional democracy" to a nation that had a fifty-five-year history of constitutional government and twenty years of experience under universal manhood suffrage. The positive characteristics of Japan's political heritage have been obscured by a rich scholarly literature on two aspects of prewar democracy that did not "succeed": the political parties, which failed to maintain control of the cabinet, and the liberal thinkers, who were either isolated or co-opted.[2] By contrast, there has been relatively little exploration of how political activities developed among ordinary citizens in the first half of the twentieth century. Neither has there been much attention given to how urban administrators set up programs to help the poor help themselves. As a consequence, Japan's modern political history appears discontinuous. To be sure, some scholars of postwar Japan explicitly acknowledge democratic elements and tendencies in the prewar era upon which the American Occupation could build, but even they employ a vocabulary of imposition and implantation and date the history of democracy in Japan from 1947.[3] The impression of sudden transformation that this rhetoric conveys and the paucity of information on citizen activities in prewar Japan have lent credence to the notion that Japan was democratized by atomic bomb.[4]

This study of state and society in prewar Tokyo alters the conventional view of democracy in prewar Japan by shifting the focus of study from party leadership and liberalism to political participation and the establishment of welfare programs. From this new perspective we can see that in Japan it was the civil bureaucracy rather than the political parties that tutored the urban masses and included them in the polity. It was also the civilian bureaucracy that, enlarging upon work begun by private philanthropists, investigated poverty and advocated remedies for it.

Espousing the principle that the state was responsible for the well-being of all its citizens, the bureaucratic staff of the municipal government extended its functions to encompass control over employment opportunities, emergency shelter, welfare payments, the distribution of gifts to the needy, and access to subsidized medical care—all the services that the political bosses of American cities employed to secure the loyalty of the voters. Valuing participation and equitable distribution of wealth over ideological orthodoxy, the bureaucrats shared their responsibilities with a wide variety of religious and philanthropic societies as well as with the local elite.

Heretofore, the civilian bureaucracy in prewar Japan has received much less attention than have the political parties and the military. Although we know that the Home, Education, and other ministries used local organizations to convey social ideology to the provinces, we know more about what the state intended than about how these various programs actually affected the people to whom they were directed. As Carol Gluck has cautioned:

> One suspects that if a farmer had attended the meetings of the score of associations in which his membership was postulated by the Home Ministry in the years after the Russo-Japanese War, he would have had little time left to perform the social tasks assigned him by these various local and national organizations, much less to tend his fields.[5]

Moreover, as this passage on a hypothetical farmer reminds us, we have conceptualized the process of social education as one between center and periphery, between urban capital and countryside.

My examination of Tokyo shows that the government was also constantly engaged in social education in the major metropolitan area of Japan. State policies intersected at a number of points with factory employment, labor union activities, and electoral politics. Home Ministry bureaucrats, especially, fostered participation by encouraging urban citizens to organize themselves for numerous reasons and in varied ways—to promote public hygiene, to care for the poor, to improve the neighborhood, or to promote good government—on the basis of neighborhoods, gender, graduation from the same school, or age cohort. The hierarchies of neighborhood organizations, young men's associations, and district welfare committees—all of which were encouraged by the Home Ministry—provided channels through which state ideology could reach the common people.

Individuals learn, however, not so much by what they hear and read as by what they do. As Tocqueville noted about political organizations in the United States a century earlier, these organizations were in effect "large free schools, where all the members of the community go to learn the theory of association." From the time of Japan's victory over Russia in 1905 to the outbreak of war in China in 1937, the citizens of Tokyo enjoyed multiple and overlapping opportunities for political participation. In the elections held after the Diet passed universal manhood suffrage in 1925, they proved to be voters who had learned their lessons well. As advocates of suffrage had hoped, the citizens of Tokyo appreciated that their privilege was "too sacred to be subject to influence by bribes or intimidation."[6] As any American reformer would have wanted in his own city, they constituted an electorate that could not be bought and that would not be bossed.

Bureaucratic tutelage of the masses not long ago would invariably have been read as a vestige of the feudal and thus militarist past. Now, at the end of a century that has experienced the steady growth of the role of the state in political life, such bureaucratic initiative appears instead as an intriguing variant on the processes of mobilization and participation in an emergent mass society. In the past fifteen years, scholars from a number of disciplines, engaged in research over a broad geographical range, have focused on how states through their policies affect political and social processes. Studies show that, even in liberal-democratic, constitutional polities such as Britain, Sweden, and the United States, civil service administrators used their expertise to diagnose social problems and propose solutions. The state, then, was not so much absent from liberal democracies as rendered invisible by the methodological assumptions of liberal pluralism and Marxism.[7]

This study, which takes the vantage point of the urban neighborhood rather than that of the central government, promises fruitful comparisons between Japan and other industrial states of the era, especially the United States. American reformers and Japanese liberal intellectuals quested for good government in the face of similar problems: the increasing gap between rich and poor, the inadequacy of current methods of poor relief, and financial scandals involving popularly elected legislators. Whereas the federal government of the United States had no parallels to Japan's Home and Education Ministries, its large cities had governments dominated by the executive rather than the legislative branch. Many of these cities employed dedicated professionals, more loyal to their bureau than to any political party. These city managers, health commissioners, park superintendents, and other technical experts faced many of the same problems as the bureaucrats of Tokyo.[8]

On both sides of the Pacific, there was an acute awareness that institutions alone could not guarantee democracy. Lincoln Steffens, a journalist who exposed the corruption rampant in several American cities, complained that the American people had let the parties "turn our municipal democracies into autocracies and our republican nation into plutocracy." Frederic C. Howe, a lawyer, social worker, and politician, who was aware of the failings of American city government from his own experience in Cleveland, wrote in 1905 that "Liberty is not a thing of rights, constitutions, or forms; it is a matter of practice."[9] Whereas American critics lamented that the American people failed to live up to the ideals of their constitutional framework, Japanese reformers were fighting to obtain the privileges that Americans were abusing.

Nevertheless, Yoshino Sakuzō, one of the foremost proponents of universal manhood suffrage, stressed that legal changes alone would be inadequate; the quality of constitutional government depended upon the quality of the voters, their knowledge and their virtue. Advanced thinkers must assume responsibility for instructing the people. Japanese reformers and bureaucrats recognized that democracy could not develop if the people were divided by great discrepancies in wealth. Yoshino Sakuzō acknowledged that democratic governments might have to regulate the economically privileged classes, but his chief hope for democracy was that the welfare of the people should be the ultimate goal of government.[10] Nowhere was the chasm between rich and poor so apparent as in Tokyo, the city where the future bureaucrats and professors of the nation arrived as young and idealistic students, only to observe horrors such as men so afflicted by poverty that they clubbed dogs to death in order to earn a living.[11]

Japanese bureaucrats, who consciously shared American perceptions that the city was both the hope of the future and the nation's greatest social problem, availed themselves of the significant body of international wisdom that American and European scholars and reform-minded experts had accumulated on urban problems. This wisdom encompassed the education of the electorate as well as sanitation, poor relief, and parks. Japanese bureaucrats wanted an electorate more judicious than those of New York, Chicago, or Cleveland in those cities' more colorful eras. In their election purification movements, they echoed American reformers in their call for nonpartisanship as a means of defeating selfish interests. In this light, we can recast Japan's bureaucratically structured political participation as a faltering step toward mature democracy, rather than as a mere reflexive manifestation of authoritarianism.

This is not to say that Japan, or even Tokyo, actually achieved democracy in the prewar era. Even by recent definitions of democracy, which allow for various degrees of "success," the absence of responsible cabinets, the preponderance of appointed rather than elected local administrators, and the limitations of free expression made Japan in this period only a semidemocracy. In this study, however, in contrast to the long tradition that has asked "What went wrong?" I ask instead, "In this semidemocracy, what went right?"[12]

The political education of the urban electorate was one of the positive developments of prewar Japan. Broad citizen participation is widely recognized as one of the requisites for a successful democracy. Tocqueville noted with approval the profusion of associations in nineteenth-century America and concluded that a successful democracy required a citizenry experienced in civic participation in a variety of organizations.[13] Scholars readily accept that Gandhi's strategy of inclusionary participation in India provided "an important historical foundation for future democratic development." Larry Diamond, a political scientist familiar with developing countries in Asia, argues

that "The organization of the citizenry—autonomously, pluralisti-
cally, from the grassroots—both inside and outside the formal polity
is an indispensable condition for the development and maintenance
of a secure democracy."[14]

This is the first study of political organization in a large metropolitan area of prewar Japan. The major studies of the brief era of
political party cabinets have been tales of power brokering and policy
making in the central government, not of grassroots political participation.[15] The Japanese political parties never developed organized
support from commoners. Although individual politicians had personal support groups, the Japanese political parties themselves were
not organized into political machines comparable to that presided
over by the denizens of Tammany Hall in New York, which could
reach every tenement in the city.[16] Tammany Hall provided its supporters with patronage jobs, lucrative contracts, licenses for business,
and emergency funds. One might well ask whether or how, in the
absence of a political machine, the citizens of Tokyo secured such
benefits for themselves. This, however, was not the question Robert
Scalapino asked in his classic study in the 1950s.

Tetsuo Najita, Peter Duus, Gordon Berger, and Sheldon Garon
have significantly modified the picture of political parties that Scalapino presented. We now better understand the aims of the parties, their
effectiveness in linking center and periphery, and their policies. Until
recently, however, there has been little information available in English to refute Scalapino's negative assessment of the masses. Finding
the urban masses absent from the parties, he asked not where else they
might be but why they were absent. He blamed their political im-
maturity, which he assmed was the product of a premodern culture
deficient in individualism and personal responsibility.[17]

The best studies of the general organization of the citizenry in
prewar Japan have been on areas other than the major cities. In the
1970s, Richard Smethurst's work on reservists and young men's associations brought these organizations to the attention of the American academic community and showed how the military generated
support for its policies in every village of Japan. Also in the 1970s,
Gary Allinson's pioneering study of the city of Kariya traced its political life over the span of a century and related political patterns to the
economic and demographic effects of industrialization.[18]

Although Smethurst studied a hamlet and Allinson a small city, they both found a stable, hierarchical social order that was virtually impervious to penetration by either the state or political parties. The army won support from rural residents, not by creating new and separate organizations but by paralleling existing hamlet structures and thus making use of hamlet cohesiveness. The political parties of Kariya made similar use of the existing social hierarchy. Smethurst and Allinson were in agreement that the liberal rhetoric of the 1920s and the passage of universal manhood suffrage made virtually no difference in the local political atmosphere.[19] The 1930s were no worse than the 1920s precisely because both decades were a continuation of the political pattern that was established in the 1890s.

Tokyo was far different from the agricultural villages and small cities from which many of its inhabitants had come. It was, and still is, the capital city, the center of education, wealth, and culture, and the seat of power. It symbolized the powerful and privileged as opposed to the weak and the excluded. Tokyo, however, was also home to millions who, although geographically close to the architectural monuments of Japanese imperialism, resided an immense social distance from the halls of power. It is the ordinary residents of Tokyo with whom this study is concerned.

Most research on urban commoners in Japan has focused on the minority of industrial workers who joined the labor movement. Much of this literature has been what Sheldon Garon termed history "from the middle"; that is, accounts of the leaders, mergers, and splits of the unions rather than of the political activities of the rank and file.[20] Nevertheless, these works tell us much about one aspect of urban, working-class political life. Andrew Gordon's first book raised labor history to a new level by giving voice to the hopes and aspirations of urban workers in their struggles with their employers. His second book related union activities to urban mass protest and suggested that the two together constituted a dispute culture, which for a time critiqued the dominant society but then withdrew from conventional politics in despair when imperial democracy was supplanted by fascism after 1937.[21]

Whereas Gordon illuminated the political culture of urban residents who protested against the existing order, this study includes within its parameters the whole range of urban political involvement: those who engaged in strikes and disputes, those who merely watched without taking sides, and those who identified with the existing order. To his demonstration that prewar experience shaped postwar developments in electoral politics, union organizing, and patterns of disputes, I add examples of prewar precedents for local festivals, public involvement in poor relief, and citizen organization to remedy local problems.

My study of urban popular participation focuses on the urban working-class population where they lived rather than where they worked. It illuminates the political and community life of one Tokyo ward, Honjo, which employed more factory workers than any other. In my documentary on the organizational life of the city, the individual working-class residents are sometimes reduced to a blurry smudge. Even their collective voice cannot ring out with the same clarity as it does in Andrew Gordon's and Michael Lewis's studies of the urban crowd.[22] What this work does provide is a detailed portrait of the local organizational framework within which unions and socialist political parties staked out their place in imperial Japan.

"Tokyo" is an ambiguous geographical term that requires definition. Today Tokyo-to consists of twenty-three urban wards, a number of smaller cities, a county, a few villages, and some islands. At the turn of the century, much less of the area was defined as part of the capital city. Tokyo city (shi), an entity within the boundaries of Tokyo prefecture (fu), administered fifteen wards. These wards centered on the Imperial Palace (which until 1868 had been Edo Castle), and all had been part of the bustling capital of the Tokugawa shoguns. In 1932, twenty new wards, carved out of areas previously administered as counties, extended the city limits to approximately the area that, since 1947, has been organized as the twenty-three wards. The prefecture was renamed Tokyo-to in 1943, when an administrative reorganization eliminated the municipal level of government.

The ward that is the focus of this book, Honjo, was a densely settled district of small shops and factories in the easternmost section of the original fifteen wards. This ward alone, by 1917, had a population of a quarter of a million, four times that of Allinson's Kariya. It thus exemplified two of the major characteristics of cities: their dense settlement and the absence of "personal reciprocal acquaintance of the inhabitants."[23] The residents of this ward depended upon the impersonal market for work, housing, food, and medicine. Many of them were not bound by any ties of loyalty, dependency, or mutual obligation to support the existing social and political order. This was no replica of a rural village; the wards of Tokyo constituted a new political space that permitted new political behavior.[24]

Honjo exhibited all the characteristics that caused worried bureaucrats to formulate social policies: overcrowding, a concentration of factory workers, rapid population growth, industrial pollution, large numbers of transients, concentrations of poor housing, too much sewage, not enough clean water, beggars, stray children, and labor unrest. A low-lying ward, subject to flooding, it was not a prestigious address. Its residents could claim no special ties to the ruling bureaucracy. It is thus an appropriate area in which to study the effectiveness or ineffectiveness of social policy and the response of ordinary citizens to the state and its competitors.

The encounters between citizen and state that occurred in Honjo were replicated in other parts of the city. With its many factories and workers, Honjo was as close to a working-class neighborhood as one could find. Andrew Gordon, in his investigation of the working-class movement, included Honjo in the industrial area he called Nankatsu, which extended east from Honjo to the Arakawa Canal.[25] Most of this area was not incorporated into the city until 1932. For Gordon's purposes, the integrity of this area as an industrial district far outweighed the problems of lumping wards with villages and distinguishing the administrative practices of the city from those of the county. Because I am interested in civilian bureaucrats and their interaction with the citizens within their administrative jurisdiction, however, I have strictly conformed to administrative boundaries. Where it has been useful to draw data from other places besides Honjo, I have used the rest of the original fifteen wards, for which comparable data are available over a number of decades.

Its sheer size and complexity made Tokyo a new political space. In the city, there was no organic social order of the sort Smethurst found in the hamlet, which the political parties could use to absorb the voters that were newly enfranchised by universal manhood suffrage. Instead, the parties had to fight for the allegiance of these voters in a political culture shaped largely by bureaucratic initiative. By the time the Diet passed universal manhood suffrage in 1925, the Army, Education, and Home Ministries, respectively, had set up organizations of reservists, young men, and neighbors. The branches of these organizations linked the local elite, who wanted influence in the ward, municipal, and prefectural assemblies, with the new voters. Through these organizations, residents aspiring to positions of leadership could demonstrate their abilities and their commitment to the local community. The municipal social bureau, through its welfare facilities, had a limited supply of jobs and goods at its disposal; its network of district welfare facilities allowed politically ambitious residents to participate in the distribution of those goods. In short, the bureaucrats provided the kind of organization and benefits we might expect of a political party machine. They did so, however, in a much less intentional way and with much less direct influence over the contraption they had constructed.

The urban political participation of the 1920s, then, took place in conjunction with the expansion of the Japanese state. A number of scholars have already begun the work of exploring the role of the state in prewar Japan and placing it in comparative perspective.[26] For an understanding of how the state shaped popular participation the most important studies thus far are Sheldon Garon's and Dean Kinzley's, which show how certain Home Ministry bureaucrats interacted with the political parties, business leaders, and even the unions themselves to shape labor policy. Labor policy, however, was only one aspect of the social policy of the Home Ministry.

In this study, I explore a wider range of Home Ministry policies. Edwin Reischauer once suggested that the history of Japan in the 1920s and 1930s was like a large and deeply buried archaeological site where there had been only a few widely scattered probes. In my archival archaeology of political participation in Honjo, the same Home Ministry bureaucrats appear again and again, as officials in the Tokyo municipal government, as architects of welfare policy, as officers of the Japan Young Men's Hall, as supporters of a philanthropic foundation for Koreans in Japan, as advocates of election reform. Many of these individuals were identified by Garon, because of their support for labor unions, as "social bureaucrats."[27]

I suggest that we might instead think of these men as "participation bureaucrats." What linked all their varied activities together was a vision of Japan in which all subjects of the Japanese emperor, without regard for religion, ethnicity, or wealth, would share in both the benefits and the responsibilities of the empire. The establishment of publicly supported welfare facilities was an expression of their inclusive vision. Only with an understanding of that vision can we understand why the Home and other ministries induced and structured political participation as they did.

My account of political participation begins with two chapters on the history of Japanese state policy toward the urban poor, the co-operation of the state with private organizations with similar concerns, and the establishment of publicly funded welfare facilities in Tokyo. The local elite of the ward make their entrance onto the stage in the two middle chapters, which describe how local residents achieved their own ends through participation in a variety of government-sponsored organizations such as sanitary associations, district welfare commit-tees, reservist groups, and young men's associations. Only in the last two chapters do we find the unions and the elections, which the lib-eral-pluralist approach would lead us to expect in a study of political participation. This is as it should be, for only in the 1920s did these activities become legal for the vast majority of Japanese citizens.

This study of civil society starts at the end of one war and ends at the beginning of another. The Hibiya riots of 1905 symbolize dra-matically the question of how the Japanese citizenry would participate in their strong and wealthy nation. Victory over Russia established Japan as a major international power, but in Tokyo the announcement of the terms of the peace treaty that ended the war was immediately followed by three days of rioting against the government's failure to obtain an indemnity. The rioters burned and smashed government buildings, police stations, churches, and streetcars. Casualties included seventeen dead and hundreds wounded. These events marked the be-ginning of serious debate about the domestic cost of Japan's success in the international sphere. Yoshino Sakuzō, the Tokyo University professor who articulately advocated universal manhood suffrage, re-garded these demonstrations as the first instance of the participation of the masses in politics, and many Japanese historians treat this event as the starting point of Taishō democracy.[28]

The study ends with the events of 1937, the year that Japan's military activities in China escalated to full-scale, albeit undeclared, war. Japanese historians of Taishō democracy often cut off their in-vestigations in 1925, the year in which the Diet passed both universal manhood suffrage and the Peace Preservation Law. The Peace Pres-ervation Law, which made it illegal to advocate either change in the form of government or abolition of private property, provided the state with a potent weapon against the small Japanese Communist

Party, and state suppression served to keep the party minuscule. To end a study of political participation in 1925, however, would be to ignore the practical experience in electoral politics that the vast majority of Japanese citizens acquired in the era of universal manhood suffrage. Some of the institutions discussed in this book, particularly the neighborhood associations, proved useful in wartime mobilization, which might argue in favor of continuing the study to 1945. This book is not, however, an investigation of wartime mobilization. The central question here is not why independent organizations of workers, tenants, and politicians were dissolved or destroyed and state-sponsored organizations were made compulsory between 1940 and 1945. This is the story of how state-sponsored organizations coexisted and interacted with independent associations over a period of more than two decades, as they would again after 1945.

The bureaucrats, shopkeepers, businessmen, factory owners, union members, and aspiring politicians who, by their jockeying for political control, shaped the institutions of Tokyo also shaped the political future of Japan, for a significant portion of Japanese now live in large metropolitan areas where electoral politics continue to be mediated in many of the ways developed in Tokyo during the 1920s and 1930s.[29] Moreover, the citizens of Tokyo learned—sometimes on their own and sometimes from bureaucrats and political party leaders—pragmatic lessons in how to operate within a constitutional framework. The process through which this occurred is as central to modern Japanese history as the various shifts in prime ministers and cabinets. The history of this process illuminates both the importance of Japan's highly educated bureaucratic elite in shaping social policy and the legitimate claim of the people of Tokyo to a continuous political history.

By addressing a number of themes common to all industrial democracies in the early twentieth century, my study contributes in a modest way to the internationalization of history that Akira Iriye called for in his presidential address to the American Historical Association in 1988.[30] At the simplest level, it provides new information. Earlier attempts to include Japan in studies of either the state or democracy have been hampered by the paucity of material available in English on either the civilian bureaucracy or popular political participation.[31] At a deeper level, it suggests that we need to reconsider how the various components of a modern state contribute to the development of popular participation.

— *Chapter 1* —

The Setting

At the dawn of the twentieth century, Tokyo was a city of contrasts. Its status as the seat of the Japanese government and the largest city in the country was a legacy from the Tokugawa shoguns, who ruled Japan from 1603 to 1868. The city itself radiated out from the remains of Edo Castle, the shogunal headquarters. Hidden amid these ruins was the palace of the Meiji Emperor, sovereign of the new Japan. In a few areas not far from the palace, the splendor of the new Japan was readily apparent. The brick and glass buildings that housed government ministries, banks, company headquarters, and factories were visible representations of Japan's strong central government and capitalist economy. Train stations and tracks proclaimed the connection of this capital with every corner of the empire.

The vast majority of the buildings in Tokyo, however, were low wooden structures with tile or thatched roofs. Such dwellings sheltered the laborers, clerks, and shopkeepers who made up the Tokyo population of over a million. Since the Meiji Restoration of 1868, a number of new forms of transportation had wound their way through the neighborhoods of the city—jinrikisha, horse-drawn trolleys, national railroad lines, and electric streetcars. Within each home, however, the furnishings, the clothing, and the food remained much as they had been for centuries.

The institutions of the Meiji government touched upon the lives of these households in limited ways. Children attended public schools where, on major national holidays such as National Foundation Day on February 11 (Kigensetsu) or the Emperor's birthday on November 3, they dressed in their best, recited special songs, and received lotus-seed cakes filled with sweet bean paste.[1] Young men here, as throughout Japan, were subject to conscription into the army. The streets of Tokyo were patrolled by the Metropolitan Police Force, a branch of the Home Ministry.

Because Tokyo was the capital city in which diplomats presented their credentials to the emperor, it was the parlor of the nation, the front room that must be kept ready for company. Consequently, it more than any other city was the focus of national policy on poor relief. Initially, the Meiji state remained aloof from the problem of poverty. The legal system held that the household was responsible for the economic well-being of its members. Private philanthropists and religious organizations that supported orphanages, charity hospitals, and other formal institutions provided a second line of defense.

Where these measures proved inadequate, poverty was a visible embarrassment. Unemployment and petty crime wordlessly indicted the political order that had permitted their development. For urban residents, the poverty-stricken were an eyesore, an inconvenience, and a danger. Beggars and street urchins confronted the beholder with the darker side of life. Petty thieves undermined the efforts of hard-working residents to achieve prosperity. Corpses in the street, unsanitary housing, and undernourished neighbors were health hazards.

The nature of urban life thus made poverty painfully obvious. Whereas village residents might gradually reduce their caloric intake until their emaciated corpses were discovered within their simple homes, urban residents who lost their jobs lost their housing as well. They slept in parks and begged for food and money. Because urban workers were often recent immigrants to the city, they could not easily call upon their families for help in times of personal and economic crisis. Of necessity, the state created policies to deal with orphans, foundlings, the elderly, sick travelers, and beggars. Whenever possible, however, it shifted the responsibility for support to the recipient of aid or to private philanthropists.

This chapter tells the story of how government officials, journalists, philanthropists, and scholars transformed poverty from a problem of personal morality and misfortune to one of political and social significance. The rice riots of 1918 have rightly been hailed as a major watershed in the history of welfare in Japan, for it was only after the labor disputes that accompanied rapid industrialization during World War I and after the six weeks of civil unrest in the summer of 1918 that the government established a social bureau and metropolitan governments inaugurated modest programs of government-sponsored social services.[2]

Although 1918 marked the beginning of a significant increase in the level of funding for welfare, both the practical and the philosophical foundations for the policies of the 1920s had been developed between 1905 and 1918. Thus far, social policy has been most thoroughly explored in terms of bureaucratic efforts to forestall disturbances in the industrial labor force.[3] Prior to 1918, however, welfare was primarily in the hands of private philanthropists who endeavored to remedy misfortunes and fight social injustice across a far broader range of the urban population. Many of these private philanthropies were linked with Christianity. One focus of this chapter will be how, through these private charities, Japanese educated abroad and foreigners resident in Japan were instrumental in what we might term the transfer of social technology.

Meiji Social Policy

In *New Theses (Shinron)*, written in 1825, the Confucian scholar Aizawa Seishisai urged his daimyo, "Above all, we must induce the people to be filial and respectfully, to care for the elderly, the orphaned, the widowed, and others in society who have no one to depend on."[4] Aizawa assumed that the members of society would care for one another; the role of the government was simply to admonish its subjects to be mutually supportive.

As Japan set out after Commodore Perry's arrival in 1853 to strengthen itself on the pattern of the West, officials sent abroad took note of welfare institutions that Japan would have to consider adopting. Even before the Meiji Restoration of 1868, the members of the first official delegation to the United States in 1860 noted the existence of orphanages and old-age homes and the care that Americans took to educate the blind and the deaf. In 1872, Kido Takayoshi, one of the most influential leaders of the new government, admired with envy the George Washington School for Delinquent Boys, which was established to educate young men who had committed crimes. Ōkubo Toshimichi, who was a member of the same government embassy to the United States and Europe, returned to Japan with a different lesson, however; he feared that institutionalized assistance to the poor might encourage laziness.[5]

The new Meiji government established a system of poor relief that invoked Confucian ideals of filial piety to justify providing aid to as few as possible. Like contemporary systems in the United States and Great Britain, it made local governments responsible for relief. The government formally articulated its policy in the Poor Law (Jukkyū kisoku) of 1874, which remained the law of the land until the implementation of a new relief law in 1932. The law of 1874 declared that systems of mutual aid, particularly the family, should provide for the poor. Local governments were required to aid those who were unable to work because of illness, youth, or old age only if the recipient had no able-bodied family members. The government provided relief in the form of a sum of money equivalent to the price of a stipulated quantity of rice in the local market where the recipient resided.[6]

Although the law allowed urban administrators to send able-bodied individuals back to their native prefectures, it was nevertheless not adequate for the needs of a great city. The Poor Law was predicated on the assumption that the local authorities knew the relatives of the needy and could bring pressure to bear upon them to fulfill their legal responsibilities. In the city, the police often did not know the relatives of the poor. Further, the provisions of the Poor Law did not begin to address the needs of those truly dependent upon it. Where were foundlings, orphans, and the homeless elderly to eat their rice? However little responsibility the national government felt toward the helpless, the Tokyo authorities could scarcely allow beggars, stray children, and derelicts to obstruct the thoroughfares. Formal institutions for the shelter of the helpless and the employment of the able were a necessity in the city.

The Tokyo Poorhouse (Yōikuin) was the preeminent institution for poor relief in the capital. It provided shelter for paupers, orphans, and those unable to work because of physical handicaps. The inspiration for its founding was not so much to relieve the poor as to conceal them. In preparation for a visit from an imperial prince of

Russia in 1870, the authorities interned the beggars of the city in a special quarter. Tokyo prefecture established the poorhouse as a permanent facility in 1872. When the prefectural assembly discontinued financial support in 1885, private philanthropists intervened to maintain the work until the city of Tokyo took over the institution in 1889. Private funding continued to be essential for the support of the poorhouse and the increase of its endowment. The imperial household gave a substantial donation at the death of the Empress Dowager in 1897.[7]

The Tokyo Poorhouse operated on a small scale that was clearly inadequate for a city of over a million; in 1872 there were about 140 inmates and in 1885 still only about 300. By 1915, the work had expanded somewhat to include, in addition to the principal buildings for the poor, a workhouse at Sugamo for dependent children, a reformatory at Inokashira, and branches for sick children and sick paupers. Together these facilities cared for over two thousand individuals. Although the scale of the work expanded, the philosophy behind the facilities remained much the same: the able must work. The poorhouse was a workhouse as well as a shelter. Inmates could labor at making envelopes, grinding meal, making cardboard boxes, plaiting straw, printing, carpentry, making sandals, tailoring, or washing. The profits from this work were divided equally between the institution and the inmate.[8]

These facilities resembled nineteenth-century American municipally supported almshouses such as Blockley, opened in 1835 in Philadelphia. Although American cities provided public buildings to shelter the poor, they did not otherwise indulge the needy. Guardians of the poor endeavored to goad them into work and thus self-sufficiency. They tried to make institutional conditions so uncomfortable that potential paupers would be discouraged from becoming dependent on public charity.[9]

In the early years of Meiji, Japanese government officials were more concerned with the problems of Japan as a poor nation than with the poor individuals within Japan. They discouraged as much as possible dependence upon public aid. They restricted eligibility, maintained only limited facilities, supported existing facilities by endowment income and donations rather than by direct appropriations, and required the recipients of aid to work. They also duly rewarded those who fulfilled their implied ideal: economic survival through perseverance and hard work even under trying circumstances. The governor of Tokyo prefecture honored a fourteen-year-old girl who from the time she was eleven nursed her sick parents and supported them by working in a printing factory. Moreover, the chief of Shiba Ward invited her neighbors to a special meeting at the elementary school she attended to honor her filial piety. The local police routinely reported to the governor cases such as that of a fifteen-year-old boy who was supporting his mother.[10]

Changes in Social Thought

Implicit in the Poor Law was the assumption that poverty was largely the fault of the poor individual, a view that was widely shared. In *The Advancement of Learning (Gakumon no susume)*, the noted writer and educator Fukuzawa Yukichi wrote in 1872 that the poor have no cause for complaint against society or the government. The only cause of poverty is ignorance; those who wish to escape from poverty should apply themselves to study.[11]

After about 1885, some writers suggested that poverty arose from changes in society as well as from individual failings. Among the first to express this awareness were members of the Liberal Party (Jiyūtō) such as Ueki Emori and Ōi Kentarō. Others, such as Gotō Shinpei, advocated the formation of public policy to solve the problems of poverty because they were concerned about preserving the labor force of the nation.[12]

During the first session of the Diet in 1890, the home minister submitted a bill calling for a revised poor law. A Diet committee substantially revised the bill, which nevertheless was denied a second reading.[13] The revision of the bill and the debate in the Diet show, on the one hand, the nature of the support that had developed for a public relief policy. At the same time, one can see the strong forces that still opposed any such program. Advocates of both the original and the revised bill agreed that society had a moral duty toward its poor. They argued that because recent changes within society had intensified the problem of pauperism, existing regulations were inadequate to fulfill the obligations of society. The nationwide system of subsistence relief they advocated would, they said, preserve law and order and, by reducing vagrancy, prevent disease. Thus, poor relief was not an end in itself; appropriate relief in the present would prevent illness and social disorder in the future.

Under the terms of the proposed bill, the state would give relief to all adults made destitute by sickness, old age, or misfortune, to the dependent children of adult recipients of aid, and to all children with no one to care for them. Persons qualifying for aid would receive shelter, food, clothing, medical care, and burial at public expense. Children receiving aid were, if possible, to train in an appropriate occupation. These stipulations enlarged substantially upon the provisions of the 1874 law, which provided only food.

More controversial than the expansion of benefits, however, was the attempt of the central bureaucracy to exercise control over what had been a private matter. Although bureaucrats in the central government drafted the proposed law, they left the responsibility for financing and administering relief to the municipalities. The bill implicitly criticized the existing system of private charity by including stipulations intended to eliminate fraud. It strictly forbade relief in the form of cash payments and set a prison sentence for anyone who obtained relief by fraud. In their efforts to control a process they considered essential to the development of the nation, the bureaucrats sought to eliminate private charity by requiring that philanthropists hand over all money and goods to municipal authorities for distribution. Their proposed procedures resembled those of the Charity Organization Society in Great Britain and the United States.[14]

Opposition to the government bill came from two fronts, those who opposed interference by the central government in local matters and those who opposed any expansion of the existing relief program. Many Diet members believed that the central government had no right to make detailed prescriptions on relief work, especially since the financial burden of the programs would be borne by the municipalities. The legislators also resented the proposed curtailment of private philanthropy. The committee that revised the bill limited the interference of the central bureaucracy in local programs by stripping the bill of most of its detailed prescriptions.

Those who opposed expanded programs of relief argued that more generous relief would encourage laziness. Liberal Dietmen grounded in laissez-faire economic principles argued that poverty was the result of idleness and negligence on the part of the pauper. Others felt that although in the future a more generous system of poor relief might be justified, the existing level of poverty in Japan did not warrant increased expenditure. The heated debates on this subject indicate the disagreement in the society as to what constituted poverty. In the end, the Diet refused to allot funds to relieve a poverty that the members could not be sure existed.

After 1890, ideas from abroad provided a strong new thrust toward the development of a positive social policy. When Kanai Noburu returned to Japan after four years of study in Germany to assume a faculty position at Tokyo Imperial University, he introduced the ideas of the German Historical School to Japan. Kanai portrayed aid to the laboring classes as treatment of a diseased part of the organism of the nation rather than as a favor bestowed upon the undeserving.[15] He believed that Japan should adopt a comprehensive system of social legislation modeled on Bismarckian Germany in order to forestall the development in Japan of an exploited and alienated working class dedicated only to its own interests. Another political economist, Kuwata Kumazō, urged the government to pass improved relief laws. Kanai's thought was particularly influential in Japan because as a professor at Tokyo Imperial University, he was the teacher of an entire generation of bureaucrats who formulated social policy.[16]

In England, the late Victorian approach to poverty was compassionate yet rational humanity. The driving mission of reformers, philanthropists, and social critics was "to make compassion proportionate to and compatible with the proper ends of social policy."[17] Some of the manifestations of this humanitarian zeal were Charles Booth's survey of the London poor, the Charity Organization Society, and the settlement house movement.

Measured Victorian compassion, which we have already observed influencing the bureaucratic reformers of Japan, found rich expression in the Japanese press. As early as 1886, a series of articles on poor districts in Tokyo appeared in *Chōya shinbun*. The articles reflected the depressed economic conditions that resulted from the government policy of retrenchment and from several years of bad crops. In the poor districts they visited, the reporters found a few professional beggars and many carters, coolies, or peddlers who were just barely able to eke out a living. Some residents did piecework within the home. Parents sent their children out to work at the age of seven or eight, the boys as apprentices, the girls to silk-reeling factories.[18]

The articles in the *Chōya shinbun* were the first in a series of journalistic accounts of poverty in Japan. The most famous book in this tradition, *The Lower Classes of Japan (Nihon no kasō shakai)* appeared in 1899. The author, Yokoyama Gennosuke (1871–1915), described the life of the poor in Japan, both in the major cities and in the countryside. Yokoyama, on the staff of the *Mainichi shinbun,* and other reporters painted a vivid picture of a world in which some worked desperately hard simply to get minimal shelter, food, and clothing. In Tokyo, Yokoyama found men who had no regular work but stood near a hill and waited for jobs working for carters. At the request of a carter, they would push from behind for about ten or twenty blocks to earn a little money. They asserted to Yokoyama that it was stupid to have regular work and they made a virtue of having the sun on their backs and lice to scratch. Yokoyama was astonished to discover such attitudes among men who in a matter of hours would be hard-pressed to pay for food or shelter. They had no homes but slept on park benches in the summer and in flophouses in the winter. He projected that their final destination in this life would be the Tokyo Poorhouse.[19]

Some Victorian philanthropic practices were implemented in Japan by the newly constituted peerage. One such instance is the Japan Red Cross. Its predecessor, the Hakuaisha, was founded in 1877, during a civil war; the name of the organization was changed in 1886 when Japan joined the Geneva Convention. The principal work of the society was the medical relief of wounded soldiers. From its beginnings, the Japan Red Cross Society enjoyed the patronage of the imperial household. The empress made an annual endowment; in addition, she honored the organization by delivering a message at each annual convention of the society. Occasionally she visited the Red Cross Hospital and bestowed gifts upon the patients.[20]

By the turn of the century, some Protestant missionaries and their imitators were acting on the principle that philanthropy should not simply relieve individual poverty but should benefit the whole society by preventing poverty. Japanese Protestant churches first became active in philanthropic efforts in the mid-1880s when the new system of taxing agricultural land, the disestablishment of the samurai class, and the ruin of traditional crafts had reduced many to poverty. Projects of the churches included medical care, poor relief, prison reform, temperance work, education, and care of lepers, the blind, and the dumb. A visit in 1886 by George Müller, the founder of orphanages in British cities, encouraged work for orphans.[21] The early Christian efforts, like the patriotic undertakings, were for the relief rather than the prevention of poverty.

One example of the new type of philanthropic activity was the Futaba Nursery School, a kindergarten for poor children established by Noguchi Yuka in Tokyo in 1900. Kindergartens had existed in Japan since the early Meiji period, but mainly as an enrichment to the education of the wealthy. In the prospectus Noguchi prepared for her nursery school, she argued that the children of poor households, having always suffered from cold, hunger, and lack of parental supervision, might fall into crime and disturb the peace of the nation if they did not experience an educationally sound environment. Noguchi was a teacher at the kindergarten attached to the Peeresses' School, and she had many contacts among the elite. Her prospectus brought in donations from Princes Konoe and Tokugawa, from Barons Mitsui and Iwasaki.[22]

Noguchi's approach to social problems came not from Bismarck's Germany but from the United States. Her associate in her work with the poor, Morishima Mine, had just returned in 1900 from an inspection tour of kindergartens for poor children in the United States. Both women attended Banchō Church, which had been founded by American Congregationalist missionaries. Other members of this congregation had a strong commitment to social reform. Among these were Katayama Sen, director of Kingsley Hall, a settlement established by the Congregationalist mission board in 1897, and two missionaries who assisted him at the new settlement house, the Reverend D. C. Greene and Miss Florence Denton. Katayama, a recent graduate of Andover Seminary in Massachusetts, had worked for a short time at South End Settlement in Boston.[23]

Honjo Ward

Philanthropists and religious leaders established their facilities in the slums of the city. To understand how reformist zeal actually affected the lives of the ordinary residents of Tokyo, let us shift our focus from the government and the intellectual elite to one of the poorer wards of Tokyo. Honjo Ward was one of the fifteen wards created by the

Law for the Reorganization of Counties, Wards, Townships, and Villages (Gunkenchōson henseihō) of 1878. The main criteria for fixing the ward boundaries were topographical, although there was some consideration for historical connections.[24] In the case of Honjo, the Sumida River separated the ward from the central part of the city to the west, but no equally distinct lines divided Honjo from Fukagawa Ward to the south or the various villages to the east and northeast.

The name Honjo, which may be a remnant of the estate *(shōen)* system, dated back at least to the Kyōhō era (1716–1736). Over a century earlier, when Tokugawa Ieyasu established Edo as his headquarters, this area along the east bank of the Sumida River was little more than sand dunes and marshes. Only a few villages such as Ishihara, Nakanogō, Susaki, Oshiage, and Koume, can claim to predate Edo. Honjo became an integral part of Edo in the seventeenth century when the Ryōgoku Bridge spanned the Sumida River and linked it to the rest of the city. Once the government had constructed canals to drain the land, it transferred many of its direct retainers to residences in the area. Some of the more scenic spots on the eastern bank of the Sumida—Koume and Mukōjima, for instance—were popular as sites for the pavilions of the daimyo and wealthy merchants. Many of the shogun's retainers fell into straitened circumstances, however, and were little better off than the local shopkeepers who supplied their needs. By the mid-nineteenth century, Honjo was a neighborhood where the sons of samurai battled over kites and dogs on nearly an equal footing with the sons of merchants.[25]

A view of Honjo in the early twentieth century, perhaps from the vantage point of one of the bridges crossing the Sumida River from Asakusa or Nihonbashi, would present an expanse of one- and two-story buildings, broken only by occasional smokestacks or large factory buildings. Public parks and other spots of greenery were few and far between. Nevertheless, the ward could still boast a few historic and scenic attractions to lure the occasional visitor. Near the Ryōgoku Bridge stood the Ekōin Temple, established for the souls of the victims of the Edo fire of 1657. Here also was the Kokugikan where sumo matches took place. The river banks of Honjo afforded an excellent view of the fireworks display that marked the "river opening" each summer. The railroad station at Ryōgoku, opened in 1903, was the main connection for the Chiba peninsula.[26]

Honjo was above all a place to live and work. The population of the ward, which had reached 162,159 by 1905, rose to 247,533 in 1917, a population density of over 100,000 people per square mile.[27] These residents had crowded into this area not because of its desirability but because of its low cost. Honjo was a low-lying district, plagued by flooding. Although in 1920 one of the wealthiest men in Japan, Yasuda Zenjirō, still lived in Honjo, the slums and flophouses of the back alleys were more representative of the ward than was Yasuda's mansion.

The Japanese divide Tokyo conceptually into high city (*yamanote*) and low city (*shitamachi*).[28] In Edo times, the high city designated the hilly sections to the west of the shogun's castle, whereas the low city referred to the merchant quarter of the central and eastern sections. Although the boundaries of high city and low city have shifted through the centuries and are never entirely clear, in any definition Honjo has been low city, for it is geographically a place of low altitude and socially a neighborhood of commoners.

In the early twentieth century, Honjo fit the cultural image of the low city as a place of small shops and businesses, uncorrupted by modernity. In Tokugawa times, a commoner urban culture had arisen in the low city, and even now residents of Tokyo speak nostalgically of the "friendly, openhearted, unpretentious, generous, and neighborly" manner of urban commoners. Edokko, the true children of Edo, who cherished an aversion to the accumulation of wealth, survived into the twentieth century to make good use of the flophouses of Honjo.[29]

At a time when the amenities of Western life were largely the privilege of the wealthy in Japan, Honjo was in some sense a repository of traditional Japanese ways, but more as an attic than as a museum. Edward Seidensticker, with his romantic nostalgia for the low city, considers Honjo one of the "saddest victims of Civilization and Enlightenment." It had "pockets of pleasure and entertainment," but "none that would take the pleasure-seeker out of his way."[30] Factories, jinrikisha, and streetcars appeared, unaccompanied by pianos, violins, or Paris gowns. Young men out to have a good time still came to Honjo in the Taishō era for sumo wrestling and the traditional variety hall, but Honjo was not quite as historically pure an example of the low city as Nihonbashi or as culturally rich a depository as Asakusa.

Private Philanthropic Work in Honjo
from 1900 to 1911

In the first decade of the twentieth century, Honjo had four private welfare facilities that exemplified the new philanthropy. One of these was a temporary shelter. Japan's modern transportation system pumped a constant stream of rural immigrants into an unstable urban labor market. The system symbolized by the Poor Law of 1874 could not deal with the large numbers of poor individuals who had no employment and no lodging and whose relatives were inaccessible. One of the first to establish a facility to help the temporarily homeless was a Buddhist of the Ōtani branch of True Pure Land Buddhism. Ōkusa Keijitsu (1858–1912) of the Asakusa Honganji founded the First Free Night Shelter to house those who were too poor to afford even the cheapest flophouses *(kichinyado)*. The shelter also maintained an employment exchange; both the shelter and the exchange served those who had arrived in the capital with neither employment nor money for the trip home. Ōkusa founded the shelter in 1901 in Asakusa; he moved the facility to Wakamiya-chō, Honjo, in 1905. In the decade between April 1901 and December 1911, the shelter served 85,000 individuals, which demonstrates how much the city needed such a facility.[31]

In 1906 the Salvation Army established a similar facility in Hana-chō, Honjo, and at about the same time a Teetotaller Eating Place (Kinshu ichizen meshiya) nearby.[32] These facilities were characteristic of the work of the Salvation Army, which had originated in the slums of London. Army policy was to lend a helping hand to all in spiritual, moral, or temporal difficulty. The work of the Salvation Army in Japan began with the arrival of twelve British officers in 1895. Japanese workers were soon enlisted and the outposts in Honjo were Japanese rather than foreign efforts.

Like the Salvation Army work, the Laborers' Moral Reform Society was closely related to Christian evangelism. Sugiura Yoshimichi, rector of True Light Church in Fukagawa Ward, close to Honjo, founded the Reform Society. Sugiura entered St. Paul's School in Tokyo in 1880 and was baptized the next year. He was ordained deacon in the Protestant Episcopal Church of America on May 31, 1891, and priest on May 20, 1894. In 1890, even before his ordination, Sugiura began to work at True Light. True Light dated from

1877, when it was decided to establish one church outside the foreign concession. As other churches were founded, True Light, located as it was in an increasingly poor and industrial area of the city, declined in membership. By the time Sugiura took charge, the congregation had dwindled to about ten members.[33]

From the time of his arrival in Fukagawa, Sugiura ministered to his neighbors. In his early days there, he founded a dispensary for the laborers, hoping to "use their bodily salvation as a means to bring about their spiritual salvation." The dispensary benefited the neighbors, but it did not increase the membership of his parish. Finding it difficult to communicate with these laborers so different from himself, Sugiura determined in 1908 to select a few that understood Christianity and to use them to reach others. This was the origin of the Laborers' Moral Reform Society.[34]

Sugiura's object in founding the society was to help the laborers by "inspiring them with the ideal of self-respect and self-help." Self-help included practical elements of economic independence. From its beginning, the Moral Reform Society operated an information bureau to assist those arriving from the countryside in search of employment. In 1910, he opened a boarding house for men with no homes, and to enable his boarders to become self-sufficient, he supplied them with peddlers' baskets and wholesale goods. A member of the Laborers' Moral Reform Society was in charge of the peddling operation.[35]

By 1911, the society had a hundred members who met weekly in two groups for Bible study in the house of a member. Special public meetings were held on the first and the fifteenth of the month, the days that laborers generally had off from work. The police, who were at first extremely skeptical of the open air meetings of the society, became friends and helpers as they saw "thieves and ruffians converted into good men."[36]

The Japan Poor Men's Hospital (Dai Nihon kyūryōin) provided medical care to the poor. Takayama Kinai, a physician from Niigata, founded the hospital in 1898 in Hamamatsu-chō. By 1913, Dr. Takayama was plagued by debt and it seemed that the hospital would have to close. Rescue came from Watanabe Jieimon, a well-to-do merchant of Nihonbashi Ward, who donated thirteen thousand yen to reestablish the hospital in Yanagiwara-chō, Honjo. Watanabe promised to continue to provide five hundred yen per month for the support of the hospital, which had facilities for four hundred patients. Eight physicians worked under Takayama's leadership.[37]

The private philanthropies located in Honjo, like the Tokyo Poorhouse, ministered to those with neither home nor employment, those who belonged to no one. Many of the recipients of this aid had only recently arrived in the city and were not as yet really part of the neighborhood.[38] These philanthropic efforts also served the more established urban residents in several ways. The shelters supplied the bare necessities of life and opportunities for employment to strangers who might otherwise become criminals and thus a threat to the local residents.

These ministrations also assisted some members of the community who had been self-supporting until economic distress reduced them to poverty. In the summer of 1912, the residents of the shelter in Wakamiya-chō, Honjo, included sixty women and children whose husbands and fathers had deserted them when, in the face of rising prices, hard-earned wages became inadequate to support a family. Many of the women and children needed medical care as well. The medical care offered by Takayama's clinic was important to many who would have been self-supporting had they not been faced with medical expenses. Sugiura's work, especially, was more than a mere rescue station; his vision (which was shared by his bishop) was to have "a university settlement on a small scale" that would provide a place for recreation and study for the laborers in the area.[39]

The human resources and the funds for these undertakings came largely from outside the immediate neighborhood. The Asakusa Honganji presumably sponsored the First Free Night Shelter. The Salvation Army depended upon contributions from members, charitable donations from Japanese philanthropists, and gifts from supporters in Great Britain. Sugiura's church provided only half of its own support; the remainder no doubt came from the American church.[40]

The State and the Philanthropists

The Japanese government began to take a more active role in welfare work in Tokyo and the whole nation at the very end of the Meiji era. The year 1911 opened with the dramatic execution on January 24 of the anarchist Kōtoku Shūsui and several others for their supposed involvement in a plot to assassinate the emperor. The execution of the perpetrators of this Great Treason Incident illustrated the determination of the state to suppress those opposed to the existing order. At the same time, however, the government began welfare work to alleviate the social conditions that might generate such opposition.[41]

Journalists and academics alike had long warned that urban poverty might lead to strikes, assassination, and revolution. Just before the turn of the century, Matsubara Iwagorō, a reporter for the *Kokumin shinbun,* wrote of Tokyo, "A day may come when it will learn its strength, and that it need no longer hunger and suffer to provide luxury and ease for its keepers." Private philanthropy, Matsubara argued, was not an adequate remedy for urban poverty: "But there are charity organizations, some may say. So there are, but what is charity but a cloak for former robbery and neglect. In a well organized state there should be no need for charity."[42] The Great Treason Incident lent credence to the arguments of those like Matsubara who wanted state involvement in poor relief and the alleviation of social conditions.

The Great Treason Incident, with its implication that grave social disorder might be imminent, lent urgency to the solution of social problems. A factory law, long urged by advocates of state responsibility for social order, passed the Diet in 1911. The law, which did not go into effect until 1916, limited the working hours of women and children, mandated two days off per month, and required owners to support disabled workers. Government officials had first advocated state regulation of industry in order to foster national productivity. Only later did thinkers such as Kanai Noburu and Gotō Shinpei transform the mission of such a law into one to protect the weak from the ravages of industrialization and to preserve the health of the nation.[43] The factory law was an instrument of control only insofar as it restricted factory owners from abuse of their workers that might make revolution an attractive alternative to the existing order.

In addition, the national government moved quickly after Kōtoku's execution to express its commitment to alleviating economic hardship. Early in February 1911, it announced a new program of charity to counteract the growth of "dangerous elements in society." The state promised to establish labor exchanges immediately and to found charity hospitals and pawnshops in the future. The government aimed through these programs to protect poor children and to improve public morals. In November 1911, the city of Tokyo opened two labor exchanges, one in Shiba Ward and one in Asakusa.[44]

These employment exchanges embodied several aspects of state policy. That the state acted at all was an implicit acknowledgment that unemployment was not necessarily the product of laziness and that the government had a responsibility to aid those who desired work. These exchanges also marked the beginning of a state concern for urban as well as rural social problems. The government distributed the money for the establishment of labor exchanges to the six largest cities of Japan. The two labor exchanges the city of Tokyo opened in 1911 were followed by a third in Koishikawa in 1912 and a fourth in Kanda in 1914. The city explicitly stated that these facilities were for slum dwellers and all were in fact located in slums.[45] Finally, labor exchanges were an extension of the basic state policy that all should be self-supporting. What the state offered its poorest citizens in economically hard times was help in finding a job.

The most dramatic expression of the state's newfound commitment to poor relief was the announcement on National Foundation Day (February 11), 1911, that the emperor would donate one and a half million yen to medical care for the poor. The emperor's donation, supplemented by donations from the business community, became the endowment for a new philanthropic society, the Saiseikai, that was formally established on May 30, 1911.[46] The plan for labor exchanges and the emperor's donation, coming as they did within three weeks of the execution of Kōtoku, underscored the bureaucratic perception that if the state failed to alleviate economic distress, the result would be social disorder.

Bureaucratic concerns about urban poverty did not inspire the state to assume financial support for social welfare. The Meiji Poor Law of 1874 placed responsibility for economic survival on the individual and the family. In the years since 1874, there had been a growing realization among bureaucrats, academics, and journalists that in an industrializing society, individuals could become poor for reasons beyond their control. The bureaucrats, ever frugal on behalf of the state, appealed to private philanthropists to care for the victims of national growth.

Thus, the government exerted state authority to establish the Saiseikai as a private philanthropic foundation. Throughout May and June, Prime Minister Katsura held conferences in his official residence to raise money for the foundation, especially from the business community. On May 9, he entertained 190 businessmen from the six great cities (54 were from Tokyo). Baron Shibusawa spoke for the businessmen, who appointed a number of managers to raise funds in each of the six cities. This was only the first of a number of meetings that Katsura held. On June 16, the Home Ministry sent prefectural administrators detailed instructions on how to go about soliciting donations, which thus generated meetings all over Japan.[47]

The wealthy found it difficult to resist the importunity of the government and despite considerable grumbling in editorial pages, the funds were forthcoming. As was the usual practice in Japan, fundraisers announced in advance how much each individual would contribute. This practice sometimes resulted in embarrassment. As an editorial in the *Jiji* complained, "When a report finds its way to public notice that the amount actually contributed was much lower than that expected by the Managing Board, such individuals may incur, without their fault, an unenviable reputation among the mass of the people." Other editorials complained that contributions were given for political rather than charitable reasons, that the universality of the campaign did not permit the degree of self-advertisement the business community desired from its charity, and that the canvassing conducted by local officials under the direction of the prime minister and the home minister tainted the campaign with an element of coercion.[48] Whether they acted freely or from coercion, the businessmen gave out of concern for the nation rather than pity for those in need of medical care. Ōkura Kihachirō, a millionaire who had risen from relatively humble origins, explained his generous gift to the Saiseikai:

> The hoards of wealth enjoyed by the millionaires must not be thought to have been amassed by work of individuals only; on the contrary, it is the progress and prosperity of the country that they have to thank for their wealth; and for this who is primarily to be thanked but His Majesty the Emperor? Therefore it is the duty of the millionaires to do as much as possible for the sake of the country.[49]

Government support for private philanthropy, so clearly exemplified by the founding of the Saiseikai, had begun even before 1911. The Home Ministry encouraged private free medical clinics, child-care centers, and labor exchanges as a means of preventing the growth of socialism among the workers and urban poor who had begun to take part in mass action such as the Hibiya riot of 1905 and some large-scale strikes. The ministry held a national conference on reform and relief work *(kanka kyūsai jigyō)* in September 1908, at which Kuwata Kumazō spoke. By inviting reformers who had on their own initiative set up facilities to improve society, the government hoped to bring such efforts under its own control and to use them to its own credit. The next month, the wealthy industrialist Shibusawa Eiichi and others gave funds for the founding of the Central Philanthropic Society (Chūō jizen kyōkai), which brought volunteers and bureaucrats together on an ongoing basis.[50]

Often, as in the case of the Saiseikai, the support for charitable organizations came from the imperial household. The emperor and his family had, of course, long given generously to civic philanthropies such as the Japan Red Cross Society, the Red Cross Charity Hospital, and the Tokyo Charity Hospital. When the Empress Dowager died in 1897, her family gave 370,000 yen to charity, part of it to the Tokyo Poorhouse. In the early twentieth century, the imperial household began to give gifts to smaller private charities, many of them Christian. In 1905, the emperor gave one thousand yen to the ex-convicts' home operated by a Christian, Hara Taneaki, in Kanda, Tokyo. The Taishō Emperor made donations to the Salvation Army, the first in 1913. He also gave a large sum toward the enlargement of St. Luke's Hospital in Tokyo.[51]

The Home Ministry as well began in 1908 to encourage private charity by disbursing funds to deserving efforts. In that year, it gave 22,000 yen to 77 organizations. The next year gifts of from 200 to 1,000 yen, totaling 40,000 yen, were made to 117 groups. These gifts from the Home Ministry reached a peak of 65,722 yen in 1911 and then declined thereafter to about 18,000 yen in 1918.[52] The ministry gave its awards to a larger number of organizations each year. Thus, the financial support itself became less significant, but the symbol of appreciation was extended in ever-wider circles.

As these statistics suggest, the state increased its role in poor relief without significantly increasing its actual expenditures. Ogawa Seiryō has pointed out that the amount paid by the state to those entitled to aid under the Meiji Poor Law actually decreased when gifts to private charity began. At the beginning of 1908, the state gave aid to 13,090 people under the Meiji Poor Law. By the end of 1909 the number had been reduced to 3,753. To meet its responsibilities to those recipients, the state disbursed 217,000 yen in 1907 and 190,000 in 1908, but only 63,000 in 1909.[53]

The government used its involvement in private philanthropy to remarkable advantage. By holding conferences and bestowing annual awards on worthy charities, it associated itself with the good deeds of philanthropists. The creation of the Saiseikai tapped the resources of the business community to provide welfare facilities. Some companies had already endowed philanthropic institutions such as the Mitsui Charity Hospital. By soliciting donations for the Saiseikai, a philanthropy closely associated with the emperor and the government, the state appropriated the credit for the generosity of the business community. The close association of the state with the benevolence of the Saiseikai was reinforced in the large cities of Japan when policemen, indisputably representatives of the state, distributed the tickets that entitled the bearer to free medical care at the expense of the Saiseikai.[54] Finally, the emperor's words on National Foundation Day suffused the philanthropic efforts with personal warmth:

> It is a matter of deep regret to Us if any of Our subjects, suffering from illness, are helpless and cannot find the means of obtaining medical aid and on that account may have to die prematurely. For this reason We are anxious to provide means of relief to such poor, helpless people by enabling them to obtain medical treatment.[55]

All this was achieved at virtually no direct cost to the national treasury.

The achievement of the government was all the more remarkable considering that public opinion still did not accept the need for the state to provide aid for the poor. Some argued that Japan had neither the extreme wealth nor the extreme poverty of the West. Under the Japanese family system, the argument went, relatives cared for the needy and so public institutions were unnecessary. In Japan where orphan boys were taken in by temples and girls could become apprentice geisha or prostitutes or entertainers, orphanages were superfluous.[56]

The tenor of some editorials in the days following the announcement of the plan for the Saiseikai suggested that, even in 1911, state provision of medical aid still would not have been acceptable had it not been couched in terms of imperial benevolence. The *Jiji* opposed state contributions to the charitable fund on the basis that if governors asked the prefectural assemblies to make contributions to the fund, it would merely increase the tax burden on those the fund was intended to help; the same reasoning was used to oppose the formation of a charity fund by the Lower House of the Diet.[57]

It might be argued that the government supported private charities to control them. The government was much more successful in portraying itself as interested in private philanthropy than it was in controlling the philanthropists, however. The gifts of the imperial household and the Home Ministry were too small to control or to corrupt the recipients. The donations from the business community may have been somewhat less than purely voluntary, but the pressure brought to bear upon the commercial and industrial magnates was primarily social rather than political or economic. That is, in its efforts to control the masses, the government depended a great deal on the goodwill of its citizens.

By involving itself in philanthropic activity, the government was transforming private interests into public ones. This transformation legitimized expertise on poverty, poor relief, and social problems. As the example of Honjo illustrates, this expertise was often embodied in Buddhist and Christian organizations, which had hitherto been excluded from the ruling circles of the Meiji state. Just a year after Kōtoku's execution, the Home Ministry invited representatives of Shintō, Buddhism, and Christianity to a conference. The leaders assembled in Tokyo on February 25 and 26, 1912, and resolved to work together to increase the morality of the nation. Christians were overjoyed to receive this government recognition, and few spoke out against it.[58]

In retrospect, Christians have looked back on this conference as a "sad turning point," one that marked the end of outspoken Christian criticism of the state and the beginning of servile cooperation with it. Regrets over wartime silence should not, however, obscure the fact that the invitations to the conference were an extraordinary concession in 1912, not only toward Christianity but toward Buddhism as well. The invitations came at a time when the state was vitally concerned about urban social problems and when religious organizations were carrying out most of the actual relief.[59]

The Growing Crisis

World War I was the single most important factor in rendering unsatisfactory this system whereby the state bestowed benevolence but very little money upon the poor. During the war, Japan played only a minor military role, occupying German territory in China and the Pacific. Unfettered by military responsibilities, Japan experienced an unprecedented industrial boom. She supplied the warring allies with munitions and manufactures and moved into the former European markets in India, the Dutch East Indies, and China. Consequently, between 1914 and 1919, Japanese gross national product rose more than one-third. Mining and manufacturing increased by one-half. Exports nearly tripled.[60]

The price of this economic success was dislocation in the domestic economy and society. Inflation was a by-product of the boom, and while the nation grew richer, the national work force struggled to survive as wages failed to keep pace with rising prices.[61] At the same time, the working class was growing and its composition changing in directions that made it potentially more politically disruptive. The industrial work force increased dramatically from 1,450,000 to 2,480,000 between 1913 and 1918, an increase of 70 percent in five years. As heavy industry grew, male workers began to constitute a higher percentage of industrial employees. Although male workers in manufacturing did not outnumber females until 1933, with World War I the shift began from the Meiji pattern of a work force that was about 60 percent female. During World War I, strikes and work stoppages became common.[62]

The effects of the industrial boom were felt most keenly in the cities, which were already prone to social problems. The anonymity of urban life drew from other parts of the nation those who did not wish to be known: the runaway youth, the fleeing criminal, the despondent soul in search of an anonymous suicide. Moreover, it was difficult for those living in an urban neighborhood to control deviant behavior in an informal manner by withholding cooperation or by ridicule as was done in the rural village.[63] In the densely populated capital city where many residents had only recently settled, an urban shopkeeper might find that many of his customers, many of the passersby and perhaps even the family in the adjacent house, were strangers to him.

Economic fluctuations were particularly marked in Tokyo. Although the value of production in Tokyo increased by more than 50 percent between 1917 and 1918, the number of poor in Tokyo nearly doubled—reaching 29,936 households with 129,886 individuals by the end of 1917.[64] All wage earners in the city, many of them employed outside the industrial sector, suffered adverse effects from the rising prices. Employment opportunities, both real and imagined, drew to Tokyo a constant stream of new workers. Some of those migrants adjusted to urban life much better than did others.

Several American scholars, interested in the orderly development of a competent and disciplined industrial work force in Japan, have offered explanations for the smoothness of the transition. James W. White has shown that migration to Tokyo was often from small and medium-sized cities and that many came to the metropolis with industrial experience. Moreover, not everyone who migrated was employed in the industrial sector. Both James White and Ezra Vogel argue that the family mediated the move to the city in Japan, arranging ahead of time to place family members in employment.[65]

The orderly integration of the majority nevertheless left a small number of migrants with serious problems. Some failed to find employment; others were laid off during economic slumps. When those who came to the city to make their fortunes lost their source of income, the individual—and sometimes his family as well—was suddenly stranded in financial distress among strangers. Such disaster could result from sickness or debauchery or bankruptcy, of either the individual or the employer.

Some sense of the fragility of life in the city is conveyed by the survey done at the Tokyo Poorhouse on the causes of the poverty of 3,224 inmates. The investigator who established the categories clearly believed that many of the poor were responsible for their own fate. He accounted for some of the cases of poverty as follows: intemperance (324), gambling (117), immorality (201), idleness (125), dissipation (277), crime (46), and speculation (79). Presumably the government regarded tramps (392) as following a chosen calling. The categories of pessimism (179), laziness (237), and extravagance (198) suggest that even minor faults could lead to destitution. Even hardworking households could fall victim to the remaining causes: mental weakness (109), ill-health (46), accidents (73), misfortune (31), business failures (106), and obsolete trades (179). To these categories,

Yamamuro Gunpei added, on the basis of his experience with the Salvation Army:

> unhappy marriages, slavery to fashion, susceptibility to undesirable tendencies of the age, bad environment, vicious passions, pernicious appetites, ignorance of the laws of economy, conceit of ability; and vanity as to artistic capacity, failure to realize the spirit of the times, superstition and too much dependence on others.[66]

Amid this turmoil, the government continued to direct philanthropic activities. The Local Affairs Bureau (Chihō kyoku) of the Home Ministry in 1917 established a Relief Section (Kyūgoka) with supervisory authority over philanthropy, relief, poorhouses, institutions for the deaf, orphanages, and insane asylums. The next year, the government established a Relief Work Investigation Society (Kyūsai jigyō chōsakai) under the supervision of the Home Ministry. A vice-minister of the Home Ministry served as chairman of the society, whose twenty members were chosen from the academic and bureaucratic communities.[67]

The Tokyo prefectural government responded to the troubled times by actively encouraging local associations for the relief of poverty. Inoue Tomoichi, governor of Tokyo prefecture from July 1915 until his death in June 1919, was an experienced Home Ministry bureaucrat who had studied social conditions in Europe and had a longstanding interest in reform. He had been instrumental in the establishment of both the conference on reform and the Central Philanthropic Society and he was a founding member of the Relief Work Investigation Society.[68]

As governor of Tokyo, he duplicated in the prefecture the institutions that were being developed at the national level. He established a "relief section" in the prefecture in 1917, and the next year he founded the Tokyo Prefecture Charity Society (Tōkyō-fu jikei kyō-kai). The society, which changed its name to Tokyo Prefecture Social Work Society in 1920, was a semi-official organ; its headquarters were in the prefectural hall, and the governor of the prefecture served as head of the society. The members were distinguished residents of the area. Under the encouraging eye of the government, private philanthropists continued their service to the needy. In Honjo Ward, for instance, the Saiseikai opened a clinic in 1912, and in 1917 the First Free Night Shelter added a section for the care of children.[69]

Nevertheless, no less an authority than Yamamuro Gunpei of the Salvation Army wrote of Tokyo in 1914, "Notwithstanding all that is being done by the various institutions there is no danger of the poor being spoiled." In the summer of 1918, rice riots, which convulsed the nation for several weeks, gave dramatic expression to the rapid social and economic change wrought by World War I. The first disturbance broke out in Toyama prefecture on July 23. Before its suppression on October 26, the rioting spread to all but five prefectures. To put down the disturbance, the government deployed over 100,000 troops and arrested 8,185 people. The mobs directed their discontent first against the rice merchants and then against the police.[70]

The violence spread to Tokyo on August 13 when the police dispersed crowds that had gathered for a speech meeting in Hibiya Park. The *Asahi shinbun* had carried an advertisement for the meeting in its August 10 morning edition. Fearing that the meeting would disturb the peace, the authorities outlawed the gathering. Nevertheless, a crowd of seven or eight hundred gathered in the park and listened to speeches on overthrowing the cabinet, a vote of no confidence in the agriculture minister, and denunciations of the nouveaux riches. By the time the police broke up the meeting, the crowd had reached fifteen hundred. Several hundred headed toward the Ginza, shouting and throwing stones at store windows. On the next day, the police warned the public against rash behavior and admonished them not to go out at night. Nevertheless, similar disturbances occurred the next three nights. In addition to throwing stones, the crowds broke into rice shops and forced the merchants to sell off their rice at reduced prices.[71]

The immediate cause of the riots was a sudden rise in prices, especially of rice. Prices rose steeply from the end of 1917. If prices in 1917 are given a value of 100, then in 1918 prices were 230; in the same interval, wages dropped on a scale of 100 in 1917 to 68 in 1918. The increase in the price of rice, the staple of the Japanese diet, was even more dramatic. If the price of rice was 100 in October 1900, it was 109 in April 1916, 186 in July 1917, 258 in July 1918, and 329 in August 1918. This sudden rise in the price of rice was the result of inflation, a rise in the cost of producing rice, hoarding by landlords, uncontrolled speculation by merchants, the expenses of the Siberian Expedition, and ineffective government policies.[72]

The disturbances over the price of rice were symptoms of underlying social unrest that might easily explode again. The rice riots warned those who feared revolution—and encouraged those who awaited it—that widespread disturbances were a realistic possibility in Japan. The threat of revolution was all the more frightening in light of the success of the Russian Revolution the year before. Advocates of a state social welfare policy could now argue with conviction that the time was ripe for the state to provide social services. The Japanese ruling class responded in a number of ways to the riots. On August 13, the emperor gave three million yen for relief. The Terauchi cabinet resigned and was succeeded by the Seiyūkai cabinet of Hara Kei, which convened a number of commissions to consider social policy. Magazines and newspapers published arguments on democracy, universal suffrage, and the right of labor unions to organize.[73]

For the history of poor relief in Japan, the most significant of these developments was the establishment of a social bureau at the national level. On December 24, 1919, the Relief Section of the Local Affairs Bureau of the Home Ministry was renamed "Social Section," the first time the characters for "social" *(shakai)* ever appeared in the organizational structure of the Home Ministry. Several months later, on August 10, 1920, the social section became a "social bureau," independent of the Local Affairs Bureau. The responsibilities of the new social bureau included, in addition to the relief and philanthropic activities of its predecessor, the relief and prevention of unemployment. The latter was a response to the postwar slump.[74]

Up to the rice riots, the government served as a cheerleader for the family system and private philanthropists. After 1918, social welfare was an instrument of state policy. The Japanese state did not embark upon this task alone. In its awards and donations, the state had already admitted to its monopoly on expertise a varied assortment of allies—Buddhist and Christian, professional and amateur, socialist and apolitical, male and female. The new activism of the state in social work would only strengthen the legitimacy of these new interests.

— Chapter 2 —

The Social Policy of Tokyo
· City, 1919–1937

By 1919, there was a general consensus in Japan that to avoid major social and political disruption, the government had to take vigorous action to relieve and prevent poverty in the cities. The central government delegated responsibility for implementing the new social policy to the municipal governments. Tokyo city established a social bureau by the end of 1919 and soon opened a number of welfare facilities. Despite the fact that the major initiatives in public welfare occurred following an assassination plot in 1911 and large-scale rioting in 1918, the programs of the social bureau were not confined to measures that would keep working-class men from erecting revolutionary barricades in the streets of the capital. The lying-in homes and day-care centers, which might seem to be simply reinforcements of the family system, were determined efforts to ensure the maximum physical and intellectual growth of every Japanese child, even poor ones.

The main constraint on the programs of the city social bureau was its limited budget. The 1920s were economically difficult times for Japan. Per capita consumption in 1932 was little more than it had

41

been in 1922, and there was increasing inequality in living standards. Although owners and employees of large-scale enterprises, skilled workers, government officials, landlords, and professionals prospered, workers in small-scale manufacturing, employees of service establishments, and day laborers struggled to maintain their standard of living or even experienced decline.[1]

In the adverse economic conditions of the 1920s, when elected members of the municipal assembly were naturally reluctant to vote tax increases, municipal bureaucrats were advocates of public welfare programs. To extend its limited resources, the social bureau encouraged private philanthropists who were running institutions such as settlement houses, kindergartens, and medical clinics. By enlisting individual and institutional volunteers, the city legitimated them. Because the city had no means of rewarding its volunteers except to encourage their work, it had few direct means of controlling them.

The highest administrative positions in the city of Tokyo were held by civil servants and scholars who valued technical expertise. Municipal involvement in child care, employment exchanges, medical relief, settlement houses, and self-improvement for minorities greatly widened the sphere of expertise required by the city government. To meet its new responsibilities, the city hired women and sought out the advice of experienced philanthropists. Thus, to prevent poverty and the social disorder that they believed would be its necessary consequence, the municipal authorities legitimated the expertise of Christians, socialists, and other reformers who endeavored to transform Japanese society.

The Social Bureau of the City of Tokyo

On October 29, 1919, the Tokyo City Assembly voted to establish a municipal social bureau.[2] This unanimous decision masked the lingering resistance that local notables harbored toward publicly funded programs of poor relief. The next year during a session of the assembly, one member, Kosaka Umekichi, complained that the city planned to rely upon an amusement tax to support the programs of the social bureau.[3] He argued that this tax would be a hardship for the 1,700 residents of Tokyo employed in the entertainment industry. He pointed out that these entertainers were largely women and children and that it was unfair to further burden those employed in occupations known to be unreliable sources of income. Kosaka suggested a number of other possible taxation schemes and finally questioned why the tax was necessary at all. Had not the donations and efforts of wealthy benefactors such as Baron Shibusawa always sufficed to support the Tokyo Poorhouse?

In reply, the bureaucrats of city hall eloquently defended both their particular policies and the general principle of public aid to the poor. An assistant mayor explained why all alternative taxation schemes proposed by Kosaka were impractical. The head of the social bureau, Kubota Bunzō, then defended tax-supported social programs. He distinguished between "charity" (*jizen*) and "social work" (*shakai jigyō*). In charity, philanthropists and leading citizens relieved the hardship of the poor on an individual basis. When the economic system had been very simple, this system had sufficed. In recent times, however, the growing complexity of the means of production had brought into operation the law of the survival of the fittest. This fierce competition ruined even the physically and mentally able. Japan must cut off at the root this evil arising from a defective social system; failure to do so would invite revolution from below. But even without this threat, the state ought to reduce social evil as much as possible. It must not delegate responsibility for the victims of society to philanthropists alone but must act itself to provide aid.

The basic responsibilities of the Tokyo social bureau were to administer public aid, operate its own welfare facilities, and provide unemployment relief. Labor policy and social education came under its jurisdiction only briefly. Because the institutions to implement social policy were developed at the local level, they varied from city to city in their organizational structure. Osaka set up a social division (*bu*), subdivided into research and operations sections (*ka*). Kyoto had a social section. Only Tokyo had, like the Home Ministry, a separate bureau; in Tokyo, the bureau was divided into sections for employment, operations of public institutions, and welfare. By the end of March 1926, the bureau employed a staff of nearly four hundred, over a hundred of whom were office workers; many of the others were employed in the welfare facilities.[4]

Although the city assembly authorized the funds for the Tokyo social bureau, the leadership for the bureau came from civil service bureaucrats who were retired or on leave. The first head of the social bureau, Kubota Bunzō, was a graduate of the Seventh Higher School and Keiō University who passed the diplomatic higher civil service examination in 1899 and entered the Foreign Ministry. His last civil service position was as consul general in Tientsin. He could claim some acquaintance with urban problems, having attended the International Labor Conference in Washington shortly before his appointment as head of the social bureau.[5]

Kubota Bunzō was only the first in a series of civil servants who would take a turn as head of the bureau. Between 1920 and 1927, ten different men held the position, only two of them for a year or longer. Most occupants of the position were graduates of Tokyo Imperial University on leave from careers in the Home Ministry. If students at Tokyo in the 1890s, these men had probably listened to the lectures of Kanai Noburu on the German school of social policy and the responsibility of the state to prevent social unrest. More recent graduates had read liberal British social treatises. By the time Tokyo city established its social bureau, many experienced Home Ministry bureaucrats had developed specialized knowledge on labor questions and urban affairs through assignments in urban areas and through study trips abroad. Others—for instance, Yasui Seiichirō, chief of the social bureau from 1929 to 1931—became experts on social work as well as on social problems.[6]

The bureaucratic composition of the social bureau reinforced the close ties already in existence between the administration of the city of Tokyo and the Home Ministry. Most mayors of Tokyo were either graduates of Tokyo Imperial University or Home Ministry officials or both (see appendix A). One reason for the marked influence of the Home Ministry on the city social bureau was that Gotō Shinpei—who was mayor from 1920 to 1923, right after the social bureau was founded—was a former Home Minister. Maeda Tamon, one of his assistant mayors and acting head of the social bureau, had just returned the year before from one of the study tours that Gotō had established for Home Ministry bureaucrats. Maeda, along with Horikiri Zenjirō, mayor in 1929–1930, was prominent among those designated by Sheldon Garon as "social bureaucrats."[7]

One head of the Tokyo social bureau who did not come from the Home Ministry underscores yet further the close ties between the city and the centers for academic study of social problems. Yabuki Keiki (1891–1938) was a professor of religion at Tokyo Imperial University who, like Maeda, had recently studied abroad. When he assumed leadership of the bureau in 1925, he attracted to it young graduates of Tokyo. Under his leadership the bureau sought to lower the infant mortality rate.[8]

In keeping with both the state's claim to authority on the basis of expertise and the bureau's close ties to the academy, the Tokyo social bureau did a great deal of research to guide it in carrying out its responsibilities. During 1921, the bureau published studies on the poor, pawnshops, and home industries; the next year it reported on housing and employment agencies. Throughout the prewar period, the social bureau published the results of surveys on those in need of public aid: foundlings, children of poor households, part-time workers, working women, the unemployed, vagrants, and the elderly. The city also compiled lists of all institutions serving those in need. It conducted new studies as new concerns arose. For example, in January 1923, the bureau investigated the food of slum residents; in 1929, under the direction of the Christian social worker Kagawa Toyohiko, the bureau conducted a study of malcontented youth.[9]

A glance at an individual researcher provides some sense of the breadth and the depth of the bureau's investigations. Kusama Yasō's work won respect from both the subjects of his research and historians of social work for its sensitivity to the real needs of the lower classes. He described the poor of the capital as individuals who toiled from dawn to dusk just to have barely enough for the next day. His articles on the conditions of the poor appeared as early as 1920, and his numerous books included material on vagrants, prostitutes, slum residents, and workers who lived on houseboats.[10]

One stage in the development of social welfare in Tokyo began with the founding of the social bureau in 1919 and ended in 1923 with the destruction of most of its facilities in the earthquake. In its first year, the bureau announced plans to provide a central market, three public halls, a public bathhouse, a public barbershop, a lying-in home, and public dining halls. One of the first facilities to open was the Kōtōbashi Day Nursery at Irie-chō in Honjo. Formally opened in November 1921, it operated under municipal guidelines issued the same year. Under these, the facilities were open to children who were six months old or older but not yet of school age. The hours of operation were from 6:00 A.M. to 6:00 P.M. in the winter and from 5:00 A.M. to 6:00 P.M. in the summer. The only holidays were the first three days of the new year and the first and the fifteenth of each month, the customary rest days in factories. The staff instructed the children in games, songs, conversation, and crafts, providing a parallel education to that which wealthier children received in kindergartens.[11] The city thus began to offer on a broader scale the same type of facility opened by Noguchi Yuka in 1900.

Because of the bureau's interest in working women and children, it hired individuals, including women, with special expertise in these areas. Hayashi Katsu filled a position created in 1920 within the labor section. Assisted by a staff of ten, she advised the bureau on all matters relating to working women. In 1921, she directed a survey of the working conditions of women in the medium and large factories of Tokyo. Kajitsuka Yōko, who had recently returned from study in the United States, was appointed head of the Kōtōbashi Day Nursery.[12]

By the time the earthquake struck, the city had nine employment exchanges with three more under construction, two nurseries with three under construction, four health consultation facilities, one cheap rooming house with two under construction, some apartments (including public baths), and three public dining halls with one under construction. A maternity hospital was almost completed. With the exception of three labor exchanges, all of these facilities were destroyed or severely damaged in the earthquake.[13]

The disastrous earthquake occurred on September 1, 1923. The fires, which broke out immediately and raged for three days, killed over a hundred thousand people in Tokyo alone and destroyed 60 percent of the buildings in the city. The relief efforts greatly expanded publicly supported facilities for those in immediate need of work, shelter, food, and other amenities. Tokyo prefecture, Tokyo city, and the Metropolitan Police all constructed barracks for the homeless. Tokyo city used money donated by Osaka city to set up such barracks at eleven sites.[14]

The earthquake also inaugurated a new era in the development of permanent welfare facilities in Tokyo. The social welfare program that city officials planned as part of the relief and reconstruction work was considerably more extensive than before the earthquake. Officials planned fifteen labor exchanges in addition to the three that had survived the earthquake. They envisioned ten nurseries with health consultation staff, five maternity clinics, nine public dining halls, ten cheap rooming houses, seven pawnshops, and ten public baths with barber shops and laundries. Despite frustrating delays, the city had completed most of this work by 1928.[15]

The purpose of these facilities was not merely to relieve currently poor people but to prevent future poverty. The government bureaucrats believed that work on behalf of children was of essential importance in the prevention of poverty. Officials were concerned about rising infant mortality rates in Japanese cities. The nurture of children began with proper care for mothers before and after birth through maternity clinics, traveling midwives, visiting nurses, and education on child care. By 1926, Tokyo city had two maternity clinics, one in Tsukiji and one in Asakusa. After the earthquake, the city provided free milk for infants and children at a number of centers. Until August 1926, the milk was free; from that date there was a small charge. At the eight centers in operation in 1926, children's weight and height were measured once a month.[16]

The city also provided support services for poor households whose children survived the perils of infancy. By the end of 1926, Tokyo, with nine municipal day-care centers, had more facilities for mothers who had to have employment outside the home than any other city in Japan, although the average number of children in each center was only thirty-six. The nurseries continued to operate under the regulations set up in 1921. The city also provided consultation centers where doctors and nurses were available at regular clinics to assess the development of children. Nurses from the centers visited the children's homes when necessary. Tokyo had four such clinics by the end of 1926, at Kōtōbashi, Tomikawa, Tamahime, and Tsukiji. The city also operated two playgrounds for children by the end of 1926, one in Asakusa and one in Ushigome, and a third in Honjo was under construction.[17]

Architects of social policy turned their attention to pawnshops because pawnshops were to the poor of Tokyo what banks are to the rich: the chief source of credit.[18] The earthquake destroyed many pawnshops, and this was the reason given for the establishment of five municipal pawnshops. In fact, the issue was more complicated. Investigators of the Tokyo slums in the 1890s had noted that the usurious rates charged by private lenders to people living from hand to mouth made it almost impossible for the poor to get out of debt. By pawning umbrellas, bedding, kettles, tobacco pipes, or even clothes, the poor could borrow a few *sen* for a few months at interest rates amounting to about 100 percent per year. Moneylenders charged even higher rates by the day.[19]

In the 1920s, the municipal pawnshops charged only 1.2 *sen* per month (or 14.4 percent per year), much less than the private lenders. A Public Pawnshop Law of 1927 guaranteed certain rights to the borrower. When a public pawnshop sold a forfeited pledge, the law required that any money from the sale left over after deducting the principal, interest, and commission of the loan be turned over to the pledger. As the city recovered from the earthquake, the number of public pawnshops increased; by the end of 1930, the city operated eighteen.[20]

Donations arrived in Tokyo from all parts of the world in response to news of the earthquake and made possible the establishment of new types of welfare services. Osaka city donated funds for a municipal settlement house, which opened in Koishikawa Ward in 1928. It contained office space and meeting rooms as well as bathing facilities, an exercise room, a barber shop, a dining hall, and dormitory space. In other parts of the city as well, day nurseries, night shelters, consultation services, and dining facilities were brought together in "people's halls" *(shiminkan)* or "district halls" *(hōmenkan)*.[21]

The world depression of 1930 deepened the existing financial crisis in Japan, which had begun with a domestic depression in 1926 and a bank crisis in 1927. The most immediate effect in Tokyo was a marked increase in unemployment. The city had, of course, accepted responsibility for finding jobs for the unemployed ever since it established the first public employment exchanges in 1912.

One program that the municipal social bureau developed in response to the worsening unemployment problem was a system of registering day laborers. In winter, the seasonal unemployment of urban day laborers coincided with an annual influx of workers from the countryside at the end of the agricultural season. The city began registering day laborers in 1926 to protect their interests against migrants from the countryside. In October 1929, at seven of the city employment exchanges, the social bureau began to accept registration from educated persons seeking work; 1,707 applied on the first day. The registration of educated persons was only one of several new measures the social bureau introduced in 1929 to aid urban workers. In addition to urging all day laborers to register with the city, the bureau argued that the city should store rice for emergencies, stem the flow of immigrants from the countryside, and discourage the immigration of Korean laborers.[22]

The system of registration, which provided each registrant with an annual photo-identification card, prevented one person from registering at several employment offices and then selling the extra cards for profit. The city employed the registered laborers in the construction of roads, harbors, sewage plants, and gas and electric works. The registered workers also provided a convenient source of labor for sudden emergencies such as snowstorms; in February 1932, the city hired 9,100 workers to shovel the five inches of snow that had fallen. Private employers, as well, could draw on this ready supply of workers. When a registered worker found employment through the exchanges, the municipal authorities paid his wages and then collected later from the actual employer. The registration of day laborers was not a small-scale affair. In June 1932, there were 18,470 laborers registered, and in 1931 the average number of workers seeking employment per day was 6,156.

As another way to alleviate unemployment, the city social bureau organized a Laborers' Cooperative Society. Depending upon their classification, members contributed one or five *sen* for each day that they worked; employers contributed seven *sen* for each worker employed per day. Any member unemployed for three consecutive days was entitled to collect seventy-five *sen*, beginning on the third day of unemployment, for each day that he remained out of work.[23]

The thousands of day laborers who found employment as infrequently as once every four days were hard-pressed to pay for lodging even in flophouses. Unless they found a spot in one of the municipal free rooming houses, they had no choice but to sleep on park benches or in cemeteries. The municipal rooming houses were, then, a means of poor relief for the unemployed. By 1933, the city operated two free shelters and nine where accommodations were from fifteen to twenty-seven *sen* a night. Any sober, unmarried man of uncertain income, who was free from contagious ailments, could apply for admission. The rooming houses were meticulously clean. The city provided steaming hot barley water and bathing facilities for the price of a night's lodging. Public dining halls, with meals at easily affordable rates, were attached to each rooming house. In each shelter, the city provided a workshop where lodgers could make bamboo baskets or balls of ground charcoal. Medical care and banking facilities were also available. In times of inclement weather, the city even sponsored entertainment for the residents.[24]

The facilities that served Tokyo through the worst of the depression were the ones devised in the aftermath of the earthquake by bureaucrats, academics, and pioneers of social work. Yasui Seiichirō, who headed the bureau for twenty-one months from September 1929 to June 1931 illustrated that the initial commitment of the "social bureaucrats" to tap into existing expertise on urban problems wherever it might lie continued to the end of the decade.

Yasui provided leadership to the social bureau as a member of the national bureaucratic elite, not as a native son of the capital. Born in Okayama in 1891, he graduated from middle school there before going to Tokyo to attend the First Higher School and Tokyo Imperial University. After graduation from Tokyo, he entered the Home Ministry and worked in Ibaraki prefecture until 1922, when he left for two years of study in Europe. After his return at the end of 1923, he served in Kanagawa, Tokyo prefecture, Toyama, Hyōgo, and Fukuoka. His assignments included stints in both police and administrative work, and working as head of the social section of Ibaraki.[25]

Yasui's appointment as head of the Tokyo social bureau in 1929 was facilitated by recommendations by two colleagues from Okayama, General Ugaki Kazushige and Tsugita Daisaburō. Tsugita, whose brother had been a classmate of Yasui's at Okayama Middle School, had graduated from Tokyo University and entered the Home Ministry in 1909, the same year as Horikiri Zenjirō and Maeda Tamon. Prominent among the social bureaucrats, Tsugita had supported an early draft of a labor union law and represented Japan at an international labor conference in 1920.[26] The fact that Yasui's appointment was related to his ties in Okayama and the Home Ministry reflected the extent to which the Tokyo social bureau was an extension of national politics rather than an instrument of the local elite.

Yasui came to the headship of the social bureau in an era of hope. In the first elections to the city council under universal manhood suffrage, six members of proletarian political parties had won election, and there was hope that this would be a reform council. Young members of the staff of the social bureau as well looked to Yasui to be less conservatively bureaucratic than earlier heads of the bureau.

Yasui lived up to these hopes when, shortly after his appointment, he accepted the Christian evangelist Kagawa Toyohiko, famed for his work in the slums of Kobe, as an advisor. Kagawa had expertise on Tokyo as well, having established a settlement house in Honjo after the earthquake. Mayor Horikiri took the initiative in securing Kagawa as a consultant to the city. Yasui welcomed Kagawa's advice and took pride in the fact that he was able to win city council approval for the city settlement houses that Kagawa recommended.[27]

In cooperation with Majima Kan, a physician and socialist member of the city council, Yasui undertook a daring program of birth control. He and Deputy Mayor Shirakami (another graduate of Tokyo) announced in fall 1929, in the midst of deep concern about unemployment, that birth control information should be made available at the municipal health consultation offices to families already having children. This stance reflected Yasui's conviction that the city had a responsibility to prevent poverty as well as to relieve it. This program was less successful than his recommendation of settlement houses, however. Home Minister Adachi Kenzō summoned Yasui and Shirakami and chastised them for "going too far."[28]

Yasui believed that effective social work, based on sound knowledge, would be efficacious in improving Japanese society. His cooperation with socialists such as Kagawa and Majima arose from his respect for their expertise. He also treated as knowledgeable colleagues the experienced staff of the social bureau, and he brought new talent into the bureau, recruiting bright young university graduates such as Isomura Eiichi, later a professor at several universities. One anecdote, told to illustrate the respect in which Yasui was held, illustrates equally well the importance he placed on meeting the needs of urban citizens. In 1930, imperial advisors worried that the desperate homeless and unemployed in the streets might pose a threat to the emperor during a tour of the city planned for the celebration of the completion of reconstruction after the earthquake. Yasui promised a solution to the problem, which was to hire every available person on the streets on the day of the imperial procession.[29] Even as a one-time temporary measure, Yasui's solution demonstrated his reliance on economic relief rather than political control, temporary employment rather than preventive detention.

When, in 1930, Tokyo celebrated completion of reconstruction from the earthquake, the social welfare facilities were strained to capacity. According to the national census returns for 1930, based on data collected on October 1, in Tokyo alone there were 1,799 individuals who passed the night in parks or other open places. About 5,000 people in Tokyo eked out livings as ragpickers. The municipal rooming houses, with a capacity of 1,500, could scarcely begin to shelter the estimated 20,000 homeless.[30]

The employment exchanges, systems of registering workers, and the free night shelters, however well run and appropriate to the conditions of the depression years, could not serve all of the unemployed, nor could they solve all the economic problems of any one unemployed person. The poverty-stricken of Tokyo may not have risen up in revolution, but they did engage in crime. Kusama Yasō, anxious to convince the public that poverty was a serious problem, quoted police court statistics to show that the destitute and unemployed committed a majority of the petty crimes in the city. The number of petty offenses in Tokyo increased from 43,000 in 1921 to 151,000 in 1930, a year of high unemployment.[31]

By the late 1930s, the national economy had improved somewhat and Japan's deepening involvement on the continent following the Manchurian Incident of 1931 had absorbed much of the surplus labor force. By 1936, over 80 percent of those seeking work in Tokyo were finding it, as opposed to about 65 percent in 1932. In 1936, fewer people ate in public dining halls than the year before.[32]

In the 1930s, social welfare work took place within a new legal framework. A new relief law, passed in 1929, went into effect in 1932. This law required local governments to provide assistance to children aged thirteen or less, adults aged sixty-five or older, pregnant and nursing women, and others unable to sustain themselves because of illness or physical or mental handicaps. Where possible, the state would provide the aid to recipients in their own households rather than in institutions. Aid might include living expenses, medical care, costs of childbirth, and funeral expenses. The local officials charged with providing this aid were further enjoined to make use of volunteers known as district welfare committee members to prevent either overpayments or fraud.[33] These volunteers (discussed in detail in the next chapter) are another instance of the state sharing its burden, and thus perhaps inadvertently its authority, with the ordinary citizenry.

The new law went into effect just as the economic situation of the nation improved. In Tokyo prefecture, the number of recipients of aid declined steadily from 49,795 to 15,303 people between 1933 and 1940. The number of elderly and handicapped recipients remained roughly constant, while the number of children and pregnant and nursing women needing aid dropped to less than one-fifth of the 1933 level.[34] The improved condition of women and children undoubtedly reflected the generally improved economic conditions. It should be noted, however, that children and their mothers were primary objects of social policy from the 1920s on. The new relief law of 1929, with its provisions for childbirth and medical care, both mirrored and further stimulated this development. In Tokyo, the number of clinics in the city for expectant and nursing mothers increased from twenty-six in 1932 to thirty-two in 1936, and in 1936 there were more child-care facilities in the city than the year before.[35]

Private Philanthropy and the City, 1918–1923

The social welfare work of the city of Tokyo supplemented but did not replace existing philanthropic establishments. The city welcomed welfare facilities operated by a wide variety of religious and civic organizations, each with a purpose of its own for caring for the poor. By investigating, cataloguing, and subsidizing such facilities, the city extended a small measure of control over the private philanthropies, but these gestures at the same time bestowed a degree of recognition and legitimacy upon any who were willing to join the state in its battle against urban poverty. Among these allies were some who espoused philosophical and political principles somewhat different from the state orthodoxy. In settlement houses enjoying government sanction, young Christians and university students taught all who would listen about socialism and the labor movement.

Private philanthropic efforts were highly varied, small- scale, and sometimes short-lived undertakings that defy analysis on a citywide level. The various social work facilities established in Honjo Ward by private philanthropists between 1918 and about 1937 provide a manageable sample of the types of philanthropy directed toward the urban poor. A number of private philanthropic organizations responded to the economic difficulties and social disturbances in Japan at the end of World War I.

Those already at work in Honjo redoubled their efforts. The Laborers' Moral Reform Society of the Reverend Sugiura opened a section for the care of children in 1920. The efforts of Deaconess Knapp and the Women's Auxiliary of Trinity Cathedral made possible the erection of a kindergarten for the children of women employed as day laborers. Sugiura then used the building at night as a free shelter for men. In 1919, the Salvation Army set up a settlement in Yanagishima Umemori-chō, Honjo, with funds entrusted to it by the Tokyo Prefecture Charity Society. This project differed from the earlier work of the Salvation Army in the ward because it served the residents (especially the children) of the area, not transients.[36]

In 1919, after consultation with Mr. Merle Davis of the YMCA, the members of the Tokyo Circle of the Foreign Auxiliary of the Women's Christian Temperance Union decided to build a settlement house in Honjo. They rented land in Matsugura-chō in June 1919 and purchased it the next year. The purpose of the project was "to keep the children off the roads, to help build up their moral character, to model them into good men and women, and to provide for all those things which go to make up a happy childhood." These American women envisioned a settlement that would include a dispensary, a kindergarten, a day nursery, classrooms, and dormitories. Americans in Japan raised money for the project through an orchestral concert at the Imperial Theater in November and a Christmas bazaar in the Ginza in December 1920.[37] Mrs. A. K. Reischauer chaired the board of directors, and Kubushiro Ochimi of the Japan WCTU was a member of the board. It was she who named the settlement "Door of Hope" (Kōbōkan).

The work of the settlement began when a matron began making calls in the area and holding meetings in a rented building. As soon as the women purchased land, they opened a playground. By 1922, they had started a day nursery and a kindergarten in a rented building. The Honjo Ward Assembly cooperated with these American women by donating twelve thousand yen for the erection of a building, which was still under construction when the earthquake struck in 1923.

The Sanikukai, a medical unit of the Tokyo Imperial University branch of the YMCA, founded the Honjo Maternity Hospital in 1918 in Yanagishima Umemori-chō. The medical work of the Imperial University YMCA group began in the summer of 1917 when a number of medical students opened a clinic for the poor near the university. The founding of the Sanikukai represented the extension of this work to a much poorer area in Honjo. The project was backed by Yoshino Sakuzō, a professor and one of the directors of the Imperial University

YMCA, and by Kinoshita Seichū, an obstetrician and gynecologist on the faculty of medicine. This maternity hospital did not limit itself to obstetrics; Tokyo prefecture credited the Sanikukai with the care of over one hundred preschool children and the relief of over two hundred impoverished individuals during 1922.[38]

Earthquake and Recovery

The earthquake and fires that devastated Tokyo in September 1923 marked a major turning point in the history of social welfare in the city. The physical destruction of the capital, followed as it was by years of economic depression, made relief work more urgent than ever. The enormity of the disaster brought donations for use in Tokyo from other parts of Japan and from all over the world. The city used much of this money to establish permanent social work facilities. Some of the money went directly to private organizations (to religious denominations, for instance). In other cases, the city bestowed a portion of the funds it received upon private undertakings. The result was that private philanthropy expanded greatly, in close cooperation with the government.

Honjo provides a particularly appropriate subject to study how earthquake relief affected the practice of private social work, for no ward in the city was as heavily damaged and thus so in need of relief. The force of the vibrations was stronger in Honjo than in any other ward. Fire broke out almost simultaneously in ten or twenty places. Strong winds from the sea to the south fanned the flames, and the area had neither large open spaces nor tall concrete buildings to act as firebreaks. Many in Honjo sought refuge from the flames on one of several bridges crossing the Sumida River. On reaching the bridges, they found that large crowds on the opposite side had likewise been pressed toward the river by approaching fires. Refugees from both sides of the river crowded onto the wooden structures, all but one of which eventually burned as first the household goods of the refugees and then the bridges themselves caught fire.[39]

One particular tragic incident in Honjo made the death toll for this ward unusually high. Fire and police officials advised residents of Honjo and nearby Fukagawa Ward to gather for protection from the fires at one of the few large open spaces in the ward, a site in Yokoamichō formerly occupied by the Military Clothing Depot. About four o'clock on September 1, one of the many whirlwinds resulting from the heat of the fires developed on the upper reaches of the Sumida River. Whirling around the fiercely burning Higher Polytechnic School on the Asakusa side, it swept across the river, through the compound owned by the wealthy Yasuda family, and into the site of the Military Clothing Depot. The flames quickly spread to the luggage and clothing of those in the crowd, and within seconds, the entire area became a sea of fire. Some forty thousand perished.[40]

Tanno Setsu, who later married the communist worker Watanabe Masanosuke, was a worker at the Seikō Watch factory in Honjo in September 1923. Workers at Seikō had two days off a month, the first and the fifteenth, so Tanno was not at the factory but was busy getting ready for a political meeting later in the day when the earthquake struck just before noon on September 1. Many years later she recalled, "The entire earth shook in a horrible fashion. The muck of the Kameido sewer rose up in waves. The house before me collapsed." On September 4, when she ventured out to visit Watanabe in prison, she encountered devastation everywhere:

> I got as far as Ryōgoku Bridge, but it had burned down. I was told that Yodogawa Bridge had burned down too, but that they had placed some planks over the river and it could be crossed. I went there, but the river was filled with corpses, and I was too scared to try to cross it. I then went to the army's supply depot. There, scorched corpses were piled in large mounds. I felt ill seeing them, and I returned to the office sick and exhausted.[41]

The destruction and misery wrought by nature were compounded by human fear. Rumors spread that Koreans were about to invade the earthquake-stricken area. Noma Seiji, the founder of the Kodansha publishing firm, wrote a decade later:

> All Japanese men, women, and children instantly armed themselves against the marauders who—as we were persistently told by police and soldiery who ran from street to street to warn us against the peril—had poisoned wells, set houses on fire, raped women, butchered children, robbed and disembowelled refugees, and perpetrated other nameless crimes.

Terrified Japanese killed thousands of Koreans.[42]

In Kameido, near Honjo, Tanno Setsu heard rumors about Koreans, and the men camping out with her in the office of the Nankatsu labor union took their turn at twelve-hour shifts as volunteer guards. Nevertheless, they themselves became victims of the terror. The police arrested six men, simply because they were staying in the headquarters of a socialist labor union. None of them was ever seen again, the police disposing of their enemies in this emergency as they could not do legally in ordinary times.[43]

The earthquake killed approximately one-sixth of the residents of the ward. Some of those who perished were preeminent citizens such as Kyōgoku Takamitsu of the House of Peers; Yasuda Yoshio of the banking family; Yamauchi Hidekazu, head of the Aioi-chō Police Station; and the principals of two elementary schools. Fire swept over 95 percent of the surface of the ward, and 220,018 people lost their homes. The disaster destroyed the ward office, three of the four police stations, the telephone office, the two public libraries, and the Kondō and Umaya Hospitals. Familiar landmarks vanished, such as the Ekōin and Hoonji Temples and the Ushijima Shrine. Of the nineteen elementary schools in the ward, only Ushijima School remained standing. The outer walls of the Kokugikan, where sumo matches took place twice yearly, soared starkly above the rubble. On December 31, 1923, there were only 901 buildings in the ward.[44]

Many residents of the ward took advantage of the government's promise of free transportation and left the city. The owners of spinning and weaving factories throughout the city sent their female employees back to their native places. When the elementary schools of Honjo reopened on October 15, enrollment was only 26 percent of the pre-earthquake level, an indication that families as well as single workers had left the ward. Even as late as November 15, the 99,386 people living in Honjo represented only about one-third of the population there before the earthquake.[45]

Most of the organizations that had social work facilities in Honjo before the earthquake resumed their work as soon as possible. The First Free Night Shelter set up by the Asakusa Honganji in Wakamiya-chō was open again by December 15. At the site of their settlement in Yanagishima Umemori-chō, which was destroyed in the earthquake, the Salvation Army set up a nursery. By October 29, the Sanikukai had reestablished at their Yanagishima site a nursery and supply depot for pregnant women, infants, and nursing babies. The Honjo clinic of the Saiseikai, which was destroyed by fire, was operating again by the end of the year. Sugiura Yoshimichi and the Episcopal church established a restaurant in Hayashi-chō 78 in August 1924 to provide good food to the poor of the neighborhood. The restaurant also distributed tickets that entitled the bearer to free food. The Foreign Auxiliary of the WCTU began a kindergarten and a day nursery in a temporary building erected on their site in Matsugura-chō.[46]

These organizations already established in Honjo received imperial, state, and foreign aid. The imperial household made donations to the Sanikukai, to the First Free Night Shelter, and to Kinshi Hospital at Yanagihara on September 16, 1923, and the Laborers' Moral Reform Society on October 6. It also made a grant of two thousand yen to the Salvation Army, which was at work throughout the city. The Rotary International Relief Fund gave ten thousand yen to the Sanikukai Hospital.[47]

Three of the organizations that came to Honjo on the occasion of the earthquake—the Bethany Home of the United Lutheran Church of America, the Honjo Industrial YMCA, and the Tokyo University Settlement House—illustrate two interrelated but contradictory trends in social work in Tokyo in the 1920s. On the one hand, the government increasingly initiated, planned, regulated, and funded private welfare facilities. On the other hand, some of the private philanthropies with government support educated local workers to question the existing social order, from either Marxist or Christian perspectives.

Cooperation between the Tokyo prefectural government and American Lutheran missionaries, for example, transformed a temporary relief effort into the Bethany Home for Women with Children. The October 1923 issue of *Foreign Missionary,* a publication of the United Lutheran Church, appealed to its readers to donate funds for earthquake relief so that the missionaries could "give a clean and convincing demonstration of the sympathy and effectiveness of Christian charity." At its meeting in Kyoto on September 29, 1923, the mission executive committee made the Reverend A. J. Stirewalt, the only full-fledged Lutheran missionary living in Tokyo, a committee of one to administer their relief funds. Stirewalt decided that rather than duplicate the perfectly adequate immediate relief measures of the government, the Lutherans should establish facilities to help the earthquake victims through the coming winter. After surveying the situation with a Japanese colleague, he concluded that those most in need of aid were widows with children and the elderly. The Lutherans decided to establish two homes, one for each group.[48]

Stirewalt worked closely with the Japanese government to obtain land, buildings, and equipment. The National Sunday School Association secured the use of land owned by the Spanish legation in Azabu Ward. Tokyo city erected barracks donated by the city of Osaka. Tokyo city and Tokyo prefecture both provided equipment. The home for widows with children, which opened in late December 1923, provided day care so that the women could go out and work. When necessary, the home supplemented the income of the residents.[49]

In February 1924, officials of Tokyo prefecture asked the Lutherans to make their work permanent. The officials promised lumber, kindergarten equipment, land rent for six months, and money toward construction costs. Some of the funds that Tokyo prefecture received from the Home Ministry for the project were a gift of the American Red Cross. The three two-story buildings that were erected on leased land at Yanagihara-chō 3–36, Honjo, could accommodate thirty-nine families, a matron, her family, and two kindergarten teachers. The buildings faced a wide boulevard with a streetcar line and thus were visible to the community at large. The Lutherans invited local residents to meetings, permitted them to put their children in the day nursery, kindergarten, and playground, and admitted them to the work department and laundry.[50]

The Tokyo University Settlement House was the project of the New Men Society (Shinjinkai), a student group at Tokyo University. The students funded their settlement house with money received from the Tokyo city government in appreciation of their relief work after the earthquake. They chose Yanagishima Motomachi, Honjo, as the site of their work. This was in the same neighborhood as the Sanikukai Maternity Hospital, maintained by fellow university students belonging to the YMCA. Suehiro Izutarō, the law professor who conceived the project, admired the English university settlements he had observed while studying in Europe, and he had long hoped to do social work in Honjo, which he regarded as the most oppressed working-class district in Tokyo.

Better than any of the earlier settlements in Japan, the Tokyo University Settlement replicated Toynbee Hall in East London where young graduates of Oxford lived in order to bridge the social gulf between rich and poor. Samuel Barnett, the founder of Toynbee Hall, believed that the poor were as capable as the rich of appreciating the very best in life. In his speech at the ceremony celebrating the completion of the buildings on June 6, 1924, Suehiro echoed this theme. He stressed that in order for there to exist unity between knowledge and labor, the fortunate few with education must share their wisdom with the less fortunate masses. The settlement house provided an opportunity for such sharing as well as for practical research on the slums of the city.[51]

Like the English and American social settlements it was modeled after, the University Settlement provided a wide range of programs and facilities, including adult education programs, a medical clinic, a small library, and an orphanage. The University Settlement Labor School, which opened in the fall of 1924, soon became the largest and most successful of all the left-wing labor schools in Tokyo. The medical students who were members of the New Men Society operated a free medical clinic for the settlement. The University Settlement continued to serve Honjo until February 1939 when, in the wake of a series of arrests of students active in the settlement, the Ministry of Education ordered the students to disband.[52]

The Honjo Industrial YMCA was essentially the project of the noted evangelist and social worker, Kagawa Toyohiko. Educated at Meiji Gakuen, Kobe Theological School, and Princeton Seminary, he had by 1923 gained considerable fame in Japan for his service in the slums of Kobe, his writings on the sufferings of the poor, and his activism in the labor movement. When Kagawa heard of the earthquake, he headed for Yokohama immediately, sailing from Kobe on September 2. He surveyed the stricken cities of Tokyo and Yokohama and then set out on a speaking tour to raise money for relief. He returned to Tokyo with seventy-five hundred yen raised at forty meetings.[53]

During this second visit, Kagawa Toyohiko decided to assist the community most damaged by the earthquake by restoring the branch the YMCA had established in 1919 in Kameido, just outside the city limits, to serve the Kōtō area of Tokyo, which included Honjo and Fukagawa. He planned to establish a settlement to provide activities and education for those living in the area. On October 18, he decided to use as his headquarters the land in Matsugura-chō, which the

WCTU had purchased for their settlement house. The next day he pitched five tents provided by the American Red Cross, through the Sunday School Union. Members of the YMCA had set up relief work in Kamezawa-chō, Honjo, and the leaders of the YMCA wished to continue work in the Kōtō area. Because Kagawa had raised most of the money for the settlement at his evangelization meetings, the YMCA entrusted its work to him.[54]

By the end of 1924, the Honjo Industrial YMCA operated two night shelters, an employment service, a kindergarten, a medical clinic, and a labor school. The larger of the two night shelters, the Reimeiryō, located in Matsugura-chō, could accommodate fifty. The other, the Konichiryō, at Kita Futaba-chō 89, held thirty-five. Matsumura Shinko ran the employment exchange, Akamatsu Tsuneko the kindergarten, and Majima Kan and his younger sister, Hisako, the clinic. Akamatsu Tsuneko, the sister of the socialist Akamatsu Katsumaro, was afterwards active in the labor union movement. Majima, who had studied at Nagoya Medical College and in the United States, came to Honjo from Kobe where he had been working with Kagawa in the slums. Other projects added to the Industrial YMCA included the Kōtō Consumer Union, formed in April 1927 with 180 members, and the Nakanogō Credit Union, established in 1928.[55]

Both the Honjo Industrial YMCA and the University Settlement maintained labor schools where intellectual reformers introduced ideas challenging the existing social order to this working-class neighborhood. Both schools opened in 1924, the Industrial YMCA's in May and the University Settlement's in September. The "school" of the Industrial YMCA consisted of lectures given on Saturday afternoons. An audience of about fifty listened to talks on subjects such as the labor problem, the women's problem, the history of the labor movement, and unemployment. The labor school of the University Settlement was somewhat more formal. Students paid a small tuition fee and attended classes for up to three hours on Monday, Wednesday, and Friday evenings for three-month sessions. Usually there were about fifty students. Lecture topics included labor law, history of the social movement, politics, economics, and the labor movement.[56]

Both schools, then, acquainted their students with the workings of the labor movement. At the Honjo Industrial YMCA especially, the lecturers themselves were men who had served the labor movement, even in the face of arrest. Kagawa held various offices in the

Kobe branch of the Yūaikai, the labor confederation founded by Suzuki Bunji in Tokyo in 1912, and he played an important role in the
formation of the Kansai confederation of the Yūaikai in 1919. In
1923, he had been one of the leaders of a major strike in the shipyards
of Kobe; as a consequence, he spent over a week in prison. Murajima
Kaerino, who spoke at the labor school on labor and the women's
problem, was a newspaper reporter who had engaged in a sabotage
incident at the Kawasaki Shipyard in Kobe. The lecturer on the history
of the labor movement was Akamatsu Katsumaro, a member of the
New Men Society of Tokyo University and an officer of the Sōdōmei,
the successor to the Yūaikai. He had aided labor struggles in Kyūshū
and Hokkaidō and had taken part in the Kobe dock strike.[57]

These labor schools encouraged the labor movement and thus
potentially divided the neighborhood along economic lines. Support
of the labor movement, however, did not disqualify the schools' efforts as social work; neither did association with these organizations
place one beyond the pale. The government repeatedly recognized
Kagawa's achievements, and government employees Yusa Hashihiko
of the Tokyo Regional Employment Office and Otake Torao of the
Shiba tax office worked side by side with him in Honjo in 1924. The
labor school of the University Settlement remained open until 1932,
when it closed because of declining interest; it would be seven more
years before government oppression would close the remainder of the
Tokyo Settlement in 1939.[58] The government supported private social
work out of conviction that people who received assistance in their
economic difficulties would be better able to contribute to society.
Secure in its conviction, it allowed considerable freedom of thought
and speech among the practitioners of social work.

The commitment of the Home Ministry to social welfare found
further expression in the social services performed by semi-official organizations that received direction and funds from the ministry. The
residents of Honjo were the beneficiaries of a number of these projects. In May 1924, the Home Ministry founded an organization,
which it called the Dōjunkai, specifically to carry out social work for
those crippled by the earthquake. The home minister served as head
of the society, and the head of the social bureau served as the head of
the board of directors. In 1931, the Dōjunkai maintained two housing
units in Honjo, the Yanagishima Residence and the Nakanogō Apartments.[59]

The Patriotic Women's Society (Aikoku fujinkai) began in 1901 as a voluntary society to care for wounded soldiers and bereaved families, but it was soon able to secure support from both the War and Home Ministries. The society began to support social work in 1917, directing its efforts mainly toward women and children. By 1934, the association had 159 social work facilities throughout Japan. The organization established a settlement house in Sotode-chō, Honjo, in 1924. The settlement provided an employment exchange and lodging for women, a kindergarten, a children's health consultation center, and a library. The opening ceremony provided an occasion for some of the leaders of the society to visit Honjo. Among those in attendance were the educator Hatoyama Haruko, Mrs. Motono (later president of the society), Baroness Megata, and Baroness Ijūin.[60]

Another organization that provided social welfare facilities in Honjo was the Sōaikai. Made up of Koreans willing to work within the framework of Japanese rule of Korea, the organization sought to promote harmony between Japanese and Koreans and to articulate Korean interests in Japan. The founder was Pak Ch'un-kum, a construction foreman. When many Koreans were laid off in the economic recession of 1921, he organized the society to provide food and shelter to the needy workers. The Sōaikai soon won government support. All of the officers of the association were Korean, but many prominent Japanese—especially military men and bureaucrats such as Maruyama Tsurukichi and Akaike Atsushi who had served in Korea—were advisors.[61]

The government and the Sōaikai entered into close cooperation in the chaotic days of the 1923 earthquake. On September 4, the Metropolitan Police invited leaders of the Tokyo branch of the Sōaikai to a meeting where it was arranged that, starting on September 10, the prefectural government would employ Korean laborers to work on cleaning up the Tokyo streets. Officials hoped that extensive press coverage of these labors would convince the public that, in the words of an earlier pamphlet, "the majority of Koreans are well behaved and are not engaging in any sort of violent behaviour." Over the next six months, hundreds of Koreans per day took part in this project. The Sōaikai was thus the instrument of cooperation between Japanese officials and upper-class Koreans to control lower-class Koreans and incorporate them into the Japanese empire. The nature of this cooperation ranged from sponsoring Korean folk songs and dances on

National Foundation Day to providing the police with information on labor organizers.[62]

The Sōaikai was the official sponsor for a number of memorial services for the Koreans killed in the earthquake. The society held services at a temple in Koishikawa in December 1923 and at the Japan-Korea Hall in Nihonbashi in September 1924. The fact that Korean workers planned a separate service in Taihei-chō, Honjo, suggests that either the Sōaikai did not have a monopoly on Korean activities or that they were holding class-differentiated memorial services.[63]

The Sōaikai opened a night shelter at Taihei-chō, 2–1, Honjo, in January 1924. By 1931, the Sōaikai had a clinic, an employment exchange, and emergency housing in their headquarters in Honjo. By 1936, the clinic and employment exchange had disappeared, but the Sōaikai continued to provide emergency housing in Honjo and to maintain a nursery.[64]

The Sōaikai built these facilities in Honjo because after 1923 that was where many of the Koreans in Tokyo lived. The Japanese annexation of Korea made possible Korean migration to Japan. During World War I, the labor shortage in Japan, occasioned by the sudden prosperity of Japanese industry, attracted to Japan many Koreans made landless by the land registration policies of Japanese administrators in Korea. Beginning in the 1920s, a steady flow of unskilled Korean workers were migrating to Japan and competing with the lower strata of the Japanese work force. By the end of 1923, the Korean population in Japan had reached 80,000 and it doubled again in the next two years.[65] The number of Koreans living in Tokyo rose from 301 in 1919, to 1,880 in 1921, and 2,234 in 1922. Within the city, the immigrants were distributed fairly evenly among the fifteen wards; 6 percent of the Koreans in Tokyo lived in Honjo in 1921, and 8 percent in 1922.

After the earthquake a relatively large Korean population became a distinguishing characteristic of the ward. Whereas in 1919, Honjo could claim only the negligible total of fourteen Koreans, there were 2,554 in the ward in 1931 and 4,055 in 1936. The number of Koreans in Honjo was no longer simply indicative of the growing number of Koreans in the capital; rather, it became an index of the changing position of Honjo vis-à-vis the other wards. Honjo was one of the areas most severely damaged by the earthquake, and thus not a desirable place to live. The Korean laborers in Tokyo were indigent aliens.

The former farmers, unskilled and disliked, could get only the grueling, low-paying jobs that native Japanese workers disdained.[66] Thus, as their numbers in Tokyo increased, they banded together in fire-ruined Honjo. After 1923, Honjo became home to over one-fifth of the Korean population in the city.

The extent to which the Japanese state expanded its role in the relief and prevention of poverty is demonstrated by the Tokyo social bureau. On the eve of the rice riots in 1918, the only social work administered by the city, apart from the Tokyo Poorhouse, were four labor exchanges. By 1937, the city supported inexpensive lodgings, public dining halls, pawnshops, labor exchanges, settlement houses, hospitals, and clinics, including several for expectant and nursing mothers, infants, and parents needing information on their children's health. The achievements of the Tokyo social bureau reflected national policy. In the new legal framework provided by the Poor Relief Law of 1929, the government gave aid to more people in the 1930s than it had in 1908 and 1909. Whereas under the Poor Law the government supported only 13,090 people in 1908 and a mere 3,753 in 1909, after 1932 the number receiving aid was always over 100,000 and rose as high as 236,000.[67]

These figures only hint at the total effect of government policy. The various welfare facilities set up after 1918 made available to many who were not receiving direct government aid a much wider variety of services than earlier. Rooming houses, public dining halls, and employment exchanges provided relief for the homeless and unemployed. Public pawnshops, public baths, and day-care centers made the survival of economically marginal households more likely. Public and private organizations carried out sound preventative measures: adequate prenatal care, proper information on child rearing for mothers, good nourishment for children, and supplementary education for the children of the poor.

No social policy, of course, can completely eliminate poverty and tramps in the streets. Even after Japan began to recover from the depression, complaints about tramps in the city persisted. In 1933, officials of Asakusa Ward installed huge electric lights to eliminate dark corners in the parks and temple grounds where tramps might sleep at night. In 1936, foreign residents still complained about beggars in the temples and shrines and on busy streets. In 1939, in response to reports in American newspapers that Japan's military involvement in

China had increased the number of beggars in Japan, the Metropolitan Police Force of Tokyo attempted to remove all beggars from the streets.[68]

The essence of modern social policy is that it treats poverty as a problem rather than as an unfortunate destiny.[69] In Japan, the funds for social programs came in several waves: unemployment exchanges in 1912 after the Great Treason Incident; public markets, subsidized bathhouses, and day care after the rice riots; and a wide variety of facilities after the earthquake. Although each spurt in welfare spending followed an incident that involved—or potentially threatened to produce—political disorder, the gradual erection of a social welfare structure was not merely a temporary expedient to achieve political control. Rather, social bureaucrats and the social work establishment used political crises to establish programs based on deep and broad concern for the Japanese citizenry.

The social policy of Tokyo was not monolithic. The social bureau built upon a foundation of expertise provided by private philanthropy, and it continued to share its burden. There was some differentiation in function between the public and private sectors. By the mid-1930s, the city provided most of the facilities in Tokyo for the immediate relief of the hungry and unemployed. The city operated twenty of the twenty-five public dining halls and the state controlled two-thirds of the labor exchanges. On the other hand, the city operated only seven of the forty charity hospitals, eight of the eighty-two clinics, and four of the thirty-two institutions for expectant and nursing mothers. In 1936, the city ran only two of the nine settlement houses in Honjo Ward.[70]

Private efforts to relieve poverty widened the degree of participation in the existing social order. Buddhists, Christians, and leftist labor union activists provided the same kind of services as the municipal social bureau and government-related philanthropies such as the Patriotic Women's Society and the Sōaikai. Moreover, social welfare work incorporated the work of several dissident and underprivileged elements in the population—women, Koreans, and labor activists, for instance.

Direct government support for welfare did not diminish the state's support for private philanthropy. In the 1920s, government support of private social work was more generous than ever. The total amount given annually by the Imperial Household and the Home Ministry to private philanthropies on National Foundation Day was considerably higher in the decade after 1923 than in the decade before. Beginning in 1923, the combined amount was always over two hundred thousand yen, whereas until the regular imperial grants began in 1921, the Home Ministry grants were never more than one-third of that amount. The Home Ministry grants declined in amount and became secondary to the ever-increasing imperial grants.[71] Having the grants bestowed by the Imperial Household linked private philanthropy more explicitly to the imperial state than did funds from a bureaucratic ministry.

The concept of a family state, headed by the emperor, was reinforced when imperial gifts were made on family occasions such as weddings and funerals. On the occasion of the wedding of the Crown Prince in January 1924, the Imperial Household presented one million yen to the prime minister to found a trust, the Keifukai, to support private social work organizations. Private donors added to the trust; Harada Jirō, a billionaire of Tokyo, gave three million yen. The imperial court made use of the imperial wedding not only to provide for the future of private social work, but also to recognize those who had worked in the past. The court granted silver cups and a total of eighteen thousand yen to ninety individuals in appreciation of their work in social and educational endeavors. It also gave silver cups and gifts of two hundred yen each to 250 individuals who had been engaged in social work for fifteen or more years. On December 27, 1927, in connection with the funeral of the Taishō Emperor, the Imperial Household donated funds to eight social work projects, six of them in Tokyo.[72]

At a more practical level, the larger imperial grants compensated for the fact that it was impossible to secure support for private philanthropy through the Diet. One attempt to obtain funding for private social work through the Diet began in 1921 when the Social Work Research Association recommended that the Diet appropriate money for a trust fund to support private social work. Finance Minister Ichiki Otohiko submitted a special finance bill for the purpose to the Forty-sixth Session of the Diet on March 19, 1924. The Diet referred the bill to committee, where it died. Kimura Kanuemon, a Diet member from Osaka, made a second such attempt when he submitted a similar motion on March 24, 1923. Kimura feared that since the establishment of public social work, private undertakings were at a disadvantage in the competition for funds. He argued that the government should support social work that coincided with its own social policy and should recognize the past contributions of private social workers to the nation. This bill, too, failed in committee.[73]

Japanese social policy was successful in projecting an image of a benevolent state. The state did not spend a great deal on social work, but it spent conspicuously. When the emperor donated relief funds, capital for charitable endowments, and rewards for private philanthropists, the press reported his actions. His generous gifts—to the victims of disasters and to the poor—clothed state aid in the compassionate raiment of a father giving to his children. The emperor personally rewarded the private philanthropists who served the needy. In Tokyo, the facilities of the municipal social bureau scattered throughout the city attested to the concern of the state for its weakest members.

Although the Japanese imperial institution can quite legitimately claim a history of a millennium and a half, the image of a benevolent emperor caring for all his children was a modern construct, one intended to make more palatable the economic hardships that came as by-products of rapid industrialization. Some Japanese historians have quite rightly pointed out that the government policy of expansion abroad in fact caused a number of the social problems the state then prided itself on having solved. Such deception was not peculiar to Japan; Hazen S. Pingree, mayor of Detroit at the turn of the century, came to realize that "the fundamental flaw of most charity work was that it freed entrepreneurs from demands for just wages."[74]

Japanese social policy was, however, more than mere window dressing. In turning their attention to the weakest members of society and instituting measures that would guarantee the economic livelihood of the poorest Japanese citizens, the social bureaucrats were instituting policies of economic development and inclusion that reformers in other parts of the world equated with the struggle for democracy. In the United States, Jane Addams said that "the essential idea of Democracy" was to identify with the common lot. Half a world away in India, Gandhi claimed to be a democrat by virtue of his "complete identification with the poorest of mankind."[75]

— Chapter 3 —

Residents Leading Residents

W hile the bureaucrats of the Home Ministry pondered how to shape urban society, the residents of Tokyo banded together to solve their own problems. Local organizations varied in size from a few individuals with common interests to self-government associations that included everyone in the neighborhood. Two networks of organizations in Tokyo that tackled peculiarly urban problems were the neighborhood associations and the district welfare committees. It was these local organizations that served as schools on the benefits of civil associations. Despite rhetoric implying great antiquity, these organizations exemplified the inclusiveness of modern citizenship. Their cooperation with the police and the ward office in matters of health and local improvements established channels through which local leaders could press their interests upon the bureaucracy. Government investigations and regulations did little more than impose the appearance of central control.

Neighborhood Associations: Organization and Activities

The term "neighborhood association" is used here, not in the usual American sense of an assortment of local organizations, but as a translation of a specific Japanese term *chōkai* (sometimes expressed *chōn-aikai*), which means literally "association of those living within the *chō*." There is no exact equivalent in the English language or in the Western perception of the urban landscape for the Japanese term *chō*.[1] Westerners have organized the grid formed by city blocks by naming the streets and avenues that are the lines of the grid; the Japanese name the spaces formed by the intersections of the major thoroughfares. These named spaces are the *chō*. The heads of all households in one of those precisely defined areas were members of the neighborhood associations.

Chō originally meant "town," and the term was in use long before the sixteenth century when Tokugawa Ieyasu established Edo as his castle town. In Edo, as in other castle towns of the era, the word *chō* designated areas of the city where merchants and craftsmen lived. Workmen of a particular occupation, for instance carpenters or innkeepers, who lived in a single area provided their *chō* with its identity and sometimes its name. Landowners *(jinushi)* and house agents *(yanushi)* administered the *chō*, which was a religious and recreational as well as an occupational and residential unit. In the festival of the Sannō Shrine, each *chō* in Edo competed to have the best decorations and costumes. The *chō* were hierarchical communal groups, sometimes analogized as family, with the landlords as parents and the tenants of the back alleys *(tanako)* as children.[2] After the Meiji Restoration, the government divided all land in the newly named capital of Tokyo into *chō*, some of the larger of which were further subdivided into *chome*.

At the opening of the twentieth century, the fifteen wards were the lowest level of formal administration in Tokyo city. The *chō* existed as defined locations within the ward, but they had no legal status and no officials, either elected or appointed, with any binding authority. Nevertheless, the *chō* served certain administrative functions, for instance as an essential part of the mailing address and as a basic unit for the formation of police, school, welfare, and military reserve districts.

The neighborhood associations included as members the heads of all households in a *chō*. In some *chō*, membership was also open to those who owned offices, shops, factories, land, or buildings there. Usually, simply moving to the *chō* and paying dues entitled a resident to membership, although a few *chō* required introduction by two members or a vote of the officers. A sliding scale of dues in some *chō* made membership more readily attainable. In one *chō* in Honjo, the dues were two yen per month for major landlords, one yen for those with only one house, and three sen for those renting.[3]

The payment of dues underscores the fact that membership in the neighborhood associations was open and voluntary. Residence in the *chō* made one eligible for membership regardless of one's occupation, native place, or income, but residence in the *chō* and neighborhood association membership were not synonymous. The household head had to pay dues as a visible symbol of his willingness to join with his neighbors to work for the common good. Disobeying rules or failing to pay dues could be grounds for expulsion.

The policy of open, voluntary membership suited well the ever-changing population of Tokyo. If the neighborhood associations had restricted membership to those whose ancestors had been in the area for generations, the policy would have barred a sizable portion of the population from joining. In fact, there were numerous examples of heads of neighborhood associations in Tokyo who were born in other prefectures.[4] Most had come to Tokyo as adults. Thus, the neighborhood associations not only included migrants to the neighborhood but enabled such newcomers to exercise leadership in the community. The open membership of associations transcended distinctions in social status without by any means erasing them. The neighborhood associations were not social clubs. They usually met as a whole only once a year. These meetings were fairly large; in 1933, the average number of members in a neighborhood association in the original fifteen wards of the city was 276.[5] The open membership policy simply meant that the efforts of all household heads would be welcome in carrying out activities to improve the neighborhood. The assessment of dues on a sliding scale, although it permitted all residents to join, reinforced the economic hierarchy of the neighborhood.

The activities sponsored by the neighborhood associations made the *chō* more pleasant places to live in. At the simplest level, they formalized ordinary neighborliness: recognition of the joys and sorrows of nearby families and a helping hand in times of trouble. The associations gave small sums of money to families in the *chō* who celebrated a wedding or a birth or who suffered illness or death. When young men left for or returned from military service, the associations presented them with a flag or a small gift. The associations encouraged all children to attend school and thus prepare for productive lives. By mediating quarrels, the associations spared their members legal expenses and future bitterness.

The neighborhood associations organized Shintō shrine festivals and patriotic celebrations. Association members collected offerings and decorated the portable shrine used by the young men of the area to carry the deity through the streets. Neighborhood associations were instrumental in organizing the ceremonies, athletic meets, lantern parades, and entertainments held throughout the city in 1928 in celebration of the coronation of the Shōwa Emperor. In 1930, when the city of Tokyo celebrated its reconstruction from the earthquake of 1923, the neighborhood associations of Honjo Ward organized a lantern parade.[6]

A number of association activities contributed to the safety and upkeep of the *chō*. At night, members patrolled the area watching for fires or robbers, and by day they posted signs encouraging safety. All who lived in the *chō*, especially those who depended upon customers for income, wanted the streets in good condition. The associations were diligent in watering the pavement to settle the dust, putting up signs, and decorating street lamps. They were particularly active in matters relating to sanitation. They helped in the dredging of sewers, the cleaning of toilets, the disposal of waste, the extermination of mosquitoes, the administration of immunizations, and the inspections of homes for cleanliness.

By the mid-1920s, neighborhood associations had enrolled most of the residents in most parts of Tokyo. By 1925, there were some wards where every *chō* in the ward was included within one neighborhood association or another.[7] Further, residents joined in great numbers. By October 1, 1933, 77 percent of the households in the city (this was the expanded, thirty-five-ward city) were enrolled in neighborhood associations. The contribution of the neighborhood associations to the life of the city was considerable, even when measured in cold economic terms. In 1935, the total budget of all the neighborhood associations was equivalent to one-eighth of the tax revenue raised by the city.[8]

Origins

Modern Japan was heir not only to some of the largest commercial cities in the world but also to a rich tradition of urban, self-governing units. In fifteenth-century Kyoto, a *machi* (written with the same character as *chō*) was a row of houses. The term also represented a social entity, the residents of the households facing each other from the two sides of a street. The members of the *machi* were mutually responsible and mutually liable for fire and crime prevention and protection. In the sixteenth century, townsmen representatives *(machi sōdai)* virtually governed Kyoto.[9]

The Tokugawa political order, although it by no means permitted urban autonomy, depended upon townsmen and their self-governing units for the administration of the cities. In Osaka, predominantly a merchant city, townsmen administered the civilian sectors of the city. They conducted inquiries, transmitted communications, collected taxes, regulated commerce, and kept records. Even in a castle town such as Kanazawa, townsmen serving as city elders *(machidoshiyori)* played a significant role in managing urban affairs. Their duties included processing the complaints and petitions of townsmen, checking tax receipts, and assisting in the investigations of crimes. The city elders were assisted by inspectors *(yokome-kimoiri)* and ward representatives *(machi-kimoiri)*. In Edo, the *chō* were the administrative units held mutually responsible for surveillance and safety.[10]

Japanese conventional wisdom holds that neighborhood associations are very old and descended from even older and more venerable East Asian institutions. The five-man groups *(gonin gumi)*, the system of town elders *(machi sōdai)*, town managers *(sewanin)*, justices of the peace *(toshiba)*, young men's groups *(wakashūkai)*, and the local religious associations *(ujiko shūdan)* are among the institutions that are sometimes invoked as the pre-Meiji forerunners of the neighborhood associations.[11] This list includes both urban and rural institutions, informal local groups as well as bureaucratic controls imposed from above. The neighborhood associations were, of course, heir to the rich tradition of cooperation between bureaucrats and urban residents that these premodern organizations exemplified, but they were not direct lineal descendants of Edo administrative units.

The Meiji government abolished the Edo forms of self-government and took over many of their functions—tax collection, registration of births, local security, and fire fighting, for instance. The single most important instrument in this transformation was the Metropolitan Police Force, established on January 15, 1874, on the model of the Paris prefecture of police.[12]

Even if some remnants of the Edo system persisted, they did not exist in exactly the same place as before, if they were organized on the basis of the *chō*. That is, there was considerable discontinuity between the Edo *chō* and the *chō* of the fifteen wards of Tokyo city. In 1872, the land belonging to the shogunate and to the feudal lords was combined with traditionally commercial and residential *chō;* there were also occasional mergers thereafter of smaller *chō* into larger ones. Major revisions of the *chō* boundaries took place in some parts of the city as part of the restoration of the capital after the earthquake. Very few of the *chō* in the 1930s, then, had boundaries corresponding to any one Edo *chō*.

Further, specific evidence offered as proof that the neighborhood associations were directly descended from Edo institutions does not stand up well under scrutiny. Those claiming feudal origins for the neighborhood associations cite replies to a survey done by the city in 1933. The questionnaires asked, among other things, the date of the founding of each neighborhood association and the motivation for its founding. In their replies, several neighborhood associations asserted that their founding was related to one of the Edo forms of local organization such as five-man groups, town elders, or town managers. One factor that compromises these replies as proof of a direct connection between the Edo institutions and the neighborhood associations is the number of years intervening between the end of the Edo system of government and the time the questionnaires were filled out in the 1930s. It is unlikely that any association head of the 1930s had actually been active in any of the Edo units of self-government. These replies, then, may simply mean that the leaders of the 1930s believed they were continuing an older tradition of self-government. Some leaders may even have exaggerated the antiquity of their association in order to enhance its prestige.[13]

Let us examine a case from Honjo Ward. Tokuuemon-chō claimed descent from the system of city elders *(machi sōdai)*. By the time the city published this claim in 1934, Tokuuemon-chō no longer existed; on September 1, 1933, the northern section had become part of Tatekawa-chō 3- and 4-chome, and the southern part had been incorporated into Kikukawa-chō 2-chome. The Tokuuemon-chō that had existed prior to 1933 had been formed in 1872 from the merger of Honjo 1- and 2-chome, and the land of the Tanuma family.[14] Thus, whatever element of the tradition of city elders the Tokuuemon neighborhood association may have preserved, it certainly had not preserved it within exactly the same boundaries.

In fact, in this case, the claim of Edo origins for the neighborhood association may well really have been an assertion by the Uchida family of its continuous leadership in local affairs since the Edo period. The same man, Uchida Yasuuemon, appears to have headed the neighborhood association throughout the 1920s and 1930s. Uchida was born in Tokyo in 1854, and he may have lived in this neighborhood since birth. He (or a predecessor of the same name) served in the Honjo Ward Assembly in 1889. When the city redrew the *chō* boundaries in 1933, he became head of the neighborhood association in Tatekawa 3-chome.[15]

The bureaucratic authors of ward histories and guides to neighborhood associations asserted the antiquity of the associations in order to establish indigenous origins for relatively recent and modern institutions, which from the authors' point of view performed many useful functions. City officials welcomed help with inoculations, cleanliness inspections, and road repairs and were grateful when the associations dutifully sent representatives to patriotic festivities. Urban bureaucrats were pleased to have inclusive community organizations that could synthesize in the city the communal spirit of the rural village.

The neighborhood associations, however, were neither revivals of the urban past nor urban versions of the village. As noted above, there was virtually no continuity between these twentieth-century institutions and their putative Edo ancestors. The neighborhood associations were different in form and function from all of their Edo predecessors. The neighborhood associations were voluntary and inclusive of all households in the area. The membership of the Edo institutions was compulsory and usually limited to landowners, homeowners, and estate managers. In Edo, even the five-man groups may not have included tenants, who made up 60 percent of the population. Some scholars now stress that the five-man groups were more than mere control mechanisms. For the people enrolled in them, they served the same functions as family in matters relating to marriage, adoption, inheritance, and the guardianship of minors.[16] This sort of private matter (which one would certainly decide among members of one's own class) was precisely the kind of concern from which the neighborhood associations held themselves apart.

The Tokyo neighborhood associations emerged from the interaction between local voluntary organizations and the government. After the Meiji leaders abolished the Edo forms of local organization, the landlords and estate managers, through their ties with their tenants, continued to dominate the local affairs not subsumed under the Metropolitan Police. In the new Meiji order, there was no formal mechanism for carrying out certain activities that defined the community. Thus, from time to time, groups of residents organized on an ad hoc basis to carry out a shrine festival or to see young men of the neighborhood off to war. A fire in Kanda in 1881 inspired the residents of neighboring Shitaya Ward to set up an elaborate system of fire watches, for example. Many local organizations simply defined themselves as friendship societies. Such local groups sometimes organized on the basis of the *chō*. They had a wide variety of names, and they tended to have specialized and limited functions.[17]

The relationship between Shintō shrine associations and neighborhood associations was complex. In Shintō, shrines had spiritual responsibility for the residents within definite geographical limits, and the shrine associations consisted of the residents of the district where a particular deity was worshiped. Residents made small monetary gifts for the annual festival. The evidence suggests that the neighborhood associations absorbed the shrine organizations rather than that the shrines begat the neighborhood associations. Many neighborhood associations assisted in shrine festivals. In a survey by the Tokyo Municipal Research Council in April 1925, 112 of the 260 neighborhood associations of Kyōbashi, Ushigome, and Nihonbashi wards answered a question on their relationship to shrine associations. In 73.1 percent of the cases, the neighborhood association had taken over the activities of the shrine association.[18]

Despite numerous vague assertions that festivals were an important reason for organizing neighborhood associations, very few associations actually claimed descent from a shrine association. One reason for this discrepancy is undoubtedly that shrine districts generally encompassed more than one *chō*. Honjo, for instance, which had only twenty-one shrines in 1896, had three or four times that number of *chō*.[19] Once some force within the *chō* had generated a neighborhood association, the shrine could make use of it. The shrine, however, which had a territory larger than the *chō*, could not initiate a *chō*-level organization.

In the same era when local residents were sporadically organizing themselves on their own initiative, the prefecture could simply mandate new organizations into existence. In a law that went into effect on July 1, 1900, Tokyo prefecture prescribed the establishment of sanitation unions in each city and village to prevent the spread of disease and to disseminate knowledge of sanitation. Tokyo prefecture had established such unions on the ward, village, and city level during the cholera epidemics of 1886 and 1890. The prefectural authorities were not, however, the inventors of this political form. In the 1880s, political organizations had sought out experts on public health, and participants in the People's Rights Movement of the 1880s had organized themselves as sanitation unions. By 1892, a national association of sanitation associations was wealthy enough to contribute to Japan's first laboratory for infectious diseases.[20] The prefecture, then, in issuing its law of 1900 was simply regularizing and co-opting a type of local organization that had sprung up under volunteer auspices.

The significance of the regulation of 1900 for the future of local organizations in Tokyo was that it designated the *chō* as the basic unit of organization within the cities and required the head of every household to join. Many of these sanitation unions eventually withered away for lack of funds, although the law that required them remained the same. Nevertheless, their creation established the form that the neighborhood associations would take: an organization composed of all household heads in the officially designated *chō*. A number of ward histories suggest that the neighborhood associations developed from the sanitation unions. By the 1920s, most sanitation unions had become part of a neighborhood association.[21]

Gradually the functions of the various shrine and friendship associations were assumed by organizations having the form of the sanitation union. No doubt patrons of the local shrine, merchants hoping for better local services, and traditional local leaders all saw the advantages of a form that obligated every household in the *chō* to join. If nothing else, high membership would increase the income from dues. It is not clear whether friendship and patriotic organizations adopted this form or whether sanitation unions took on a number of additional functions.

The Russo-Japanese War spurred the growth of local associations. In this unprecedented national crisis, urban residents of both genders and all ages poured their energy into making condolence calls and providing aid for the families of soldiers away at the front. According to the Shitaya Ward history, residents organized themselves for these activities through the sanitation unions, now reborn as neighborhood associations. *Chō* organizations first used the term "neighborhood association" *(chōkai)* in Waseda-chō, Ushigome Ward, in 1900; in Nezu Shimizu-chō, Hongō Ward, in 1906; and in Yanagihara 3-chome, Honjo Ward, in 1906.[22] One indication that these multi-purpose neighborhood associations with broad membership had become common by 1921 is the fact that a magazine article of that date criticized the newly established district welfare committees of Tokyo as inappropriate foreign imports and suggested that the neighborhood organizations ought to have been used instead. In Shitaya Ward, by the end of 1922, there were enough neighborhood associations to justify linking them together in a formal league *(rengōkai)*.[23]

The Great Kantō Earthquake of 1923 provided the impetus to spread the neighborhood associations to every part of Tokyo. The associations proved their value as civil defense organizations through their activities on the day of the disaster and during the period of disorder that followed. Where formal associations already existed, the members assembled to fight fires and evacuate those in danger.[24] The associations served as vigilante and mutual aid associations as residents searched for bodies among the wreckage and ashes and tried to protect their few remaining possessions from looters.

Neighborhood associations were invaluable in administering relief programs in the weeks following the disaster. The fires had destroyed both the landmarks that defined addresses and the records that showed who belonged in the neighborhood. Only longtime residents knew who should get what. Through October 31, the Honjo Ward Office used neighborhood associations to distribute food. Where associations did not already exist, local leaders formed them. In Kayaba-chō, Honjo, which had no neighborhood association, a local resident, Kitamura Zensan, fetched supplies from the ward office and distributed them in the neighborhood. Twenty-three others joined Kitamura to provide watch patrols. They obtained cleaning supplies from the ward office and distributed them. Eventually, Kitamura provided funds for the formal creation of a neighborhood association.[25]

Even in districts less directly damaged by the earthquake, the enormity of the total disaster drew neighbors together into mutual support groups. In Koishikawa Ward, "the fear and horror brought by the Great Earthquake and Fire caused people to strengthen solidarity and provide local security. These associations continued to exist even after the earthquake and eventually became permanently established chōnaikai. Today there is almost no town which does not have chōnaikai." In an introductory essay to a collection of neighborhood association regulations, an author described the origins of the association in the residential district of Minami-chō, Ushigome, where he lived:

> The quake at last shook the residents of Minami-chō out of their isolated habitations and into the streets where they greeted those they chanced to meet with concern and asked after each other's safety. Slowly a sense of solidarity began to grow among members of the neighbourhood. There were worries about fire and concern about security at night as well as problems involved in food rationing, and as the residents worked out who would take turns each night to take the cart to pick up ration rice at the ward office or perform other jobs, somehow we achieved agreement, assigned jobs and collected money as necessary. In the process, a sense of community feeling at long last began to emerge. . . . Realizing that the earthquake disaster had brought us an unexpected gift in our new-found community feeling, we decided to make our association permanent.[26]

Unquestionably, the earthquake stimulated the creation of neighborhood associations. In their answers to the survey in 1934, 21 percent of the associations in the old section of the city gave the earthquake as the impetus for their founding. More were founded in the five years between the beginning of 1923 and the end of 1927 than in any other single five-year interval.[27] After 1923, neighborhood associations existed in virtually every *chō* of the original fifteen wards, and these neighborhood associations were voluntary. Although the government directive on sanitation unions provided their form, and the government relief policy at the time of the earthquake hastened their proliferation, the initiative for the founding of the neighborhood associations and the commitment to their perpetuation came from the local residents.

Leadership

Who were the local residents who led these associations? What were their economic interests? What were their ties to the wider society? By the mid-1920s, when the city authorities began their regular investigations of the associations, the general pattern was to have a head, an assistant head, and several directors. From five published lists of the heads of associations in Honjo, it is possible to draw a profile of the citizens who provided leadership to the associations. Custom varied from neighborhood to neighborhood as to the tenure of the heads. Although a few men held office continuously from 1925 to 1935, there were many areas where a different individual served as head each year. The number of associations in the ward fluctuated slightly. For the approximately seventy-eight associations, a total of 221 names are available. Of these 70 percent (or 153) can be identified by occupation.[28]

The outstanding characteristic of the leaders of the neighborhood associations in Honjo was their close connection with small-scale economic activity in the ward, usually within the particular *chō*. Nine of the association leaders were landowners and seven were landlords; thirty-nine were heads of factories within the ward.[29] Twelve were doctors and one was a dentist. An additional fifty-two were wholesalers or proprietors of shops, pawnshops, or bathhouses. Thus, well over half the leadership (or 120) derived their livelihood through the proprietorship of small individual enterprises, which it would have been inconvenient to move. These were the households that most needed a clean, safe, and orderly environment, and the heads of such households provided an overwhelming proportion of the neighborhood leaders.

In general, the officials of large factories and banks in the ward did not lead the neighborhood associations. In many cases, the managers of branches in Honjo did not live in the ward. In 1935, of fifteen officials of nine different branch banks in Honjo, only three lived there.[30] The owners of some of the factories were businessmen with property in many parts of Japan who had no particular reason to live in Honjo. Even those factory owners and bank managers who did reside in the ward seem not to have bothered with neighborhood affairs. The managers of several of the large factories—Great Japan Beer, Kurihara Spinning, and Hattori (Seikōsha) Watch, for instance—lived within their factory compounds but did not become leaders of neighborhood organizations.

Also absent from the rosters of the neighborhood leadership were company employees, wealthy doctors and lawyers, and entrepreneurs with investments throughout the city and nation. The Japanese sociologist Yazaki Takeo has noted this occupational pattern in the neighborhood associations throughout the city. He explains that those whose jobs took them to the central part of the city, whether as company men or government bureaucrats, devoted most of their energy to their employers. Often new to the city, they had little time for contact with their neighbors, especially since they knew that they might well be transferred soon to another city. The custom of erecting high walls around residences reinforced this independence from community life.[31]

Perhaps most important, there were virtually no bureaucrats or educators to be found among the leaders of the neighborhood associations. So the associations were not, in actuality any more than in origin, a simple extension of the leadership of the police, the ward office, or the educational hierarchy. The leadership of the neighborhood associations reflected the essentially local orientation of the institution.

The Neighborhood Associations and the Government

The nature of the neighborhood associations in prewar Tokyo has been obscured because the national government used the same term for the local organizations it mandated by law in 1940 as part of the wartime mobilization of the Japanese people. In 1940, the Home Ministry issued a directive entitled "Outline for the Organization of Neighborhood Associations and Village Associations" (Burakukai chōnaikai seibi yōkō), which ordered all towns, villages, and cities without such organizations to establish them immediately. Those areas in which associations already existed were to incorporate them into the local government apparatus. The Home Ministry issued its directive on neighborhood associations in conjunction with the establishment of the Imperial Rule Assistance Association (Taisei yokusankai). It listed, among the aims of the associations, dissemination of national policy and the achievement of a controlled economy.[32]

The neighborhood associations that had developed in Tokyo in the early decades of the twentieth century were incorporated into the national mobilization program. The city government had in fact already enlisted the neighborhood associations of Tokyo as support on the home front during the emergency created by the China Incident. In its proclamation of April 17, 1938, the city invoked the ancient traditions of the nation in its call for stronger local self-government to foster harmony and welfare at home.[33]

Although the neighborhood associations of Tokyo were absorbed into the war effort and although their form was adopted as the local unit for urban mobilization throughout Japan, they were not created as instruments of war. They did, however, owe their uniformity to the policies of urban administrators, and both before and after the China Incident, they worked closely with the city government. The question arises, then, whether the neighborhood associations were the instrument of neighborhood influence on the government or the means of government control over the neighborhoods.

The working relationship of the neighborhood associations with the municipal government, the police, and the ward office developed from a long tradition of private responsibility for the physical maintenance of urban neighborhoods and the preservation of social order therein. Until the Meiji Restoration of 1868, the ruling authorities had depended almost entirely upon local leadership for the governance of urban residents. Although after the Restoration the Metropolitan Police and the city government assumed many of what had been local responsibilities, local residents remained interested and involved in improving conditions in their neighborhoods. By the turn of the century, there were ward-level educational associations, physicians associations, and sanitation societies that sponsored various programs. Honjo Ward, for instance, had an educational society and a physicians society.[34]

School-related associations, based on school districts, were on an intermediate level between the ward and the neighborhood. Several of the schools in Honjo—Chūwa, Yokokawa, and Kikukawa, for instance—had such societies. In 1911, the Chūwa Society for the Encouragement of Learning, founded in 1900, gave one thousand yen toward the cost of an asphalt exercise area at the Chūwa School. In 1923, the society also sponsored a seaside school in the summer.[35] Such school-related associations, which improved the physical plant of the schools and provided special programs, must certainly have required cooperation with the Ministry of Education.

In periods of economic crisis, the local elite and the government worked together to carry out relief measures. In the summer of 1912, the high price of rice was causing some to go hungry, and a rice broker in Fukagawa gave one *shō* of rice to each of three thousand needy individuals within one of the police districts of the ward. That summer, the Honjo Rice Merchants Guild distributed rice among the poor of Honjo. The guild rented vacant houses as distribution centers, where they gave free rice to all who presented the special tickets that the police had distributed to the poor. In 1918, at the time of the rice riots, the government enlisted members of the Tokyo Prefecture Charity Association to supervise the bargain selling of rice.[36]

Neighbors sometimes cooperated with each other in order to protest the actions of the state. In 1890, angry property owners of Shitaya Ward objected strenuously to the plan of the Japanese National Railroad to construct a line at ground level from Ueno to Akihabara. More than three thousand signed a petition to the government authorities. In 1893, residents of Shiba Ward raised a number of arguments against an infectious disease laboratory and hospital proposed for their neighborhood. In 1913, landlords, landowners, and residents of three neighborhoods in the same ward feared that a new streetcar line would hurt their businesses. A deputation of fourteen, representing a thousand residents, took their message directly to the chief of the electric bureau.[37]

Sometimes the community rallied to urge officials to act on their behalf. Ward assembly members from Asakusa personally visited the headquarters of the Metropolitan Police Force on behalf of residents near Asakusa Park who wished the police to take action against prostitutes who were soliciting in the neighborhood. Apparently, the assembly members were effective messengers. A few months later, eleven plainclothesmen, detailed to clean up the street, arrested twenty-three women in the park and sentenced them to prison for "loitering on public ground."[38]

Occasionally, residents directed their ire toward private industry. In February 1911, residents and businessmen of Fukagawa Ward complained about the smoke and ash emanating from the Portland Cement factory. They claimed that the ash constituted a health hazard when it fell on rice, barley, and other articles of food that were displayed for sale in shops. The neighbors went so far as to demand the removal of the factory. After several weeks of negotiation, the company agreed to leave the area by 1916.[39]

To the degree to which the neighborhood associations can be considered successors to the political agitators disguised as sanitation societies of the late nineteenth century or to the spirited neighborhood protests of the early twentieth century, the authorities succeeded in taming their beast. In the years following the earthquake, the neighborhood associations often worked with the authorities, and they rarely became instruments of citizen protest. The heads of the associations met with the ward heads to plan the local festivities that were carried out in connection with public events such as the coronation of the Shōwa Emperor (1928) and the ceremonies marking the completion of the reconstruction following the earthquake (1930). Some associations worked with the police in carrying out the twice-yearly great cleaning and other projects connected with sanitation.

The formation of networks *(rengōkai)* of associations within each ward facilitated cooperation between the voluntary neighborhood associations and the formal administrative apparatus. By 1935, fifteen of the thirty-five wards of the expanded city had such networks at the ward level. The first of these ward-level networks was formed in Shitaya in 1922, even before the earthquake. The network for Honjo was founded in April 1931.[40]

An examination of the form and activities of the Honjo network gives some idea of how the networks assisted administration. First (and perhaps most important), the ward head was head of the network, and the network had its headquarters inside the ward office. Thus, the networks linked the administrative hierarchy with that of the voluntary neighborhood associations. The entire network met only once a year, but the directors *(riji)* met monthly, thus giving the ward head regular contact with the neighborhood associations. The activities of the network included providing recreation for health workers and collecting money for the unfortunate, such as the victims of natural disasters in the Kansai region and those suffering from bad harvests in the northeastern part of Japan. The network was also the arbiter of disputes between different neighborhood associations. Networks directly aided the ward office in collecting money for trees along the roads, evaluating the members of the district welfare committees, and conducting the national census.[41]

Because of these cooperative efforts, the municipal government was eager to have up-to-date information on the condition of the neighborhood associations. The city made official surveys in 1928,

1934, and 1935. The municipal assembly also took an interest in the associations. A committee to investigate the neighborhood associations and to develop a policy regarding their form and their limits was appointed in September 1929.[42]

In general, the governing authorities had a positive attitude toward the associations. Municipal publications stressed the importance of the neighborhood associations, both for the proper development of the city and for the happiness of the citizens. Bureaucrats fretted that the associations had never been officially recognized and that there was no regular system of cooperation with the ward offices; that is, the bureaucrats wished to institutionalize the system of cooperation that had gradually evolved. The neighborhood associations themselves, however, were not problems. They were highly valued for their role in local self-government and for their close connection with the everyday life of the citizens. They represented a mutuality of interest among residents that could never exist on a ward or city level.[43]

Thus, the municipal government strongly endorsed the concept of neighborhood associations. It used the associations to carry out certain of its own policies. The associations did not, however, become arms of either the municipal or the national government until after the outbreak of war with China. The projects on which the administration and the associations worked together prior to 1937 were nearly always matters of health, compassion, and recreation rather than overt social and political control. The government was becoming involved in the concerns of the associations, which is quite different from the associations' becoming the creatures of the government. Street decorations, cleanliness inspections, and national festivals did little to impede labor unions, socialists, right-wing fanatics, or even corrupt politicians.

District Welfare Committees: Origins

The district welfare committees *(hōmen iin seido)* were the product of cooperation between the Home Ministry and the local elite. Their purpose was to enlist the local elite to aid in the administration of poor relief. In Tokyo, the municipal social bureau—once it was established in 1920—bore responsibility for poor relief, and one of its first acts was to organize a system of district welfare committees. Through these committees, the social bureau recruited and supervised hundreds of volunteers who investigated neighboring households that received public aid or that might potentially need supplementary support.

The committees were not peculiar to Tokyo, nor were the ones set up there the earliest examples of the system. Some authorities cite, as the first fully developed example of this system in Japan, the district welfare committees that Hayashi Ichizō, governor of Osaka, established in that prefecture in October 1918. Other authorities hail as the pioneer effort the public welfare advisors *(saisei komon)* that Kasai Shinichi, governor of Okayama prefecture, appointed in May 1917.[44]

Kasai and Hayashi organized their committees out of the same concern for social order that had inspired the creation of the Tokyo social bureau. Kasai feared that the poor might turn to suicide, crime, or worst of all, socialism.[45] Ogawa Shigejirō, a scholar who helped Hayashi set up committees in Osaka, regarded the committees as Japanese counterparts of the American system of probation, parole, and big brothers, all three of which used close supervision, sometimes by volunteers, to prevent antisocial behavior.[46]

Ogawa Shigejirō's writings on the Osaka district welfare committees provide a window into the thought of one of the architects of the committee system. In Osaka, the system began with 527 committee members for 35 districts, most of them in industrial areas. The first committee members were individuals who had done relief work during the recent rice riots, and the geographic units corresponded to existing school districts. Through their committee work, responsible citizens would prevent future riots by getting aid to the truly needy without accidentally selling relief rice to the undeserving, as had occurred during the rice riots. Civilian committee members could secure information on the needy (and thus potentially revolutionary), without provoking the resistance that would be inevitable in a police survey of the neighborhood. At the same time, the committee members could provide surveillance over individuals released from prison or out on bail or parole, habitual criminals, delinquent youth, prostitutes, and the unemployed.[47]

Ogawa believed that the gap between rich and poor existed not because the poor were lazy but because they spent beyond their small incomes. Ogawa's solution was to bring the poor under the supervision of the middle class, from which all 750 Osaka committee members came. The relationship between the committee member and his charges, which should develop gradually through a series of visits of the committee member to the poor household, should be an ideal Confucian one—like that of a parent to a child, an elder brother to a younger brother, a lord to his retainer, or a friend to a friend.[48]

Ogawa was oblivious to the economic conflicts inherent in the relationship between the middle class and the poor households he wished to entrust to their care. The members of the middle class he most highly recommended for membership on the district welfare committees were those who had regular contact with the poor: doctors, religious leaders, pawnbrokers, druggists, rental agents, and the keepers of rice, fish, vegetable, and charcoal shops. It does not seem to have occurred to him that a householder with a small income might well blame the excess of his expenditures not on his own lack of wisdom but on the unreasonably high prices of the shopkeepers, high rents of the rental agents, and the high interest rates of the pawnbrokers.[49]

Apologists for the district welfare committees cited precedents from both Japanese tradition and European and American social work. Inevitably, they mentioned the five-man groups (gonin gumi) of Tokugawa Japan.[50] The connection is tenuous. The five-man groups did include elements of mutual aid, but the Tokugawa government required commoners to enroll in them in order to establish joint responsibility for tax payments and crime prevention. They were thus scarcely voluntary. In the modern district welfare committees, by contrast, there was no surveillance or joint responsibility among equals; rather, the affluent supervised the poor and committee members suffered no punishment for crimes committed by those under their supervision.

The modern district welfare committees in Japan bore a somewhat stronger resemblance to their most often mentioned European precedent, the Elberfeld System (named for the German city in which it was first introduced in the 1850s).[51] In Elberfeld, the first volunteers to engage in poor relief were members of the city council. These unpaid officials were held responsible for the proper use of the community resources placed at their disposal. Wise stewardship required thorough examination of each dependent, continued careful guardianship throughout the period of dependence, and constant effort to enable the recipient of aid to regain economic independence.

The municipal council delegated its responsibilities to distinguished residents, whom it appointed "visitors" *(armenpflegern)*. Each was responsible for calling on four or fewer households, keeping constantly informed of their needs, and exerting a beneficial influence over the family. Several such units formed a district, and the visitors of each district met regularly to decide on the amount, type, and duration of assistance to be given. The superintendent of each district served as liaison with the managing board. The municipal council chose the members of the board, who in turn appointed the visitors whom they supervised. All positions except that of the chairman of the board were honorary rather than salaried. Nevertheless, the board made special efforts to recruit for service citizens of modest means: tradesmen, mechanics, and the better class of laborers.

The Elberfeld System was simply one example of a practice that was widespread in Europe and the United States in the late nineteenth century. In the United States and England, "friendly visiting" brought system and science to the existing custom whereby women of wealth and social position gave moral instruction and material aid to the worthy poor. The traditional charitable lady of wealth had delivered baskets of food; the more modern friendly visitor brought scientific information about nutrition. Friendly visitors entered the homes of the poor to try by personal influence and practical suggestion to improve their condition. The visitors investigated claims for aid and referred the needy to appropriate agencies. In the United States, by the turn of the century, many volunteers were directing their energies to the settlement house movement and paid staff began to assume the tasks of volunteers. By 1920, the professional caseworker had displaced the friendly visitor in New York.[52]

The Japanese adaptation of these Western forms reflected Japanese values in several respects. Because Japan was not nearly as affluent a country as the United States, there was a practical element in instituting an elaborate system of volunteers in Japan, just at the very time that professionally trained and paid social workers were replacing such volunteers in New York. The institution of this system coincided, not with what W. Dean Kinzley has termed the Japanese "discovery of poverty" in the nineteenth century, but with the state assumption of responsibility for social policy following the rice riots of 1918.[53] The Japanese bureaucrats, then, created a system of volunteers in Japan in order to supervise closely the economic conditions of the urban poor, and to do so without expending additional state funds. Invocation of the German model enabled Japanese men to recruit male volunteers without any mention of the fact that in England and the United States most friendly visitors were women, a fact that was well known in Home Ministry circles.[54]

Implementation in Tokyo

The first effort to introduce district welfare committees to Tokyo proved abortive. In 1918, the Tokyo Prefecture Social Work Society proposed to use its own members to investigate poverty and carry out relief work. This prefectural network was abolished in 1922, not long after the much more effective municipal system went into operation.[55]

The real beginning of district welfare committees in Tokyo was in December 1920, when the Tokyo municipal social bureau created six districts in Fukagawa Ward and four in Shitaya Ward and thus inaugurated permanent district welfare committees. The bureau established the first committees in areas where workers with low incomes lived. In 1922, the system expanded, almost to its full size, with the addition of nineteen new districts, including six in Honjo.[56]

The main purpose of the district welfare committees was to investigate and improve living conditions in Tokyo. The head of the municipal social bureau chose distinguished residents of a district to be committee members. Each member of the committee served two years.[57] In general, the police district defined the geographical extent of the welfare district, but officials modified this rule to accommodate the terrain or local custom. For instance, Honjo Ward, with only four police districts, had six welfare districts. The two welfare districts that Shiba Ward established in 1922 apparently did not follow the boundaries of the police jurisdictions, for in 1934 the two districts were reorganized as three to make them conform to the police system.[58]

Every district had about ten committee members. These men chose from among themselves a committee head and a deputy, and they met once a month with the committee head presiding. The heads of each district, in turn, formed an assembly with the head of the social bureau as its chairman. Regulations permitted the appointment of councillors and advisors. Police chiefs, ward heads, the heads of the local medical societies, and other local notables served as councillors.

The advisors, men with academic knowledge or practical experience in district work, planned improvements in the system.[59]

The committee members recorded information about households receiving aid on cards, thus coining a new term for the poor: "card class." Investigators classified the households in one of two categories of poverty. In the first class were those unable to exist without help from public or private agencies. In the second class were those households that were just barely able to maintain economic independence.[60] Each district had an office, where the cards were kept, and one salaried employee who took responsibility for the office records, communication among the committee members, and liaison with the city social bureau. In addition to their investigative work, the committee members also took responsibility for the unemployed and the health of pregnant women, nursing women, and children. They provided advice on household management and child rearing, free medical care for the sick and wounded, and protection for juvenile and elderly victims of abuse. They mediated disputes, relieved poverty, lead the improvement of public morals, and promoted improvement in the quality of life.[61] In other words, the district welfare committee members shared all of the responsibilities of the social bureau.

The 1923 earthquake temporarily halted the progress of the committee system. Most of the twenty-nine districts in 1923 were in the low city, the area most damaged by the earthquake. In Fukagawa Ward, fire destroyed almost all of the district offices, and officials did not complete the investigation necessary to reestablish the card system until 1925. Between 1925 and 1933, the system grew to include the affluent wards of the old city. Each of the remaining wards established one district; Hongō in 1925, Azabu and Ushigome in 1928, Akasaka in 1932, and Nihonbashi (the last of the original fifteen wards to establish a district) in 1933.[62]

After the earthquake, the committee system was even more important in Tokyo as a means of extending aid to the needy. In December 1924, committee members helped administer a gift from the imperial household for medical treatment of the poor. The committee members distributed tickets entitling the needy to free care from local physicians, and they took general charge of the patients. This responsibility was thenceforth part of the annual year-end duties of the committee members. In 1929, the committee members began administering a loan fund, which advanced capital for worthy enterprises.

Beginning in 1930, each district office stored rice to distribute when rain, snow, or any other natural disaster prevented the poor from working.[63]

The responsibilities of the committees were further expanded in the 1930s. The Relief Law, which the Diet passed in 1929, made the district welfare committees an integral part of the relief system. In 1933, the district welfare committee system in Tokyo extended its services to people living on boats in the city's waterways. Other types of social work—in people's halls and day nurseries, for instance—came under committee jurisdiction in 1934.[64]

As far as the district welfare committees functioned in accordance with their stated goals, they served the social bureau well. Volunteer labor extended the range of the bureau's services. Each poor family received aid (for instance, year-end gifts and medical benefits) that significantly exceeded the simple rice allowance stipulated in the Meiji Poor Law. In addition, the investigative work of the committees extended both the control and the benefits of the social bureau to several times the number of households actually receiving relief. In 1931 (when the city still consisted of but fifteen wards) only 5,961 households received relief, but 29,667 households were enrolled in the card class and were thus under the supervision of committee members.[65] The investigative work of the committees deterred fraud and abuse of state benevolence and thus enabled the state to make the best use of its expenditures on aid payments and welfare facilities. The committee members were also the crucial link between the city's welfare facilities and the potential users of those services.

Conflicts of Interest

The extension of poor relief into the neighborhoods would translate into direct political control of the poor only if the members of the district welfare committees shared the goals of the social bureau. At the national level, district welfare committee members dramatically expressed their solidarity with the Home Ministry by lobbying for implementation of the Relief Law passed by the Diet in 1929. When their pressure on Finance Minister Inoue Junnosuke proved ineffective, they petitioned the emperor. Satō Aizō, chairman of the first district of Honjo, and 1,115 others from throughout the country signed the petition, which was presented on February 16, 1931.[66] In this case, then, the district welfare committee members constituted a new interest group in national politics.

By and large, however, the members of the Tokyo district welfare committees were not dutiful employees of the social bureau. Rather, they were volunteers, residents of the community with economic and political interests of their own. The district welfare committees were, in fact, local organizations. Responsible property owners, with the approval and blessing of the city, gathered together on a regular basis to investigate and regulate the lives of the local poor. As duly constituted local philanthropic bodies, the committees contributed to the corporate life of their neighborhoods. Some engaged in relief work following the earthquake. When the Shōwa Emperor was enthroned in 1928, each district welfare committee in Honjo undertook a special project. Most committees distributed relief tickets to the poor, but one committee showed movies and gave mirrors to several shrines in the ward.[67]

The local character of the committees remained intact, and the bureaucracy was never able to impose total uniformity on the volunteers. There was considerable variation from the general rule of thumb that each district should have ten committee members—most of them had more: in 1934 the three districts in Shiba had 25, 13, and 23; in 1932 the four districts of Shitaya had 18, 21, 12, and 30; in 1938 the two districts of Kyōbashi had 32 and 31. Even within one district, there was often variation from year to year in the number of members for the district. It is not surprising, then, that some district committee members had far more households under their care than did others. In 1936 in Shiba Ward, each committee member had over a hundred households to care for; in Nihonbashi, the number was closer to sixty.[68]

Despite these anomalies, the institutional arrangements created the impression that the bureaucrats controlled the volunteers. The municipal social bureau initiated the committees. The social bureau or the city or the ward bureaucracy at all times retained control over both the appointment of volunteers and decisions on aid. In each district, there was a paid employee who was responsible to the city administration rather than to the committee.[69]

Nevertheless, the district welfare system was never free from the suspicion that the funds and the activities of the committees were being used for political ends. Bureaucratic supervision and paid employees proved weak bulwarks against self-interest. The guidelines for the Tokyo district welfare committees stipulated that the members be men with substantial time and wealth who had lived in the district for several years.[70] In point of fact, the members of district welfare committees were often proprietors of local businesses. They were the keepers of shops that sold aluminum goods, tobacco, medicine, Western clothing, secondhand clothing, sake and rice, or they were the heads of transport or printing or precious metals companies or the owners of restaurants or doctors in local private practice. Some were wholesalers of sake or fish. So close was the connection between local business interests and the committees that there were even instances of business owners who lived outside the ward who nevertheless served as district welfare committee members in the place where their business was located.[71]

These local businessmen invested their time in district committee work because they expected that the onerous tasks would bring them direct or indirect rewards. They were willing to join hands with the municipal administration to maintain social order because the existing order worked to their benefit. The same community of interest with the local neighborhood that inspired them to become district welfare committee members might equally motivate them to run for the municipal or prefectural assembly or to support a neighbor who was doing so. As a member of a legislative body or the friend of a member, they could win advantages for the neighborhood. Not surprisingly, some property-owning district welfare committee members ran for political office; many served in ward assemblies, and a few reached higher representative bodies such as the prefectural assembly.[72]

Those outside the system, particularly those who had their own agenda for mobilizing the working classes, were quick to point out the potential conflict of interest. Majima Kan, a proletarian political party member from Honjo to the municipal assembly, soon after his election in 1929 inquired in the assembly about the procedure for selecting welfare committee members. He told the mayor that he had heard that these positions were limited to men with no political connections, but he wondered whether this was actually possible.[73] In fact, Majima was quite right; there were committee members who engaged in partisan politics.

To benefit from the local connections inherent in the welfare committee system, a candidate for office need not serve on the district welfare committee himself. According to a 1933 article in a Tokyo newspaper, political candidates who refrained from serving as welfare commissioners simply encouraged their campaign workers to fill the positions. The duties of a committee member, which included calling on the poor, easily served as a cover for house-to-house solicitation of votes. Under such circumstances, the year-end charitable distribution of goods became almost indistinguishable from vote-buying. Later the same year, in response to such charges, the municipal social bureau established a committee to oversee the selection of district welfare committee members.[74] It is doubtful, however, that any single committee could resolve the underlying differences between the aims of the bureaucracy and those of the volunteers.

The political proclivities of the district welfare committees were an unintended consequence of using the middle class to mediate the gap between rich and poor. In his early advocacy of the welfare committees, Ogawa Shigejirō envisioned the warmth of personal friendship overcoming all resentments and animosities and perhaps drawing the poor into the ranks of the middle class. His plan, of course, placed the poor squarely under the control of the middle class. There could, however, be no guarantee that the local middle class and the bureaucracy would always have the same aims. Ogawa wanted the middle class to help preserve social order in the nation as a whole. The shopkeepers, landlords, and pawnbrokers whom he recommended for membership on the committees because of their daily close contact with the poor had a vested interest in the existing economic order of the neighborhood. The poor should not be allowed to perish, because then they would cease to buy food, pay rent, and take out loans. Whereas the district welfare committee members would certainly not like to see their clientele organized into a class-based movement, their more immediate concern was for social, political, and economic advantages such as prestige in the neighborhood, votes for local elections, and steady customers.

An example from literature provides additional evidence that the district welfare committees were more effective in preserving the tyranny of the local elite over the poor than in ferreting out dangerous thoughts. In a story by Miyamoto Yuriko written in 1938, Tsutomu, a young man engaged in leftist political work, brought his entire family to live in Tokyo. When his younger sister developed tuberculosis and required hospitalization, the family had no other alternative but to turn to an uncle who worked in a ward office. Through his government connections, they were able to get a district committee to provide medical care for the sister.[75]

Miyamoto was herself part of the leftist movement in the 1930s, and we can trust that her story reflects the experience of the politically suspect rather than the police, of the beneficiaries of public aid rather than its providers. One significant point in Miyamoto's story is the implication that, without connections, the free medical care of the district committee would not have been available. Another implication is that, although Tsutomu had suffered police arrest in the past and was under constant surveillance from the police for his proletarian activities, the police had not bothered to communicate this to the district welfare committee, whose services were available to him as long as he had connections. Obviously the district welfare committees were not an effective part of the police surveillance network. The most unbearable part of the sister's illness and death was not any observable connection between the district committee and the police, but the overbearing attitude of the uncle's third wife. Thus, the help from the district welfare committees was available only at a price, but the price was enduring the arrogance and superior attitude of relatives with money and connections, not enduring police surveillance.

The neighborhood associations and the district welfare committees each operated through a partnership of government cooperation with local volunteers. In the case of the neighborhood associations, the original impetus came from local concerns, but the government eventually succeeded in standardizing the groups and linking them into hierarchies in touch with the local government. The district welfare committees began at the initiative of the municipal social bureau, but they retained an independence that permitted members of the committees to purchase votes or tyrannize their relatives. Within these institutions, there remained a great deal of room to maneuver.

The links that neighborhood associations and district welfare committees provided between politically ambitious local leaders and the poor resembled the connection between political machines and the poor in American cities. In both Japan and the United States, local leaders could provide the poor with access to medical care, connections to get jobs, and goods such as rice and coal. In the United States, the machine, which asked only for loyal votes in exchange for benefits, provided a welcome alternative to charity societies, with their narrow definition of need. The contrast between the warmth of political largess and the coldness of public charity in the United States reflected ethnic divisions; the machine politicians were, like the poor, immigrants from Ireland, Italy, Germany, or Bohemia, whereas the members of the local charity societies were usually native born and Protestant.[76]

In ethnically homogeneous Japan, the political parties never established the equivalent of the American ward and precinct committees. They did, however, welcome into their ranks elected representatives who had used service in neighborhood associations or district welfare committees to secure a local electoral base. Inadvertently, the Japanese bureaucracy provided the political parties with the mechanisms to link welfare benefits with votes. In Chicago, an aspiring politician joined the party and served a long apprenticeship before he achieved elected office. A. J. Cermak, mayor of Chicago from 1931 to 1933, started his political career by tacking up tax notices, joining fraternal organizations, and founding a neighborhood improvement association.[77] In Tokyo, neighborhood associations and district welfare committees provided a similar educational experience for the politically ambitious. The parties then absorbed the most successful graduates of these schools of civic association.

— Chapter 4 —

National Networks in the Neighborhood

The peculiar characteristics of Japan's largest cities, which inspired bureaucrats to establish social welfare facilities and foster urban community organizations, did not exempt cities from programs designed for the entire country. In the decade following the Russo-Japanese War, the officials in the various ministries of the Japanese state stumbled over each other in their efforts to preserve the best customs of the past and prepare each citizen to better contribute to future national development. Local organizations linked to the central government were invariably the bureaucratic means to the ideological end. As with the neighborhood associations, bureaucrats invoked traditional Japanese institutions to justify the hierarchies of local branches that formed a pyramid extending upward through ward, city, and prefectural organizations to the national level. Often these hierarchies also served to bring under government control voluntary associations that had sprung up at local initiative. Two of the most pervasive of these networks were the Imperial Military Reserve Association and young men's associations.

In the city, where a high turnover in the local population had destroyed most vestiges of traditional village organizations, these branches and associations were not simply new names for existing patterns of organization; rather, the national models brought new forms to a growing and diverse population in need of structure. Local voluntary committees may spring into existence at the behest of government officials, but they neither continue in existence nor operate effectively unless they meet the needs of the volunteers. The local units of the reservists and the young men's associations penetrated below the lowest administrative unit, the ward, and involved the residents of the *chō*. The new organizations that they created within the neighborhood were concerned with local needs. At the same time, these local units brought the national concerns of their parent organizations right into the neighborhood. Although it has been an axiom of modern Japanese history that these hierarchies mobilized the population of Japan for nationalistic and militaristic ends, the local branches remained local organizations and were used for local ends. Activities included not only overt demonstrations of patriotism but also recreation, education, and even electoral politics.

The Reservists

The Imperial Military Reserve Association (Teikoku zaigō gunjinkai) was a private association founded in 1910 by the Army Ministry in order to broaden its support within Japanese society. Even when it became an official organization *(chokurei dantai)* in 1936, the service ministers directed the local reservist branches rather than commanding them. Although from its beginning the association invited men enlisted in the navy to join and although a naval commander, Yoshikawa Yasuhira of Chōshū, was among the officers who planned the organization, the navy did not officially participate until 1914 and even thereafter remained a minor force in the organization. Because the army was four times the size of the navy, veterans of the navy made up only about 2.5 percent of the membership and only about a quarter of the headquarters staff positions.[1]

The new organization made full use of its close connection with the imperial institution, and the opening ceremonies for the association took place on the emperor's birthday, November 3, 1910. Prince

Fushimi, a member of the imperial family, served as president. But it was the army minister, Terauchi Masatake, who, as the first chairman of the association, gave the keynote address.[2]

The guiding force in establishing the reservist association was Tanaka Giichi of the Army Ministry. Whereas some generals wanted a reservist organization strictly limited to veterans, which could be used for post-service training and for the emergency recall of ex-service men, Tanaka envisioned an association that could be an instrument of social education. He made membership in the association voluntary and extended eligibility for membership to all who had passed the conscription physical regardless of whether they had served on active duty.[3]

A number of factors inspired Tanaka and his associates to found the Imperial Military Reserve Association in 1910. One was a desire to preserve the sympathy and pride for their army that the Japanese had demonstrated in the Russo-Japanese War. These military leaders feared that decadent and materialistic influences from the West would corrupt the moral fiber of the Japanese people. They also were intensely concerned for Japan's national security in an increasingly hostile and complex international environment.[4]

Although the Army Ministry remained very much in control of the headquarters of the Imperial Military Reserve Association, it was not possible in a voluntary organization to exercise control down to the grassroots level. The regiment was the basis for the chapters *(shi)* of the association and the branches were at the city, ward, or village level. Since the wards of Tokyo were divided between two separate regiments (Azabu and Hongō), there was no municipal unit intervening between the regiment and the ward.

The architects of the Imperial Military Reserve Association built upon a foundation of thousands of local martial and veterans groups that had sprung up at local initiative throughout the country, some as early as 1877 but most after the Sino-Japanese and Russo-Japanese Wars. Many of the eleven thousand such groups in 1910 were military in their activities rather than in their membership; that is, local leaders, whether veterans or not, joined together to perform services for soldiers from their local area. These groups performed the same sorts of duties later taken on by the reserve branches and subunits: seeing off soldiers, welcoming them back, and consoling bereaved families.[5]

The capital city produced many such groups. Residents formed martial societies in a number of Tokyo wards during the Sino-Japanese War; only later did they formalize their organizations. For instance, in Azabu Ward, the Azabu Ward Martial Society (Azabu-ku heijikai) held its founding meeting in 1900. The head of the society was the ward head, and several members of the ward assembly served as the executive committee. Hongō, Nihonbashi, and Asakusa wards had similar organizations, also dating from the Sino-Japanese War. During the Russo-Japanese War, local relief organizations proliferated. In Azabu, an association for the relief of families of soldiers sent a monthly allowance to the bedridden parents of an only son serving in the military.[6]

In Tokyo, the ward-level branches of the Imperial Military Reserve Association seem to have paralleled rather than replaced the existing martial societies. In 1934, of the fifteen wards in the old part of the city, six were contributing to some sort of military society in addition to the ward branch of the reservist society. Azabu Ward was not one of those, but the Azabu Ward Martial Society, formally constituted in 1900, continued in existence until 1940.[7]

Branches of the Imperial Military Reserve Association appeared in every ward in Tokyo soon after the formal opening ceremonies on November 3, 1910. Membership in reservist branches was voluntary and the members chose their leaders from among themselves, but effective administrative guidance speeded the process. The Asakusa Ward history provides us with a glimpse of how the civilian authorities of the wards organized a voluntary association in accordance with official guidelines. The ward head called upon Hagino Kitarō, a local resident with the rank of first lieutenant in the infantry, to head a committee to form a ward branch. Hagino became the first head of the branch when it held its opening ceremony on December 4. Thus, the ward heads, employees of the Home Ministry, exercised the only effective supervision of the local branches. The regulations of the Asakusa branch enjoined members to cooperate with the ward office and with the police, both of which were under the jurisdiction of the Home Ministry. Usually the office of the military reserve branch was inside the ward office.[8]

Each branch was further subdivided into squads (han). Asakusa had fifteen, Azabu twelve, Koishikawa four, Kōjimachi ten, Kyōbashi nine, Nihonbashi seven, and Shiba six. Each squad, in turn, could be divided into teams *(kumi)*. In Honjo, the *chō* was the unit of organization for the seventy-six teams listed after the earthquake.[9] In all wards, the subunits of the reservist association respected *chō* boundaries. The definition of squads by *chō*, with every *chō* assigned to a squad, meant that there was a designated squad for everyone who had passed the conscription physical. This pattern indicates that the definition of reservist subunits was not left to the whim of local organizers.

In Tokyo, actual enrollment never realized the high numbers possible in this organizational format. The average Tokyo branch enrolled only from 15 to 20 percent of the men between the ages of twenty and forty in the ward. These figures reflected the mobile population, the diversity of occupations, and the looser social organization of the city in comparison with agricultural villages. A smaller percentage of young men passed the conscription physical in nonagricultural wards of Tokyo than in the countryside, but the difference in physical fitness was not nearly as great as the difference in enrollment.[10]

Factories provided an alternative to residential neighborhoods for organizing reservist units. When Tanaka traveled to Europe in 1914, the German chief of staff, Erich von Falkenhayn, lectured him on the efficacy of factory branches. First set up in Japan in 1915, such branches numbered 257 by 1926, and 567 by 1937. Since in 1924 Tokyo alone had 375 factories employing thirty or more workers, factory branches were far from encompassing all industrial workers. Usually they existed in large establishments such as the Ishikawajima shipyard, the Tokyo Matsuzakaya department store, and the Ōmiya yards of the national railroad.[11]

The regular activities of the Honjo reservist branch were speech meetings, target practice, and welcome and farewell parties for those entering or leaving the services.[12] The speech meetings and the target practices provided the "continuing education" Tanaka had envisioned. At the same time, both the practical activities and the parties were occasions for young men of the ward to gather and reaffirm their membership in that particular urban community. The Honjo branch and its subunits formed an organizational mechanism for members to participate in events of municipal and national importance. On May 15, 1930, when the city of Tokyo celebrated the completion of its reconstruction following the earthquake, for example, the reservists sponsored a lantern parade for the children of the ward and distributed cakes afterward.[13]

The branches and subunits of the Imperial Military Reserve Association constituted potential allies for either side in local civil disturbances. Government officials and major capitalists presumed that the reservists were their allies and called on them for support against strikers and rioters. In the rice riots of 1918, the reservists proved unreliable allies. About 10 percent of those indicted for rioting were reservists, including thirteen from Tokyo. Even when they proved reliable, the reservists were not necessarily effective. In Fukuoka, officials of the Mitsui mines who organized local reservists on behalf of the company, found that the workers treated the reservists like strike breakers. Reservist participation in the riots was more common in the countryside than in the city. In agricultural villages, a high proportion of those eligible joined the reservist organization, which was then, in effect, an organization of the adult males of the community. In some villages this was an economically homogeneous group who perceived their interests to be threatened by outsiders. Thus, it is not surprising that individual reservists led their community in resistance to those held responsible for the unreasonably high price of food.[14]

The 1923 earthquake created a situation in Tokyo where all residents shared a common affliction. Under these circumstances, reservists, together with young men's and neighborhood associations, engaged in watch patrols and relief work. In Honjo, reservists fought fires, cared for the wounded, facilitated communication, patrolled the area, distributed food and water, repaired roads, and directed traffic. The Honjo reservists, who operated as *chō*-level teams, no doubt overlapped in membership with the neighborhood associations.[15]

The earthquake sharpened awareness of the importance of local groups. In September 1924, reservist organizations in Kanda, Azabu, Hongō, Akasaka, and Yotsuya wards discussed the advisability of creating a permanent organization in Tokyo to help the police and the army in times of calamity or emergency. The principal aims of the organization, tentatively named the Keikyūtai, would be to maintain order and to protect life and property. In March 1926, the Tokyo municipal assembly unanimously passed a motion to provide financial support to ward-level branches of the Imperial Military Reserve Association. The resolution, which praised the reservists for their watch patrols and traffic direction, made particular mention of the invaluable assistance the reservists provided after the earthquake.[16]

Tanaka founded his national association in part to preserve the vanishing virtues of the rural community, but local units sometimes acted upon the worst as well as the best impulses of Japanese folkways. In 1922, *burakumin*—the descendants of the outcast communities that were officially liberated in 1871—founded a society to work for their own betterment, which they called the Suiheisha. In the 1920s, Suiheisha members occasionally accused reservists of insulting behavior, and indeed, reservist groups sometimes engaged in organized opposition to outcast organizations. In Tokyo, similar prejudices were no doubt responsible for the slaughter of Koreans in the aftermath of the earthquake by self-defense groups that included military reservists.[17]

The leaders of the ward branches and the neighborhood subunits of the Imperial Military Reserve Association were local residents. Neighborhood leaders extended their interests to include military activities; military officers did not come into the ward or the neighborhood to control local activities. Although the first two heads of the Honjo branch were military officers, the third head, Matsuda Kōsaku, who served from 1922 into the 1930s, was first and foremost a leader of the local community. A veteran of the Russo-Japanese War, he was a landlord and head of his neighborhood association. Nobusawa Torajirō, head of one of the squads in Honjo when the earthquake struck, was likewise deeply rooted in the local community. He was concurrently a member of the ward assembly and head of his neighborhood association.[18]

In Honjo and other Tokyo wards, then, the Imperial Military Reserve Association created new organizations at the ward and neighborhood level. The activities of the branches and subunits included lecture meetings on military topics and various types of drill, but the local activities of the branches and subunits were at least as important as the specifically military activities of the associations. The local units provided both needed services and an arena, a most welcome one in the impersonal city, for participation in local affairs. The reservist groups extended membership to some men who, since they were not heads of households, would not have been eligible to belong to their neighborhood associations. Further, those migrating to Tokyo were familiar with the Imperial Military Reserve Association in other cities and in their native villages and therefore felt comfortable associating with the local urban branch. The local elite of the wards and neighborhoods provided the leadership for these nominally national units. Whatever the intention of the founders of the Imperial Military Reserve Association, the effect in the ward was to strengthen the ties of the urban dweller to his urban neighborhood.

Young Men's Associations

In the early twentieth century, the term "young men's association" *(seinendan, seinenkai)* referred to voluntary organizations, usually in rural areas. The term acquired a more formal meaning on September 15, 1915, when the Home and Education Ministries issued a directive to regulate such organizations.[19] The directive declared that young men's associations were important for both the Japanese nation and local communities. Under appropriate local leadership, such associations were to create healthy and loyal citizens through moral cultivation.

The bureaucratic leaders of the young men's associations claimed for their organization direct descent from the *wakamonogumi* of the Tokugawa era. The *wakamonogumi* were informal associations of village men in their productive years; a man was a member from his adolescence to his retirement.[20] Because the groups were informal, there was tremendous geographical variation in terminology, age restrictions, and activities, but generally the men carried out village projects such as building roads, thatching roofs, policing the village, and preparing for festivals. The groups fostered friendship and recreation; some even played a role in the selection of marriage partners.

In fact, the local associations formalized in 1915 had more recent origins. From about 1890, educators founded young men's associations to extend the educational process beyond the required years of elementary school. Intended as instruments of education, the pre-1915 young men's associations were composed mainly of recent graduates of elementary schools rather than of all able-bodied males in the village. The Sino-Japanese and Russo-Japanese Wars stimulated the proliferation of such groups. Meanwhile, the Tokugawa *wakamonogumi* had long since disappeared, and state-supported fire brigades and police forces had taken over functions such as fire watch and night patrol.

After 1905, both the Home and Education Ministries took an interest in informal young men's associations as a means to educate future national citizens. Yamamoto Takinosuke, an elementary schoolteacher in Hiroshima prefecture, brought the young men's associations' potential for extending education to the attention of Home Ministry officials, many of whom were already interested in guiding the youth groups into a nationwide hierarchy as part of the Local Improvement Movement (Chihō kairyō undō). In 1906, both the Home and Education Ministries published pamphlets on young men's organizations, and in the next two years, both ministers addressed the prefectural governors on the importance of the associations. In 1910, Komatsubara Eitarō, the minister of education, honored over eighty young men's groups that had rendered distinguished service to the nation.[21]

Tanaka Giichi, the founder of the Imperial Military Reserve Association, supported the formation of a national youth association. When he observed the education of youth in Europe and the United States in 1913 and 1914, he was most impressed by the orderliness of the German groups. He urged the Japanese government to invest Japanese young men's groups with similar unity, order, and capacity for training and inculcation of morals. Upon his return to Japan, Tanaka worked with representatives of the Education and Home Ministries to develop a national young men's organization. Originally, the directive was to come from the army as well as the home and education ministers, but the name of the army minister was omitted lest his signature create the impression that the young men's associations were designed to advance the cause of militarism.[22]

A notice by the vice-ministers of the Home and Education Ministries, which accompanied the 1915 directive on young men's associations, mandated policies distinctly different from those of the traditional *wakamonogumi*. The *wakamonogumi*, as informal organizations including adults, had been self-governing and any officers of the group came from within its membership.[23] The directive set an upper age limit of twenty for the young men's associations, thus eliminating adult members. At the same time, the directive recommended village heads, elementary school principals, teachers, police, Buddhist and Shintō clergy, and military reservists as appropriate leaders for the associations. The youthful members, firmly under the control of non-member adults, were to provide for their own expenses.

The Home and Education Ministries continued to guide and fund the young men's associations. In 1920, the Home Ministry provided 540,000 yen.[24] Through the Home Ministry, the young men's associations participated in the building of the Meiji Shrine. Both the Home and Education Ministries sponsored the Japan Young Men's Hall, which was built within the grounds of the Meiji Shrine.

Tazawa Yoshiharu was the single most important individual in the creation of the Japan Young Men's Hall. In 1915, the Home Ministry appointed Tazawa head of the bureau for construction of a shrine for the Meiji Emperor, who had died in 1912. This appointment forged the crucial link between Tazawa, who had a personal interest in the moral education of the youth of Japan, and the young men's associations designated in the 1915 directive. Tazawa invited young men's associations throughout Japan to assist in building the shrine, and 15,000 individuals from more than 280 groups accepted. After their work each day, the young men heard lectures on moral culture before retiring for the night to barracks provided by the shrine construction bureau.[25]

The opening ceremonies for the main building of the shrine took place on November 1, 1920. On the recommendation of Tazawa's bureau, the Home and Education Ministries jointly sponsored a National Young Men's Association visitation to the Meiji Shrine. They invited one representative from each county, city, or ward young men's association to come for a week beginning November 21. There were 697 participants. On the third day of the visit, at the same time that the branch representatives worshiped at the shrine, all three million members of the young men's associations were encouraged to pause in their fields, factories, and shops where they worked and to turn toward Meiji Shrine in worship.[26]

The Japan Young Men's Hall developed from the visitation of the representatives to Tokyo. When the young men paraded before the Imperial Palace, the Crown Prince made a brief speech. The youths themselves decided, it is said, that their associations should construct a building in one corner of the grounds of the shrine to commemorate the Crown Prince's speech. Each member of the young men's associations would contribute one yen toward the construction. The Home and Education Ministries authorized the establishment of the Young Men's Hall on September 2, 1921, in time for the return of the Crown Prince from Europe the next day. Within the Home Ministry, the strongest supporters of the project were Tazawa and Tago Ichimin. Prime Minister Hara overcame the reluctance of the education minister to participate. The founding directors were Tago, Akashi Yoichirō (a bureau head in the Education Ministry), Konoe Fumimaro, and Tazawa.[27]

The opening ceremonies for the Japan Young Men's Hall took place on October 26 and 27, 1925. The Imperial Household bestowed a gift of one hundred thousand yen. Later, Tazawa recalled with pride that the guests included Prime Minister Katō Takaaki and the heads of the two other major political parties, Tokonami Takejirō and Tanaka Giichi. On the evening of October 26, Tazawa made a thirty-minute radio broadcast on the history and the future of the young men's associations.[28]

Tazawa's vision of the young men's associations was that the local branches should be classless, encompassing landlords and tenants, capitalists and laborers. He expected the groups to inculcate general morality. In contrast to Tanaka, he had no desire to emphasize a special brand of military culture, and he successfully resisted Tanaka's efforts to forge closer institutional links between the young men's associations and the reservists. Tazawa thus rejected both socialism and militarism. He was, however, no less a patriot for having rejected militarism. The moral development of the youth of Japan for which he strove all his life included reverence for the unique national essence of Japan, the unbroken imperial line.[29]

The instrument that formally linked local young men's associations into a national network was the Japan League of Young Men's Associations (Dai Nihon rengō seinendan), for which the inaugural ceremony took place in April 1925 in Nagoya. The Tokyo City League of Young Men's Associations first proposed such a network at the general meeting of the National Urban Young Men's Associations in Osaka in July 1921. At first, the Home and Education Ministries, which were already sponsoring the Japan Young Men's Hall, opposed such a league. Negotiations over the next few years among the Home Ministry, the Education Ministry, the Japan Young Men's Hall, and members of the committee for the establishment of the Japan League resulted in the Japan League of Young Men's Associations, which was closely linked to the Japan Young Men's Hall. Of the twelve members of the board of directors, half were selected from among the directors of the Japan Young Men's Hall. The other half were elected by the council of delegates of the league. The council of delegates consisted of the elected representatives of the prefectural and metropolitan leagues. Each prefecture and each of the six large cities of Japan elected one representative to the council.[30]

The leadership of the league was overwhelmingly civilian. The first director was Ichiki Kitokurō, later minister of the Imperial Household and president of the Privy Council, who as home minister had issued the directive on the young men's associations in 1915. After an interval with Maruyama Tsurukichi (a Home Ministry bureaucrat) as acting director, the financier Inoue Junnosuke was director from 1926 to 1929. His successor, Gotō Fumio, was a former Home Ministry bureaucrat, as were his successors, Tazawa Yoshiharu and Kōsaka Masayasu.[31]

The city was not merely an afterthought in the formulation of national policy on young men's associations. To be sure, Yamamoto Takinosuke was thinking of village youth when he urged the revival of *wakamonogumi*. To the extent, however, that the national leaders of the young men's associations sought to compensate for the disruptions of modern industrial life and to prevent the spread of dangerous thought, the city was in the front line of the struggle. The provision in the Japan League for direct representation of the six major cities of Japan in the council of delegates reflected the concern of the leaders of the league for urban young men's associations. If the only purpose of the young men's associations had been to reach rural youth, the cities could easily have been represented through the prefectures in which they were located.

The leaders of the Japan League of Young Men's Associations had considerable experience with urban problems. Although many of these leaders had been born in rural areas, nearly all had come to Tokyo for their education and had remained there since. Several officers had held positions in the administration of Tokyo city or in organizations concerned with urban problems. Tazawa Yoshiharu provides a good example: his first two jobs after graduation from Tokyo Imperial University were in Shizuoka prefecture, first in the prefectural office and then as head of Abe County. In 1915, however, he returned to Tokyo as head of the construction bureau for the Meiji Shrine. His appointment in 1920 as executive director of the Harmonization Society (Kyōchōkai), a position he was to hold until 1924, placed him in the center of government policy on urban industrial problems. In 1919, the rice riots of 1918 and the many labor disputes of 1919 inspired the government to create the Kyōchōkai to bring together labor, capital, the government, and the scholarly world in order to reduce the class tensions in Japan. In 1922, Tazawa attended the Fourth International Labor Conference in Geneva as the representative from Japanese labor, albeit without the full support of the labor unions themselves. His deepest involvement with urban problems came in October 1924 when he became assistant mayor of Tokyo, a position he held for a year and nine months.[32] His duties included a month as head of the social bureau of Tokyo city. His urban responsibilities provided a new arena for his activities on behalf of the young men's associations; as assistant mayor, he served as assistant head of the Tokyo League of Young Men's Associations.[33]

Tazawa was by no means the only link between the administration of Tokyo city and the Japan League of Young Men's Associations and its close associate the Japan Young Men's Hall. Maruyama Tsurukichi, a director of the Japan League from 1924 on, also served for four months in 1926 as head of the social bureau of Tokyo city.[34] Later, from July 1929 to April 1931, he was head of the Metropolitan Police Force. Gotō Shinpei, an advisor to the Japan Young Men's Hall, was mayor of Tokyo in the early 1920s. One of the men who served him as assistant mayor, Ikeda Hiro, was a director of the Japan Young Men's Hall. Ikezono Tetsutarō was a director of the league from 1925 to 1929; during his years within the city of Tokyo he served as chief of the social education section, head of Asakusa Ward, and head of Yodobashi Ward.

Bureaucratic concern for youth extended to young women as well as to young men. In November 1926, the year after the Japan Young Men's Hall opened and the Japan League of Young Men's Associations took shape, the Home and Education Ministries issued a directive on young women's associations. A year later, Tokyo prefecture and the city government issued similar directives. In Ushigome, the ward head initiated the young women's associations and each school principal in the ward headed a branch made up of the female graduates of his school who were between the ages of thirteen and twenty-four.[35]

Young Men's Associations in Tokyo

In Tokyo, the implementation of national policy on the standardization and control of young men's associations required not merely the transformation of existing organizations but the creation of youth groups where virtually none had existed before. That is, because Tokugawa *wakamonogumi* and their successors were rural rather than urban phenomena, in the city, organizers had no traditional base from which to build. In 1917, there were six occupational young men's associations in Tokyo city and a handful of geographically based units. Shiba Ward, for instance, in 1920 had three young men's groups centered on the *chō*; the oldest of these had been founded in 1904, during the Russo-Japanese War. None of those indicted in Tokyo in the rice riots of 1918 claimed to be members of the young men's associations, probably because so few young men belonged to the associations. Moreover, the only associations from Tokyo prefecture that assisted in the building of the Meiji Shrine were from outside the city.[36]

Local groups proliferated in Tokyo city only after the municipal authorities lent their support to the program. Despite Tanaka Giichi's enthusiasm for the 1915 directive, educators (rather than either military officers or the officials of reservist organizations) created the young men's associations of Tokyo. In 1919, the city of Tokyo appropriated 2,300 yen for research on the education of youth. The researchers recommended that the young men's associations be used to educate the youth of the city. The mayor then asked the advice of the Association of Tokyo City Principals and the Tokyo City Young Men's Education Investigation Society as to how young men's groups could be formed in Tokyo. In June 1920, the city assembly voted to budget thirty thousand yen for the support of young men's associations. Shibusawa Tokusaburō, head of the education section of the city of Tokyo, became chair of the Committee for the Establishment of Young Men's Associations. The committee encouraged existing youth groups and elementary schools to participate in the young men's associations and suggested that local leaders create new associations in the various wards.[37]

This was the real beginning of the young men's associations of Tokyo. Of 118 local associations in the city that were surveyed in 1930, only 12 claimed to have existed prior to 1920. However, 35 gave 1920 as their founding date, 16 gave 1921, and 16 gave 1922. In Honjo, all of the 50 groups in the ward in 1925 had been founded in 1920 or thereafter. In Kyōbashi and Nihonbashi Wards as well, all the associations dated from 1920 or later. In Ushigome, the ward branches made no claim to have participated in the building of the

Meiji Shrine, but they were sufficiently organized in November 1920 to welcome and provide assistance to the representatives of young men's associations who came as part of the nationally organized visitation to the shrine.[38]

The vast majority of branches, then, came into being with or in the wake of the Tokyo City League of Young Men's Associations, which was founded in July 1920. The head of the citywide league was the mayor, and the head of the ward-level young men's association was the ward chief. This overlap between the urban administration and the young men's associations was not merely nominal. Two men who represented the Tokyo League in the negotiations for the formation of the Japan League of Young Men's Associations, Osako Motoshige and Ikezono Tetsutarō, were one after the other head of the social education section of Tokyo city.[39]

Not surprisingly, given the role of school principals in organizing young men's associations in Tokyo, many of the 216 local branches in 1920 were based on school districts and headed by the school principals. Shiba Ward had twenty branches based on elementary districts, and in later years a number of elementary-school-based branches in Shitaya and Nihonbashi Wards claimed 1920 as their founding date. In Honjo, the branches centered on schools were without exception headed by the principal of that school. Some school branches were school alumni associations under new names; in Honjo, the male alumni group of the Narihira Elementary School became a young men's association branch in 1920.[40]

The regulations of the Tokyo League reflected the peculiarities of urban life. To be sure, Tokyo youth shared national aims such as fostering the constitutional spirit and furthering the national destiny. The adult leaders offered their young members a number of practical precepts: be physically fit, abstain from liquor and tobacco, go to bed early so as to rise early, and read. Particularly suited to the urban locale were the strictures on respect for public property and thoroughfares and the admonition to exercise civic virtue on the trains.[41]

Young men's associations took root and grew in Tokyo. In 1920, the 216 groups had 45,640 members. Between 1920 and March 1923, there was a slight increase in groups in Tokyo to 263 and a great increase in membership to 92,105. After the earthquake, the number of groups increased greatly to 509, whereas the membership grew only slightly to 109,282. The apparent discrepancy between the large number of new groups and the very slight increase in members was the result of conditions in Tokyo after the earthquake. The need for relief work stimulated the proliferation of local organizations at the same time that the devastation of the earthquake reduced the actual population. These figures may well exaggerate the actual number of members; they include a large number of school-based groups, many of which existed on paper only.[42]

The purpose of the young men's associations was to educate their regular members, male residents under the age of twenty, but not all young men of the appropriate age group belonged to an association. An official of the Japan League of Young Men's Associations estimated on the basis of the 1930 census that only about one-third of the youth eligible for the young men's associations actually belonged. He gave absence from home for work or study as reasons that a young man might be unable to join. In Tokyo prefecture in 1930, only 12.7 percent of the youth eligible to join the young men's association actually did so; by 1936, the percentage for the prefecture had risen to 17.2. In 1936, however, of those within the city limits, only 15.6 percent belonged.[43] This figure, based on the expanded thirty-five-ward city, gives us only a vague notion of what the percentage was for the original fifteen wards, such as Honjo, in the center of the city. A very rough estimate is that young men in the city joined the association at about half the rate for the nation as a whole.

The reasons for this difference are not difficult to find. In the villages, those who had graduated from elementary school and were still in the village were automatically members of the young men's association. Rarely was there an adult male in the village who had not graduated from the same school as the others his age. All worked in agriculture and shared the same days of rest. In the city, there was no automatic membership for anyone; one became a member after accepting a letter of invitation.[44] The letters no doubt went to the sons of those who led the associations: shopkeepers, owners of small factories, physicians and dentists in local private practice. In any urban neighborhood there were young men who had come from other wards and other prefectures and who shared no common past with the longer-term residents of the area. Those between the ages of fourteen and twenty worked at all the various occupations to be found in the city. Some had the first and the fifteenth of the month as days off,

whereas others were free on Sundays. There was thus no natural, spontaneous community on the basis of age.

The young men of the capital who did become members of a local
branch gained access to the various publications of the young men's
associations. In 1922, the Japan Young Men's Hall took over an existing publication and renamed it *Young Men (Seinen)*. In April 1927,
in turn, the Japan League assumed the educational responsibilities of
the Japan Young Men's Hall. The league added a pamphlet, entitled
Young Men's Card (Seinen kaado), in October 1929. The publication
was simply written and very reasonably priced; twelve issues a year cost
only fifteen *sen*. In 1930, the league began publication of the *Japan
Young Men's Newspaper (Nihon seinen shinbun)* to supply news of the
various branches. The influence of these publications should not be
exaggerated. The league's magazines competed with commercial publications such as Kodansha's *King,* which at fifty sen an issue was more
expensive but which claimed circulation of over a million.[45]

The Tokyo League of Young Men's Associations added to the
mass of newsprint that could potentially have arrived at the home of
a member with its official publication *Tokyo Young Men (Tōkyō no
seinen)*, said to be controlled by Ikezono Tetsutarō. Arima Yoriyasu,
Ikezono's opponent within the Tokyo League, issued a rival publication, *Imperial Young Men's Association Report (Teikoku seinen
danpō)*. Some ward branches published their own newsletters; the one
in Ushigome appeared twice a year.[46]

Membership in the young men's associations also provided urban
youth with opportunities to compete in sports. Beginning in the fall
of 1924, the young men's associations sponsored an athletic meet in
connection with the Meiji Shrine festival. From 1926 to 1939, the
contest was held in alternate years; in 1939, it again became an annual
event. At first, members competed only in track, kendo, and sumo.
Swimming was added in 1929. The fact that three former participants
in these contests represented Japan in the Far Eastern Olympics in
1926 shows that the competition was serious. The Japan League established medals for those who broke records or in other ways compiled especially outstanding records at league-sponsored events.
Members from Tokyo could easily get to Meiji Shrine and compete
in these contests, sometimes quite successfully. In 1937 members
from Tokyo won prizes in the relay race and the judo contest.[47]

It was equally easy for Tokyo branch members to join in events
sponsored by the Japan League of Young Men's Associations and the
Young Men's Hall. Many of these events centered on members of the
imperial family. When Crown Prince Hirohito returned from a trip to
Europe in September 1921, the Education Ministry held a two-day
meeting for the representatives of the young men's associations who
had gathered at the dock to welcome him. In June 1924, the Japan
Young Men's Hall sponsored a celebration of the marriage of the
Crown Prince and the representatives of the young men's association
who attended sent a congratulatory message to the couple. After the
death of the Taishō Emperor in 1926, members of the young men's
associations gathered in Tokyo for two days in February 1927 to
honor his spirit. When the Shōwa Emperor was enthroned in Kyoto
in November 1928, the Japan League held its general meeting there.
The general meeting of the Japan Young Men's Hall in May 1934
included the celebration of the birth of Crown Prince Akihito.[48]

The Tokyo League and its branches sponsored additional activities. In February 1921, forty-eight thousand members of Tokyo
young men's branches staged a lantern parade in Hibiya Park to honor
the Crown Prince on his departure for Europe. When the Taishō Emperor was ill in December 1926, members of the Ushigome branch
prayed for his recovery at the Akasaka Shrine. On the occasion of the
enthronement of the Shōwa Emperor in 1928, the ward-level chapters
of the young men's associations each held celebrations. In Honjo, the
young men held an athletic meet and led a lantern parade through
the streets of the ward.[49]

In Shiba Ward, one encouragement to local activities was the establishment of a ward-level Young Men's Hall in Shiba Park. Donations for the building came from the branches and from local businessmen. One of the many money-raising projects undertaken by the
young men was an outdoor concert at the Hibiya bandstand. Once
finished, the building was used for citywide as well as ward activities.
Whereas a separate hall was unusual, ward-level support for young
men's associations was not. In 1934, all of the wards of the expanded
city gave financial support to the local young men's association.[50]

Perhaps precisely because membership in urban young men's associations was limited, often requiring graduation from a given school
or a letter of invitation, the activities of the urban chapters were more
explicitly patriotic and less integrated into ordinary life than in the

countryside, where young men's associations emphasized study and individual development. Flags and uniforms identified the city branches and their members as they participated in highly visible activities such as traffic management and lantern parades.[51] High visibility was more characteristic of *chō*-based associations than of school-based ones. The Ushigome branch chose uniforms, flags, and official branch lanterns in 1924 only after the establishment of several *chō*-based associations.[52]

An outline of the annual events of the Ushigome Young Men's Association, drawn up at the end of the Taishō era, shows that the branch sponsored about two events a month. Often these were speech meetings commemorating a holiday: National Foundation Day, Emperor Jinmu Day, Army Day, Navy Day, Self-Government Day, and the Emperor's Birthday. The young men of the ward made two or three outings a year, including one to Ise Shrine. In addition, they participated in martial arts and athletic meets.[53]

The Ushigome activities are consistent with the general picture of the Tokyo branches provided by a survey conducted by the Japan League in 1930.[54] Educational activities usually took the form of speech meetings, debates, brief courses, and moral culture societies. A few groups had educational movies and field trips. Many activities promoted physical fitness: outings, contests of military skill, exercise, mountain climbing, baseball, swimming, table tennis, sumo, tennis, camping, gymnastics, and basketball. Service to the local neighborhood included night watch, fire protection, traffic control, and sanitary work. That is, the young men's associations functioned to a certain degree as an auxiliary police force. Nearly all these activities had both recreational and social aspects. As young men studied, participated in sports, and worked together, they strengthened their bond to each other and to their neighborhood or school district.

Neighborhood and Nation

Historians of Japan commonly assume that the reservists and the young men's associations played a major role in the mobilization of the masses in the cause of ultranationalism in the 1930s. According to this view, the associations reinforced the conformist in-group at the local level and linked it to the bureaucratic structure of the central government. This linkage is predicated upon the relationship of a rural village to the political center. Tokyo—where there were no organic units comparable to the rural village in which reservist and young men's associations could embed themselves—invites reconsideration of the relationship among the military, the government, and the local branches.[55]

The central government made good use of the reservists and the young men's associations to increase participation in activities of symbolic importance to the nation. Both the Home and Education Ministries encouraged members of the associations to participate in events connected with the imperial institution. The Japan Young Men's Hall had its origins in the shrine bureau of the Home Ministry, which included young men's associations, young women's associations, reservists, firemen's federations, Boy Scouts, and schools in the removal ceremonies for Ise Shrine in 1929.[56] The Education Ministry, for its part, sent notices to young men's and young women's associations to encourage them to participate in the thirtieth anniversary of the Imperial Rescript on Education in 1920. On National Foundation Day in 1928, reservists and young men's groups marched from six sites to Nijūbashi to pay their respects to the emperor. In 1938, on the same holiday, there were celebrations at parks throughout the city and members of the young men's associations gathered in front of the imperial palace and then visited the Meiji Shrine.[57]

For most of its existence, the Imperial Military Reserve Association, which prided itself on its patriotic activities, consciously held itself aloof from partisan politics. The Imperial Rescript to Soldiers and Sailors warned members of the military not to "meddle in politics."[58] When the Meiji Emperor issued the rescript in 1882, abstention from politics was the normal state of affairs for Japanese subjects, for there were not as yet any national elections, and when the first Diet was elected in 1890, the suffrage was limited to about one percent of the total population. The passage of universal manhood suffrage in 1925, however, which allowed all adult males to vote and thus participate in politics, changed the relationship of the reservists to politics. The extension of suffrage coincided with the depression, international competition among communist, fascist, and democratic regimes, and an era of turmoil in China and thus in Japan's continental policy. In this era of considerable dissension over economic, political, and diplomatic issues, the reservists, long socialized to be patriotic, could not help but feel involved in the national crisis.

From the army's point of view, it was essential that the reservists and others supportive of the military be properly informed on national issues. The military reserve hierarchy was one means that the army used to propagate its views. In 1934, it distributed copies of a pamphlet on the essence of national defense to all reservist associations as well as to army divisional and regimental headquarters.[59]

The Imperial Military Reserve Association itself provided information on various issues. In 1932, the Christian educator Nitobe Inazō gave a series of lectures in Ehime at the invitation of the prefectural authorities. One of his remarks was interpreted by the press as an attack on the army. The Imperial Military Reserve Association responded by issuing a pamphlet outlining the controversy. The pamphlet, while acknowledging Nitobe's rights to his pacifist point of view, questioned the propriety of his expressing his notions in a time of national crisis. The effect of the pamphlet, which quoted many of the angry accusations against Nitobe, was to keep the controversy alive.[60]

The urban branches that received these pamphlets, however, were not simply passive and obedient receptors of political wisdom. The regular activities of the military reserve branches maintained for their members an identity with the military and the imperial institution even as they acted as neighborhood service organizations. That is, association activities legitimated the participation of civilians (albeit reserve military civilians) in national affairs. During the 1930s, reservists demonstrated and petitioned against ratification of the London Naval Treaty of 1930, for the Manchurian settlement, in favor of withdrawal from the League of Nations, and in support of leniency for the assassins of Prime Minister Inukai.[61] They did so not because of orchestrated central campaigns but out of a sense of responsibility to their army, their emperor, and their nation.

The importance of the reservists as makers rather than mouthpieces of association policy is illustrated by the Minobe crisis of 1935. On August 27, 1935, the Imperial Military Reserve Association passed a resolution condemning the constitutional theories of Minobe Tatsukichi, a professor just recently retired from Tokyo Imperial University. Richard J. Smethurst has argued persuasively that the reservist involvement in this crisis originated in the branches of the association, not in its headquarters or in the army. Minobe's "organ theory" had first become a public issue several months earlier. On February 7, 1935, Etō Genkurō, a member of the Lower House of the Diet, in an interpellation of Home Minister Gotō Fumio, suggested that the government had been remiss in not censoring Minobe's works. On February 18, Baron Kikuchi Takeo made a speech in the House of Peers, which reiterated these accusations. Ten days later, Etō filed charges of lèse-majesté against Minobe in Tokyo District Court.[62]

These initial attacks on Minobe escalated so much in the following months that, by September, Minobe found it prudent to resign all his public positions, including his seat in the House of Peers. The cabinet, which initially had supported Minobe, twice issued statements condemning the organ theory, once in August and once in October. The Minobe crisis culminated a series of right-wing attacks on liberal scholars and resulted in a new era of press controls. The escalation of this crisis was marked by popular agitation of such intensity that virtually no newspaper or interest group came to Minobe's defense. Some of this agitation came from local reservist units, which "held meetings, passed resolutions, and dispatched petitions, telegrams, and even delegations to Tokyo to pressure the government."[63] The reservists acted, however, not on orders from the army or from the headquarters of the Imperial Military Reserve Association but under the direction of local leaders, many of whom were members of ultranationalist organizations such as the Meirinkai, to which both Etō and Kikuchi belonged. One example of local ultranationalist leadership in Tokyo was Lieutenant General Okudaira Shunzō of the Azabu Ward reserve association. The Meirinkai was soon joined in its efforts to mobilize the masses by the Seiyūkai Party, which convened a mass rally in Hibiya Park on July 31 to castigate the Okada cabinet for its failure to clarify the national essence.[64]

The Minobe crisis, then, arose not so much from state oppression as from the vigor of civic associations, in this case right-wing ones. In order to educate and incorporate ex-soldiers, the Home and Education Ministries had included reservists in the pageantry of the state, thus legitimating their presence on the political stage. Universal manhood suffrage had given ordinary men the vote. The Imperial Military Reserve Association and the ward administration that had financed and housed the branches provided institutional form, publications, meeting times and places, and mailing lists. Contrary to the best-laid plans of civilian and military bureaucrats, the members of the branches used these resources not to acquiesce to academic expertise on constitutional issues but to agitate against such expertise on the basis of an antiforeign superpatriotism. Once the situation had developed, neither the state nor the parties invoked liberal principles to defend Minobe's right to opinions that the reservists found offensive. The state thus acquiesced in the tyranny of the majority, or at least of the noisy. The fact remains that the Minobe crisis was largely a case of oppression from below rather than from above.

In contrast to the reservists, who built on a foundation of locally organized military support groups, the young men's associations of Tokyo were almost entirely bureaucratic creations. The majority were headed by school principals who acquired their responsibilities when the Education Ministry appointed them to their current jobs and would leave them in an instant if offered a promotion. Although local branches often extended the age limit for regular members from twenty to twenty-five, the young men's association, even in the age of universal manhood suffrage, remained an organization of the unenfranchised, for the voting age was twenty-five.

After the Manchurian Incident of September 1931, the officers of the Japan League of Young Men's Associations compensated for the powerlessness of their membership by lending the same conspicuous and unflagging support to the imperial troops on the continent that they had always encouraged toward the imperial institution. On November 6, Gotō Fumio, in his capacity as president of the Japan League, visited the Meiji Shrine to pray for the good fortune of the imperial troops. In November 1931 and again in April 1932, the league headquarters dispatched representatives to bear condolences to the soldiers in Manchuria and China. As the names of those killed in the Manchurian and Shanghai Incidents were published, the league sent formal condolences to the bereaved families in Gotō's name.[65]

Public meetings and special issues of the league publications impressed upon the rank-and-file members the gravity of the national crisis. The Young Men's Hall, the Japan League of Young Men's Associations, the Japan League of Young Women's Associations, and the Tokyo city and Tokyo prefecture leagues of both the men's and the women's associations jointly sponsored a meeting at the Young Men's Hall on December 12, 1931. One of the main speakers was Kumagai Tatsujirō, who had recently returned from Manchuria where he had served as the league's representative to the troops. Meanwhile, subscribers to *Young Men's Card* received in their homes a special issue on "National Defense and the Army." The league encouraged members to send condolence money in support of the troops.[66]

After the outbreak of war with China in 1937, young men's associations in Tokyo became more explicitly supportive of the military and more actively involved in matters of foreign policy. One project of the Japan Young Men's League was to collect funds for the purchase of heavy bombers. The league presented the funds in amounts that would buy two bombers at a time, one for the navy and one for the army, thus maintaining an evenhandedness with respect to interservice rivalries. On July 26, 1937, shortly after the Marco Polo Bridge Incident, the league announced a plan encouraging members to collect old newspapers (the league would arrange for their sale), contribute their haircut money, and work overtime to accumulate cash for donations. Patriotic citizens donated warehouse sites free of charge, and members of the young women's associations joined in the project. By December 9, 1937, the president of the league, Kōsaka Masayasu, was able to present the funds to the Army and Navy ministers. The league then made a second donation of a heavy bomber for each of the two military services on February 10, 1938. Members of the young men's associations attended the christening of the naval planes on March 17, 1938, and the army planes on May 30, 1938. Because both events took place at Haneda Airport, members from Tokyo had to travel only a short distance to attend.[67]

Young men's associations lent their support to the particular direction of recent foreign policy. Members participated in a lantern parade in 1937 to celebrate the signing of the Anti-Comintern Pact. The Tokyo League planned to present Japanese swords and armor to Chancellor Adolf Hitler and Premier Benito Mussolini through the German and Italian ambassadors in Tokyo on February 11, 1938, National Foundation Day. Two or three envoys of the Tokyo League were to visit Germany and Italy on a goodwill mission.[68]

These public activities encouraged the 12–15 percent of the eligible age cohort who actually joined the associations to support enthusiastically the existing government policy, just as one would expect of an organization whose hierarchy consisted mainly of school principals and ward chiefs. Nevertheless, young men's associations that were centered in the neighborhood rather than in a school had some potential to harbor political positions opposed to or at least independent of the government. Moreover, several wards deviated from the practice of having the ward chief head the young men's association. The first head of the Kōjimachi association was a member of the ward assembly. In Shitaya, the ward head recommended that the chief of one of the police stations be head of the young men's association. When Akasaka Ward inaugurated a young man's association in 1920, the ward head was in charge, but sometime after 1925, Arima Yoriyasu, a director of the Japan League, assumed leadership of the branch. Arima was also said to have influence in several other wards where the ward chief was not the head of the young men's association, namely Fukagawa, Nihonbashi, and Kōjimachi.[69]

The few neighborhood branches that propagated ultrapatriotic thought do not seem to have been the handiwork of military reservists, for there was little overlap between the leaders of reservist units and those of young men's associations.[70] Some of the heads of neighborhood branches came from the educational community. Nagasaka Yoritaka, head of the Wakamiya-chō association in Honjo, was principal of a private elementary school in the ward and a member of the ward and city educational societies. A number of leaders of young men's associations were members of their ward assemblies, and some held higher political office. Fukushima Gensetsu, head of an association in Honjo, was a medical doctor who had been in practice in the ward since 1896 and was head of his neighborhood association; he was elected to both the ward and the prefectural assemblies. Takizawa Shichirō, also the head of a young men's association in Honjo, served in both the ward and the city assemblies before he was elected to the Diet as a Seiyūkai candidate.[71]

Where young men's associations deviated from political orthodoxy, it seems to have been a product of individual political dedication and ingenuity. In Kyōbashi, some neighborhoods had more than one young men's association, thanks in large part to Gotō Takeo, the head of the Imperial Detective Agency, who was reputed to be spreading reactionary thought through the associations. Like many other association leaders, Gotō had served in the ward assembly (1913–1925) and in the city assembly (1914–1922). He ran unsuccessfully for the Diet in 1915 and 1920. His family controlled at least two young men's associations, one at the detective agency and one at their home address.[72]

In the city, then, military reserve and young men's associations were local organizations with local leadership that encouraged interest in national issues, reverence for the imperial institution, and public service at both the local and national level. Their value as conduits of official orthodoxy was limited in the city by the small percentage of the eligible population who actually joined the organizations.

For those who did join, membership could mean a wide variety of things, ranging from connection to the local neighborhood to identification with extreme nationalist views. Membership provided access to organizational structures and experience in leading volunteers. The origins of these organizations in the Army, Navy, Education, and Home Ministries and their focus on the imperial institution made it likely that any critique of the government arising out of these organizations would be from the right rather than the left end of the political spectrum. This proved true in the Minobe crisis, but the lessons instilled by organizational membership could not be limited to a particular ideology. Let us note in passing that there were socialists who distributed pamphlets through the young men's associations and rural tenant union leaders who recommended that union leaders be recruited from among the activists in the reservist association.[73]

The actual history of the military reservists and the young men's associations must be distinguished from the dreams of orderly national grandeur that their hierarchical and inclusive structures inspired. The nationalist Kita Ikki suggested that the reservists supervise the national reform he envisioned. Nagai Ryūtarō, a Minseitō Diet member, said in 1924 that he would have to use the reservists to achieve the restoration he wanted for Japan. In 1935, Diet member Kamei Kanichirō of the Social Mass Party hoped that state-affiliated groups such as the Imperial Military Reserve Association would bring political change to Japan.[74] None of these men ever reached the heights of power to which they aspired, and their dreams of using the hierarchies of the associations to realize their political ideals remained dreams, nothing more.

— Chapter 5 —

Factory, Union, and Neighborhood

In the opening years of the twentieth century, brick factories with soaring smokestacks towered above the Tokyo landscape. Their architectural dominance symbolized the set hours, arbitrary wage system, and imminent possibility of unemployment that were among the factors making urban life different from rural. It has often been blithely assumed that the factory somehow served as an urban counterpart to the rural village.[1] In fact, factories were major sites of ideological and economic conflict in Japanese society. Owners and managers met with only limited success in efforts to control their workers.

As soon as moderate and thus legal labor unions took shape in the Taishō era, they offered workers an alternative pattern of association to the usual vertical networks of the local community, and their educational programs introduced workers to theories that challenged both the state and the social and economic order of the neighborhood. In the voluminous literature that exists in both Japanese and English on the labor unions of prewar Japan, the relationship of union activities to the communities in which the workers lived and worked has remained largely unexplored. This study of Honjo shows that union activities were by no means confined to some remote headquarters but, rather, extended into the places of employment and the daily lives of ordinary workers.

Unions were thus another instrument through which urban residents were schooled in civic association. As unions sought support from other unions and from proletarian political parties and as factory owners called in the police, labor struggles provided further lessons on the benefits of association and the dangers of the authoritarian state. From these origins came the votes that elected socialist candidates to the Diet in 1936 and 1937; in a broader perspective, the activities of the unions represent the beginnings of the urban strength of the Japan Socialist Party in the postwar period.

Factories, Large and Small

Throughout the early years of the twentieth century, Honjo was one of the most highly industrialized areas of the city, whether measured by the number of workers in the ward or by the number of factories. The ward achieved preeminence as an industrial area very early in the century. In 1902, Honjo, with 58 factories, was second only to Fukagawa Ward. By 1907, Honjo had 127 factories, far more than any other ward in the city. By 1920, there were more than four hundred private factories employing ten or more workers. All of these factories combined employed about nineteen thousand workers.[2] The factories listed in government statistics ranged from workshops with as few as ten workers to huge plants employing over a thousand.

In the early years of the century there were a few large enterprises among the many small factories of Honjo Ward. Of the factories in Honjo in 1920, two employed over a thousand workers and twenty-seven others employed over a hundred. These large and medium factories were a visible and well-established part of life in the ward. Nearly half of them dated from before the turn of the century. The buildings of the largest of these factories—the Azumabashi factory of the Great Japan Beer Company, for instance—towered over the one- and two-story dwellings in the neighborhood. This particular factory, completed as part of the Sapporo Beer Company in 1903, loomed above its level site. In contrast to most beer factories, which were built into the side of a hill, this building had thick-walled tunnels above the storage areas to prevent the sun's rays from reaching the barley, malt, and beer.[3]

The writings of Nagai Kafū provide vivid images of how the factories formed part of the sights, sounds, and smells of the district. Approaching Honjo from the west side of the Sumida River, one could see the smoke from factories spiraling upward. As he walked through the ward, the main character of one story passed houses and factories:

> Mossy shingled roofs, rotting foundations, leaning pillars, dirty planks, drying rags and diapers, pots and cheap sweets for sale—the dreary little houses went on in endless disorder, and when on occasion he would be surprised by an imposing gate, it would always be a factory.

The noise of industrial machinery and the smell of industrial soot filled the air.[4]

The chief economic and social role of the large factories in the ward was that of employer. The employees were from the lower reaches of the social scale in the neighborhood. In the first phase of industrialization, from about 1894 to 1912, industrial laborers were members of the larger category of the working poor. Employment in large, private factories was characterized by low wages and long hours. Urban workers lived in slums and their economic condition was only slightly less miserable than that of unskilled outdoor laborers and jinrikisha pullers, their social status lower than that of many shopkeepers and artisans.[5]

Workers rented living quarters in the neighborhood or lived in dormitories that were in the urban ward but not really of it. The residents of company dormitories were usually women employed in very large factories. Some of the factories in Honjo in 1920 that employed a large number of female workers were Fuji Gas Spinning Company, Kurihara Spinning, Seikō Watch factory, Mitatsuchi Rubber, Kobayashi Shōten, Hirao Soap, and Yoshishiro Soap.[6]

Although in this era few workers felt themselves to be part of a particular company, firms took some responsibility for the welfare of the workers. The Fuji Gas Spinning Company had regulations giving 10 percent of the net profits each fiscal year to the staff and operatives and maintained a relief fund for workers whose annual income was less than one hundred yen. At the Seikō Watch factory, the company gave prizes for diligent and conscientious work, cared for the sick, and provided education for the apprentices. The Great Japan Beer Company established a mutual aid society for its employees in 1920 and a health insurance association six years later.[7] In the devastating floods of 1910, the Fuji Gas Spinning Company supplied food and clothing to commuting workers as well as those in the dormitories and all workers were given half pay for the days out of work during the flood. As Andrew Gordon has pointed out, however, some of these measures were enacted more to exert company control over the worker than to improve the living and working conditions of the individual employee. This was particularly true of forced savings plans.[8]

Owners and managers varied greatly in the degree of their involvement in the local community. On the one hand, some of the factory heads were outstanding businessmen who exercised authority over all aspects of an operation of which the factory in Honjo made up only one part. For instance, Hasegawa Shōgo—the head of the Train Manufacturing Company, one of the largest factories in Honjo—lived in Osaka where the main branch of the company was located. Doi Shūsaku, head of the Tokyo Hat Company, lived in Koishikawa Ward, near another factory of the company. Others, like Okazaki Kujirō, head of the Japan Bicycle Company, were connected with so many enterprises that they were little involved in the affairs of the community around their factory; Okazaki lived in Shiba Ward and in 1915 was elected to the Diet from Gifu prefecture.[9]

On the other hand, the owners of some of the large factories lived in the ward. Tsuchiya Hikitatsu, one of the founders of Mitatsuchi Rubber Company, which employed over a thousand workers, lived in Koume Kawaramachi and Hoho Seijirō, owner of a somewhat smaller soap factory, lived in Midori-chō.[10] Two others, Aoki Naoji and Kurihara Kohachi, not only lived in the ward but were also active in ward affairs. Aoki, who was head of a dyeing factory that employed more than three hundred workers in 1920, was a member of the Honjo Ward Assembly from 1899 to 1904 and from 1911 to 1913. Kurihara was likewise involved in the textile industry; in 1920, his factory in Yanagishima Motomachi, Honjo, employed 98 men and 474 women. Kurihara served in the Honjo Ward Assembly for one term, from 1918 to 1922, and in the Tokyo City Assembly.[11]

For those who were neither the employers nor the employees of these large enterprises, factories were not always ideal neighbors. Fires broke out within their confines. For instance, a blaze at the Mitatsuchi Rubber factory in 1920 seriously injured four workers. Strikes and labor disputes spilled out into the streets and occupied the time and energy of the local police. When in 1909 the police were called in to settle a disturbance among the workers at Toppan Printing, it was the fifth time their intervention had been sought.[12] Police were also involved in disputes at the Maruboshi electroplating factory in 1912 and at Fuji Gas Spinning Company in 1920. The crowded women's dormitories of the large factories provided a breeding place for disease; in the summer of 1913, nearly a hundred girls at the Fuji Gas Spinning Company became ill with what was thought to be typhus.[13]

The beer factories, which sometimes marketed their products in beer halls or gardens attached to their factories, were a happy exception to the general dreariness of industry. In 1903, the Sapporo Beer Company (one of the companies that later merged to form the Great Japan Beer Company) opened a beer garden in its Honjo factory, which was built upon the site of the estate of Marquis Satake, former Lord of Akita. In 1906, the company built a hall next to the garden. Such establishments provided a meeting place for high and low, rich and poor:

> Everyone who enters is a guest who drinks the same beer as everyone else. Jinrikisha men meet gentlemen, workers meet merchant princes, and frock coats touch army uniforms. It is a place where smiles blossom as beer and foam disappear into people's mouths.[14]

By 1920, then, many of the largest factories in the ward had been there for three decades and had become part of the topography. Looming two and three stories above the surrounding buildings as they did, they were a conspicuous and continuing part of the landscape of the neighborhood. For some, the factories provided employment, but for many others, the presence in the ward of large industrial institutions meant only increased danger from fire, disorder, and disease. In the case of factories with dormitories, the employees themselves had been recruited from outside the city and might never become part of urban society. The owners of the large factories, especially where the factory in Honjo was merely a branch of a larger concern, were often not resident in the ward and not interested in local problems. The few owners who participated in local affairs were proprietors of family firms.

The small factories, on the other hand, had quite a different relationship to the ward. Usually the owner of a small enterprise lived in the neighborhood, often in quarters attached to his business. He was linked by investment and long-standing business ties to other enterprises in the ward. His employees, too, were part of the local community; the workers lived in rented quarters in the neighborhood or in their employers' homes rather than in cloisterlike dormitories. Thus, both the owners and the employees of the small factories were very much part of the local community.

The close relationship among the small factory owner, his family, and his employees arose in part from the type of small factory to be found in Honjo. Most small factories were very small. Of the 397 factories in Honjo with between ten and a hundred employees, more than half had fewer than twenty employees. In addition, in 1920 there were 877 tiny workshops with fewer than ten workers; these shops figured in municipal statistics because they had either motor power or five or more workers. A large number of these small factories, nearly half of the ones employing between ten and twenty workers, were machine shops, which employed few if any women. Male workers in heavy industry, whether they worked under labor bosses in large plants or for the owners of small factories that subcontracted work, had a lifestyle similar in many ways to that of the artisans of the Tokugawa era; in both situations, quasi-parent-child relationships existed between the bosses and their workers.[15]

As property owners in an urban neighborhood, the proprietors of small factories participated in community affairs. They were active in local organizations. Several served in the Honjo Ward Assembly. Oguri Tomiguro, owner of a small knit factory, was elected to the city assembly in 1918.[16]

In many cases, economic interests beyond his own enterprise tied the owner of a small factory to the local community. The ownership of a leather processing shop in Matsugura Itchome, Honjo, demonstrated the interdependence of local shops. Two of the investors owned leather shops elsewhere in the ward.[17]

The employees of small factories were, either as members of their employer's households or as tenants of other premises, members of the community. In many cases, the living quarters of the owner and his family were attached to the factory. Sometimes additional quarters, perhaps on a second floor, were available for employees.[18] Employees who did not live on the premises were limited in their choice of housing to the area within walking distance of the factory or within reach by streetcar. Thus, they lived either in Honjo or in areas much like it. At small factories, festival days of local shrines or temples were holidays from work, which shows the connection between the small factories and the neighborhood, whereas at larger factories such festivals went unobserved. To be sure, workers in small factories did not necessarily remain with one company for an extended period of time. Because of fluctuating economic conditions, the owners of small factories could not always offer steady employment. Further, in the early part of the century, skilled workers were in demand and they could and did move from employer to employer.[19] Nevertheless, no matter how brief the tenure of his employment, as long as a worker was employed in one of these small shops, he was linked to the neighborhood.

For those not directly connected to the factories, the small factories blended into the general fabric of life in the ward much more easily than the large companies did. The physical appearance and the employer-employee relationship of these workshops were little different from those of small commercial enterprises. Both functioned as enlarged families and their position in the neighborhood was that of a resident household. Small factories, crammed as they were into narrow streets, were probably more of a fire hazard than were the larger factories with their fenced-in compounds. Destructive fires did break out in several places where an open fire was necessary to the work, in the drying room of a dyer, the shop of a metal caster, and an electroplating smithy, for instance. Blazes that broke out in factories were made more dangerous by the flammable nature of the materials manufactured; a fire that broke out in the workshop of a celluloid manufacturer spread quickly and consumed five houses.[20] For the neighborhood, this very real danger was a necessary evil. The large factories might be viewed as uncaring invaders; the small factories were owned by neighbors, some of whom served in the ward and city assemblies.

Labor Disputes and Labor Unions, 1905–1919

Rhetoric on the familial nature of industrial establishments could not disguise the fact that a huge gulf existed between the owners of large-scale establishments and their workers. Owners and managers differed from their employees in social status and outlook as well as in economic interests. Sometimes differences between employer and employee erupted in open conflict. One yearbook lists thirteen labor disturbances in Honjo between 1906 and 1918; there were probably many others.[21] Disputes broke out for a number of reasons. Pay was naturally one area of conflict; workers demanded increases or protested announced decreases or demanded wages they had not yet been paid. Occasionally, workers objected to changes in management or they wished their foreman fired.

Article 17 of the Police Regulations of 1900 prohibited instigating others to (1) strike, (2) join unions, or (3) engage in collective bargaining. Under these restrictions, labor disturbances resembled personal quarrels. Workers sometimes went as a group to confront the head of the company in person. For instance, in 1909, forty or fifty workers from Toppan Printing went to the home of Kawai Tatsutarō, the company head, in Shitaya Ward to demand an interview. The police, who often intervened to maintain peace, at times took the side of the workers. When two hundred dredging workers went on strike in 1912, the police chastised the leader of the disturbance but then themselves opened negotiations with the municipal authorities to secure a wage increase for the dredgers. Companies usually fired the instigators of a disturbance; this was the case with printing workers in Honjo in 1908.[22]

Such labor disturbances were discrete incidents that constituted no general pattern of resistance to the existing order. Conservative rather than radical, workers demanded no new rights or privileges but simply asked for what they felt was their due under the existing rules of society. The significance of labor disturbances changed when unions linked the participants with demands for political and social reform, which were implicit critiques of the existing government, the leading political parties, and many of the local neighborhood organizations. The first unions of lasting influence in Honjo, as in most of Japan, were those associated with the Yūaikai.

In 1912, Suzuki Bunji, a graduate of Tokyo Imperial University, founded the Yūaikai in a Unitarian church in Shiba Ward, Tokyo, for the mutual aid and self-improvement of workers. The social problems that inspired Suzuki to found the Yūaikai were the same ones that had given impetus to the development of public and private social welfare facilities. Suzuki himself had done research on vagrants in Tokyo and on the relief institutions available there. As a graduate of the law section of Tokyo University, Suzuki also had contact with the scholarly and bureaucratic advocates of social welfare facilities in Japan. Kuwata Kumazō, who was so important in spreading German social policy theory in Japan, had been Suzuki's teacher and served as an advisor to the Yūaikai. Suzuki became a member of the Social Policy Society (Shakai seisaku gakkai), which Kuwata had helped found, and several members of the society advised and aided Suzuki in his union work. Another advisor to the Yūaikai was Ogawa Shigejirō, the advocate of district welfare committees, who also advised the Home Ministry on prison reform. Like many other Japanese reformers, Suzuki was a Christian. The Unitarian church in which the Yūaikai was founded continued to give moral support.[23]

In its early days from 1912 to 1918, the Yūaikai established a presence at some of the largest factories in Honjo. Before Suzuki set up a branch in any given factory, he always secured the consent of the factory head.[24] Thus, Yūaikai branches reinforced rather than undermined the sense of identity that workers felt with their place of employment. To be sure, the society furnished the workers with new ideas about their position in society and encouraged them to improve their own situation, but at this point the reforms proposed by Yūaikai leaders were quite moderate. Although a few chapters and branches of the Yūaikai took part in labor disturbances and Suzuki Bunji mediated a number of disputes, strikes were not an activity the Yūaikai took pride in.

The opening ceremonies for the Honjo chapter of the Yūaikai took place on February 27, 1915. By 1916, membership had grown to 1,650 (1,200 men and 450 women). The Honjo chapter was made up of many branches. In the early days, there was sometimes more than one branch at a factory, but by 1919 the branches corresponded to the various factories where some of the workers belonged to the Yūaikai. The five branches that had the greatest representation among the officers of the Honjo chapter in 1919 were those at Fuji Gas Spinning, Mitatsuchi Rubber, Takeuchi Safe, Japan Bicycle, and the Train Manufacturing Company. These included four of the five largest factories in the ward. In addition, the official magazine of the Yūaikai made passing mention of new members from the Tōbu Railroad, the Narihira branch of the Gas and Electric Company, and the Seikō

Watch factory.[25] These factories, too, each employed well over a hundred workers.

Branch activities included mutual relief, recreation, education, and self-improvement. Mutual relief and recreation were particularly important in creating a group consciousness. Mutual aid consisted in part of cash payments to those who were ill or whose relatives had died, or to the families of deceased workers. It sometimes took the form of ritual expressions of friendship among union members. Union representatives visited the ill and the bereaved; when a member died, his colleagues in the union might attend the calling hours or funeral.[26]

Regular branch meetings brought members together and provided the arena for educational activities. The usual format for these gatherings was the "tea meeting" *(chawakai)*. Following the regular business meeting, someone from union headquarters gave a talk. The meetings ended with tea and cakes. New Year's parties and outings were examples of recreational activities. Both the Oshiage and the Takeuchi branches held New Year's parties in 1919. At the Oshiage party, Tanahashi Kotora from Yūaikai headquarters gave a talk, after which the workers gave three cheers for the emperor and the union and drank sake together. Several months later, the Takeuchi workers, with the factory head's permission, organized an outing to Nakayama in Chiba prefecture. Setting out from the factory, they sang as they marched to the train station. In front of the Honjo chapter headquarters, they stopped to give three cheers.[27]

One of the basic aims of the Yūaikai was to educate workers in order to build their self-respect and their ability to further their own cause. From the earliest days of the organization, Suzuki invited prominent speakers to the regular meetings that were held at Unity Hall in Shiba on the first of each month. The branch meetings extended this custom to the local level. The speakers at branch meetings were usually representatives from the Yūaikai headquarters or advisors to the organization. It seems likely that these men spoke on the same topics that they wrote about for the official publications of the union: labor problems in Japan, labor movements in foreign lands, and universal suffrage.[28]

Among those who made frequent appearances at the tea meetings in Honjo was Aburadani Jirōshichi, the head of the education section of the Yūaikai. A graduate of Dōshisha, the premier Christian university in Kyoto, Aburadani had spent several years studying in the United

States.[29] Occasional meetings of the entire Honjo chapter provided additional opportunities to educate the workers. Aburadani spoke at these larger meetings, as did Suzuki and Kitazawa Shinjirō, a young professor at Waseda University.[30]

In its early years, the Yūaikai, although it did not stand aloof from labor conflicts once they erupted, was important primarily as a mediator between the workers and the management rather than as an instigator of protest. Suzuki himself was often the negotiator. In 1916, when thirty-one workers who demanded distribution of the profits of the Hiraoka Vehicle Company were fired, Suzuki was able to secure their retention as employees. In February of the next year he negotiated a 10 percent raise for workers at the Mitatsuchi Rubber Company in Honjo; the striking workers had demanded a wage increase of 30 percent. At his suggestion, the workers shouted "Banzai!" for the company and the company officials did so for the workers. These instances from Honjo were typical of Suzuki's increasing role in labor disturbances. In the three years from August 1912 to August 1915, he intervened in seventeen labor disputes; in the next year and a half alone, he mediated twenty-seven, most of which involved Yūaikai members. Suzuki's chief motive was to dispel by his presence the notion that the Yūaikai was instigating strikes.[31]

On some occasions workers who were members of the Yūaikai did lead disturbances. On July 29, 1917, for instance, the male workers at the Fuji Gas Spinning Company demanded an increase in wages of 18 percent because of the recent increase in prices. Because the company directors were out of town for the summer, the matter could not be settled immediately. By telegram and telephone, the parties agreed that a decision would be made on August 3. The workers then decided they would not work for the intervening six days. When management ordered them out of the company recreation hall, they did not return to their work but instead marched out of the factory compound and reassembled in the grounds of a nearby temple; for the next few days, the workers reported there each morning rather than to their work at the factory. The leader of this disturbance was Akiyama Naojirō, who had been an officer of the Honjo chapter of the Yūaikai since 1916.[32]

Suzuki was in Chiba prefecture when the incident began. Upon his return to Tokyo on August 1, he met first with the workers and then with Abe, the factory head. The negotiations that followed included an interview on August 2 with Wada Toyoji, the head of the entire Fuji Gas Spinning Company. Finally, when the workers agreed unconditionally to return to work, the company announced a 10 percent increase in wages. Suzuki did not raise the issue of whether the workers should have the right to strike. In fact, in these years, Suzuki deliberately dissociated the Yūaikai from unlawful actions. The volume to commemorate the fifth anniversary of the Yūaikai stated proudly that of the tens of strikes in the nation, Yūaikai members had participated in only a few peaceful and justifiable actions. In particular, the Mitatsuchi strike was an example of courageous perseverance, which demonstrated that group action could work for orderly and gradual change.[33]

Prior to the end of World War I, then, the Yūaikai did not change significantly the relationship of the workers to the neighborhood elite. Yūaikai chapters merely reinforced the ties of the workers to their places of employment, which were, in any case, the large factories that had only tenuous connections to the local community. This was all the more true when companies responded to Yūaikai activities by extending further welfare benefits to their employees.[34] When members of the Yūaikai occasionally made demands upon their employers, they generally asked for an increase in wages. Suzuki's mediation as the representative of a worker organization was a new development, but his presence did not eliminate other mediators such as the police.

What the Yūaikai did do was to draw working-class residents of the neighborhood into civic participation. Although the owners of large factories did not reside in the neighborhoods of Honjo, the workers in Honjo factories lived not far from their place of work. The Yūaikai involved working-class-neighborhood residents in civic associations and speech meetings that had heretofore been the preserve of the wealthier professionals and merchants who enjoyed the franchise.[35]

Labor Disputes and Labor Unions, 1919–1923

In August 1919, at its annual meeting, the Yūaikai transformed itself from a friendly society to a federation of unions and changed its name to Dai Nihon rōdō sōdōmei yūaikai (Great Japan federation of labor friendly society), usually shortened to Sōdōmei. This formal change was the result of a number of developments within the Yūaikai. First, there was an influx of new leadership. Inspired by the Russian Revolution and the rice riots of 1918, bright, enthusiastic young graduates of Tokyo and other universities sought to hasten Japan's progress toward democracy by organizing labor. Second, Suzuki himself had been trying to advance the cause of labor in Japan by forming industry-based unions. The redefinition of unions as associations of workers united by their industry rather than by their company or neighborhood symbolized the growing self-consciousness of the labor movement. Finally, organizational changes within the Yūaikai permitted leaders in the large cities of Western Japan, who were more radical than Suzuki, to involve the Yūaikai in political issues.[36] The effect of these policies at the local level was to create among the unionized workers a political self-consciousness that could not easily be co-opted by the local elite.

In a larger sense, the transformation of the Yūaikai reflected the changes wrought in Japan by World War I. The rapid expansion of industry during the war increased the frequency of labor disturbances. The number of incidents jumped from 64 in 1915, to 108 in 1916, 398 in 1917, 417 in 1918, and 497 in 1919. In many of these incidents, the workers achieved their aims; at the time it was estimated that 60 percent of the strikes between 1911 and 1919 were successful.[37] As Andrew Gordon has so aptly stated, "Inflation made union activity necessary and attractive; the labor shortage and the desire of owners to avoid costly strikes made it often successful." In the intellectual realm, the Russian Revolution abroad and the rice riots at home inspired hope that the power of the masses could transform domestic politics. The labor clauses in the Treaty of Versailles bestowed international legitimacy on organized labor. By the time the Yūaikai became the Sōdōmei in 1919, Yūaikai membership was thirty thousand.[38]

Among the enthusiastic young intellectuals who joined the Yūaikai leadership were Tanahashi Kotora and Asō Hisashi, both of whom graduated from Tokyo Imperial University in 1917. Tanahashi was from Nagano, where he had graduated from the Matsumoto Middle School before going on to the Third Higher School and the imperial university. Asō, who was from Oita in Kyūshū, also attended the Third Higher School. Both had been greatly influenced by Professor Yoshino Sakuzō and his ideas on democracy. Following graduation, Tanahashi worked at the Tokyo district court and Asō became a reporter for the *Tōkyō nichinichi shinbun*. Both men took an interest in the Russian Revolution, and in the closing days of 1917, together with Yamana Yoshitsuru and other classmates, they formed the "Wednesday Society" to discuss revolution; they were soon joined by others such as Sano Manabu, another Tokyo graduate, who was to be one of the founding members of the Japan Communist Party, and Akamatsu Katsumaro, a student at Tokyo University. During Tanahashi's student days, Yoshino Sakuzō had introduced him to Suzuki Bunji. In the autumn of 1918, just after the rice riots, Tanahashi resigned from the position that could have been the first step in a distinguished career in the Ministry of Justice and joined the Yūaikai as director for the Kantō regional headquarters. Asō entered the Yūaikai in the summer of 1919 as director of publications.[39]

Under this new leadership, the Yūaikai expanded its scope of activities beyond the factory walls and into the political realm. For instance, the union circulated and in March 1919 presented to the Diet a petition for the repeal of Article 17, the article that denied workers the right to strike.[40] Working-class members of the Yūaikai could not help but notice the new concern for political issues. The August 1919 issue of *Rōdō oyobi sangyō* (Labor and production), the official publication of the Yūaikai, proclaimed on its cover in large characters, "Overcome the Evil Peace Police Law!" In March 1920, *Rōdō* (Labor), the retitled official publication, published the words to a song on universal suffrage.

The Yūaikai and fifteen other labor groups sponsored the first Japanese celebration of May Day on Sunday, May 2, 1920, in Ueno Park. Suzuki Bunji opened and closed the meeting. There was no mistaking the political content of the resolution that called for abolition of the Peace Police Act, the prevention of unemployment, and the establishment of a minimum wage. Banners covered with huge red characters, floating against a blue sky, reinforced those demands in the minds of all who attended.[41]

The impact of these developments was soon felt in Honjo. Asō and Tanahashi became frequent visitors. Even before they formally joined the Yūaikai, they brought their new ideas to the workers at chapter and branch meetings. Tanahashi spoke at tea meetings at the Takeuchi Safe Company on October 15 and November 15, 1917, and at Mitatsuchi Rubber on November 20, 1918, and January 15 and 23, 1919. When the Honjo chapter held its 1918 fall meeting at the Narihira Elementary School on Sunday, October 20, Tanahashi was one of the speakers. He made other appearances at the New Year's party at Fuji Gas Spinning Company in 1919 and at a speech meeting at Mitatsuchi Rubber on February 16, 1919, at which Asō also spoke while still a reporter. Asō also appeared at a large speech meeting of the Honjo chapter on June 22, 1919, and at a tea meeting on August 15, 1919.[42]

Honjo was the site of one of Suzuki's first efforts to create industry unions within the Yūaikai. This was the Yūaikai Spinners Union, which had its strongest support at the Fuji Gas Spinning factory. The Honjo chapter of the Yūaikai took the first step toward the creation of a spinning union when it invited all workers employed in spinning in Tokyo to an organizational meeting on March 1, 1918. The twenty-one representatives of six factories who attended took no immediate action. It was the officers of the Oshiage branch of the Honjo chapter who voted on June 6 to found a spinners union (Bōshoku rōdō kumiai) with the Fuji Gas factory at its center. The new union would consist of all Yūaikai members employed at the Oshiage factory of Fuji Gas Spinning Company.[43]

In reality, then, the spinners union was little different from the Oshiage branch of the Honjo chapter. The personnel was the same. Almost all of the officers of the Spinning Union had long and distinguished careers in the Honjo chapter. Nevertheless, the establishment of industry-based unions encouraged a feeling of unity with other workers of the same industry. This sense of solidarity with other workers was a small but important wedge between the worker and his company, who were none too securely attached to each other in the first place. Workers consciously at odds with management could easily become alienated from the local elite of the neighborhood as well.

Under union leadership, labor disturbances ceased to be spontaneous, unplanned outbreaks. Leaders planned their course of action and alternatives to it in advance. They printed up the strike demands and resorted to new methods of struggle such as picketing and sabotage. Honjo, with its many factories, was of course affected by these developments. In 1919 alone, there were twenty-three labor disputes in the ward; unions were involved in disturbances at Takeuchi Safe Company, Seikō Watch, Mitatsuchi Rubber, and Fuji Gas Spinning Company. Strikers demanded better working conditions as well as higher wages. In at least two cases, one at the Train Manufacturing

Company and one at Seikō Watch, the workers demanded establishment of the eight-hour day. What had previously been mere quarrels between employers and their employees became confrontations with the state as the police took workers into custody. One such instance was the Seikō Watch disturbance of June 1919.[44]

The 1920 strike at the Fuji Gas Spinning Company was significant in the history of the labor movement because the workers included among their demands recognition of their union. Moreover, in this strike, the quarrel between management and labor in one factory spread to the society at large. The strike drew considerable outside support, only some of it from the Sōdōmei. The rights of workers in one factory were becoming the concern of all workers. The state resisted this notion when the police stepped in and arrested several workers who were demonstrating in sympathy with the Fuji union.

The main issue in this disturbance was the right of the union to exist. There had been a branch of the Honjo chapter of the Yūaikai at this company since 1914, and the company had never before objected to its presence. In 1920, however, fearing the growing power of the union, company officials began to try to break it up. To divide the women workers, the company formed a young women's society to compete with the women's section of the Yūaikai. The company also forbade the Yūaikai to collect dues, and on June 27 they fired two officers of the Spinning Union, Akaishi Haruyoshi and Tamura Shozo. Tamura, especially, had worked for the causes of the Yūaikai and benefited from its programs for a number of years. In 1916, he contributed toward Suzuki's trip to America; two years later, when his son died, he was the recipient of money from his union.[45]

Once again, the union came to his support. Three officers, especially—Satō Yoshitoku, Ōhashi Heikichi, and Shibayama Tamakichi—rallied the workers and collected money for Tamura and Akaishi. The company opposed these activities, and on July 13, it fired Satō, Ōhashi, and Shibayama. The next morning at 6:00 A.M., the members of the union met in the company recreation room and announced a strike for company recognition of the Spinning Union. By the end of the day, the company had ordered the strikers out of the recreation room and had locked the women workers who lived in company quarters into their dormitories, out of communication with the strikers. The workers transferred their strike headquarters to a nearby restaurant. On July 15, Satō and Shibayama and three others went to the headquarters of the company in Nihonbashi and asked the company to restore the fired workers and to recognize the union.

Throughout these weeks, Sōdōmei headquarters provided support for the struggling workers. Satō, Akaishi, and Tamura visited there on July 10. The next day, Asō, Tanahashi, and Takata Waitsu came from headquarters to attend the tea meeting of the Spinning Union. When the strike was announced on July 14, Asō and Tanahashi were in attendance. On July 16, the Kantō Regional Alliance of the Sōdōmei resolved to support the Spinning Union in its strike at Fuji Gas. On the same day, Tanahashi attended a speech meeting at strike headquarters. The Yūaikai held speech meetings in support of the striking workers at union headquarters on July 16, 17, and 19.

In this dispute, the union support from outside the Fuji factory had social and ideological dimensions not present in earlier disputes in the area. Asō and Tanahashi, slightly more enthusiastic than Suzuki Bunji in their commitment to socialism and the reform of Japanese society, shared with Suzuki his Tokyo University education. Takata Waitsu, on the other hand, came to the Sōdōmei from the ranks of the workers. He was employed at the Shibaura Manufacturing Company when he first came into contact with the Yūaikai through a study group set up by intellectuals including Asō and Tanahashi in the Tsukishima district of Tokyo. Takata and others such as Yamamoto Kenzō, a fellow worker at Shibaura, were attracted to the ideas of Kropotkin and came to place more confidence in anarchist notions of direct action than did their original teachers.[46] Takata's presence at these meetings, then, represented a faction within the Sōdōmei that was more likely to press the workers on to resistance against the company. Moreover, among the non-Sōdōmei unions whose members demonstrated in support of the Fuji workers were the Shin'yūkai and the Seishinkai, both anarchist in their political approach. This new militancy did not go unnoticed by the authorities. On July 18, the police arrested five or six workers from other chapters of the Yūaikai and other unions who were demonstrating in support of the strikers in front of the main gate of the plant.

The union directly challenged state policy toward labor when it attacked the Kyōchōkai, a semigovernmental organization established in 1919. The Kyōchōkai—whose board of directors included Wada Toyoji, the president of the Fuji Gas Spinning Company—refused to mediate or acknowledge the right of the workers to strike. In a letter of July 16, the Sōdōmei queried the Kyōchōkai as to how Wada's presence on the board could be reconciled with the supposed impartiality of the organization. When the Kyōchōkai issued only pious equivocations in response, the Sōdōmei proclaimed that the incident exposed the Kyōchōkai, supposedly the instrument of harmony between labor and capital, as the protector of capitalism. The presence of the owner of Fuji Gas on the board of a supposedly neutral, government-sponsored organization was indicative of the disadvantaged position of the workers in shaping labor policy. The negative publicity from this exchange did, however, cause the Kyōchōkai to undertake a major reorganization in October 1920. Three new managing directors were appointed, in the hope that they would be more adept in dealing with labor. One of these was Tazawa Yoshiharu, who would later serve in the Tokyo municipal government and the Japan League of Young Men's Associations.[47]

On July 22, just a few days after the Sōdōmei sent its letter to the Kyōchōkai, the company acknowledged the right of the workers to organize and the strikers agreed to return to work on July 24. What had seemed an amicable settlement quickly degenerated, however. On July 23, the company fired several women workers and began pressuring union members to renounce their membership. The workers, feeling the company had again broken its word, resolved to continue the strike. The labor movement rallied behind the workers at Fuji. There was a huge speech meeting at the Kanda YMCA building on July 24 and a demonstration parade the next day. The Fuji workers themselves, however, exhausted by nine days of striking, gave up the struggle. After the company announced a bonus in honor of the twenty-fifth anniversary of the company, only thirty-seven workers kept up the fight. The Spinning Union was completely crushed.

Another instance in which union members outside the ward supported strikers in Honjo was the disturbance at Mitatsuchi Rubber in the fall of 1922. In celebration of its transformation from a partnership to a joint-stock company, the company announced that it would pay a bonus to the fifty-eight workers with ten or more years of service. The majority of the workers resented that this windfall was enjoyed by only a few. More than five hundred workers joined the Great Japan Rubber Workers Union (Dai Nihon gomu rōdō kumiai), an affiliate of the Sōdōmei.[48]

The Great Japan Rubber Workers Union was the latest incarnation of the Yūaikai branch at Mitatsuchi, which had been one of the original components of the Honjo chapter. Like the Spinning Union, it was an attempt to redefine local labor units as industry rather than company unions. The rubber union held its opening ceremony on May 22, 1921, at the Oshiage Club. Several of the leaders of the new union had been officers of the Honjo chapter of the Yūaikai since 1918. Suzuki Bunji had helped negotiate settlement of a disturbance at Mitatsuchi in 1917, and the union leadership had maintained close ties with the local branch in the intervening years. Tanahashi Kotora, Asō Hisashi, Takata Waitsu, and other leaders of the union spoke at meetings at Mitatsuchi. The union organized a women's tea meeting at the company and dispatched Tanaka Takako, an American-educated activist, as a special speaker.[49]

In the 1922 dispute, an eighteen-member executive committee of the Great Japan Rubber Workers Union presented demands to the company; when these were refused, the workers started a work slowdown on November 2.[50] When the workers met on November 5, they were promised strong support by the Tokyo Ironworkers Union (Tōkyō tekkō kumiai), the union to which Takata Waitsu, who had brought anarchist influences to the Fuji strike, belonged.

On the morning of November 6, representatives of the rubber workers union asked that Mitatsuchi distribute sixty thousand yen as bonuses to those employed less than ten years. The company announced its refusal the next day. Beginning on November 8, the laborers reported to the company but did no work. At this point, there was dissension among the workers as to whether they were really willing to resign their jobs over this issue. Meanwhile, the labor representative of the Tokyo Metropolitan Police tried to work out a settlement.

On November 9, Tazaki, the company manager, called nineteen workers—including Nemoto Komakichi, Mori Asakichi, and Ishikawa Gonnosuke—to his office and told them that, because of their opposition to the interests of the company, he was firing them without severance pay. The workers, united once more by indignation, rallied in two separate locations in defense of their representatives and resolved to go on strike the next day.

As in the case of the Fuji strike, the Sōdōmei and its affiliated unions supported the strikers. Various branches of the Yūaikai sent money and demonstrators. The Tokyo Ironworkers Union sent three representatives—Yokoishi Shinichi, Ichimura Hikao, and Nakajima Seihachi—to help organize strike activities such as peddling goods to raise strike funds.[51] The Kantō Regional Alliance dispatched Yamaguchi Taiichi and five others to aid in the negotiations with the company. Matsuoka Komakichi of Sōdōmei headquarters helped negotiate the final settlement. Other union leaders who contributed to planning sessions and speech meetings were Doi Naosaku, Tawara Tsugio, and Akamatsu Katsumaro. While most of these supporters from outside the company were part of the Sōdōmei, they represented a variety of opinions on the best strategy for the labor movement. The Tokyo Ironworkers Union and the Kantō Regional Alliance were both known for their anarchistic tendencies. It is likely that the outside leaders urged the workers on to greater resistance against the company.[52]

The first three efforts at negotiation, on November 11, 13, and 14, came to naught. The strike finally ended on November 22 when the company agreed to pay a bonus to the workers employed less than ten years and to pay fourteen days' wages and normal severance pay to the workers who had been fired. Although the workers won some concessions from the company, the cost of the victory was high. Nineteen rubber workers lost their jobs. In addition, two of the supporters from outside the factory, Yokoishi and Ichimura, were arrested.

In the disturbance at the Train Manufacturing Company in 1922, ideological conflict within the labor movement manifested itself in a struggle between two rival unions within the same company. In the summer of 1922 the only union at the plant, one with origins in the Honjo chapter of the Yūaikai, had about a hundred members. In August, conflict developed between two officers of the association, Namakata Saichirō and Ono Keiji. On August 16, Ono resigned his union office and with Matsubara, another former union officer, set out to destroy the union he had helped found. On August 30, members of Namakata's faction asked the company officials to dismiss Ono and Matsubara. When the company refused, the workers went on strike on September 18.[53]

Once again, support came from other unions. Tawara Tsugio and Watanabe Manzō, both of the anti-Sōdōmei Association of Machine Workers Unions, attended the speech meeting held at the Nippon Club in Fukagawa. Again, the cost of such support was high; on September 24, three demonstrators were arrested in front of the Train Manufacturing Company for violation of the publishing law.[54]

As a result of that struggle, there were two labor organizations at the Train Manufacturing Company: the Kakushinkai, with 780 members, mainly those who took part in the strike of 1922, and the Seibokukai, with 126 members, a group that enjoyed a close relationship with the company. In February 1923, however, the Kakushinkai dissolved and reconstituted itself as the Kantō Vehicle Workers Union (Kantō sharyō kumiai), a union affiliated with the Association of Machine Workers Unions, which had aided the Kakushinkai in its recent struggle. Consistent with the militant position of its parent association, the new union insisted that there should be only one labor organization in the company. Thus, the new union was founded with the understanding that both of the older unions would participate. Opening ceremonies for the Kantō Vehicle Workers Union were held on February 25.[55]

Difficulties in merging the two older unions lingered on long after the opening ceremonies for the new union. Negotiations on the part of the Seibokukai during April and May were met with insistence that the union agree unconditionally to the merger. When the Seibokukai met on May 19 to consider the merger, several members of the Vehicle Workers Union invaded the meeting and disrupted it. This created an irreparable rift between the two groups. The Seibokukai announced on May 21 that it would not merge with the Kantō Vehicle Workers Union but would instead become the Honjo branch of the Kantō Ironworkers Union, associated with the Sōdōmei. The Kantō Vehicle Workers Union resolved to eliminate the opposing group, arguing that the Seibokukai was a company union and that its existence interfered with the right of workers to organize. On May 22, Namakata Saichirō and twenty others went to Sasaki, the manager, and asked him to fire two officers of the Seibokukai—Andō Tarōkichi and Mukai Otogoro—as threats to peace among the workers. The company replied the next day at noon that this was a matter to be settled among the workers themselves and that the company would not fire the workers.[56]

When the company refused to do their will, the Vehicle Workers Union began a work slowdown. On May 24, after closing time, the workers gathered at the Ōjima Labor Hall, where they resolved to continue their slowdown and bury the officers of the Seibokukai. During rest period the next day, they found Mukai and three other leaders of the Seibokukai and surrounded them; no injuries were sustained only because the company officials hid the workers in an office. The company had finally had enough of the Vehicle Workers Union. At closing time that day, it announced that Namakata Saichirō and sixteen other members of the union were fired.[57]

At a meeting in Ōjima that evening, the leaders of the Vehicle Workers Union resolved to press the company for reasons for the firings. They were not satisfied with Sasaki's answer at an interview on May 26 that the workers were fired for the convenience of the company. A union delegation consisting of Numada Tetsuji and eight others met with Sasaki again on the morning of May 28 and demanded that Andō and Mukai be fired and that the seventeen fired members of the Kakushinkai be restored to their positions. Sasaki refused. When the workers heard that their demands had been refused, they walked off their jobs. They reassembled in the Ōjima Labor Hall and resolved to strike until their purposes had been realized. Various speakers expounded on the unfairness of the company. Thirty police from the Taihei Station began keeping watch on the disturbance.[58]

The confrontations that followed—between the strikers and the members of the Seibokukai who continued to work, between the strikers and the police, and between the strikers and the company— lasted for nearly two months. As the strike dragged on and the families of the strikers began to suffer, individual strikers weakened and returned to work. Threatened by these defections, the strike group became violent against the scabs who were working. One rainy evening, June 21, fighting broke out between members of the two unions in front of the Honjo chapter of the Sōdōmei in Oshiage, where about a hundred members of the Seibokukai had assembled. Three members of the Vehicle Workers Union were hurt. A week later, on June 28, Ichikawa Benjirō and seven other members of the Vehicle Workers Union entered the headquarters of the opposing union and damaged it; the police arrested some of the culprits.[59]

The bitterness between the two unions at this plant was exacerbated by ideological rifts within the labor movement. The Seibokukai was closely associated with the Sōdōmei, with its origins in friendly associations and a recent tendency among some elements toward communism. The Association of Machine Workers Unions, which supported the Kakushinkai, leaned toward anarchism. Initially, the Seibokukai struggle was directed by Watanabe Masanosuke, one of the founding members of the Japan Communist Party, and Yamamoto Kenzō, a radical worker. Both were forced to go underground when the government launched a major roundup of suspected communists in the summer of 1923, but they were replaced by Tsukamoto Shigezō and Uchida Tōshichi.[60]

Tsukamoto was a leader of the Sōdōmei in Osaka, where the headquarters of the Train Manufacturing Company was located; the workers at the Osaka plant belonged to a union associated with the Sōdōmei. During the strike the union of the Osaka plant printed and distributed pamphlets that placed the blame for the disturbance in Tokyo on the Vehicle Workers Union. Beyond providing headquarters, leadership, and printed materials refuting accusations made by the Vehicle Workers Union against the Sōdōmei, however, the Sōdōmei did relatively little to advance the cause of the Seibokukai. The Association of Machine Workers Unions played a more active part, sponsoring two speech meetings at the Kanda Youth Hall, one on June 23 and one on June 30, and another meeting in Kyōbashi on June 28. Admission was charged at some of these meetings to raise money for the families of the striking workers.[61]

With the passage of time, the strikers modified their demands. Whereas they had begun by asking that two men from the opposing union be fired and that the sixteen men from their own union who were fired be restored, after weeks of struggle, they asked only that the fired workers receive severance pay and that the other workers be paid for the days on strike. In the end, exhausted by the strike, the workers suddenly announced on July 11 that they would return to work unconditionally.[62]

In the history of the labor union movement, these struggles in Honjo stand as mileposts in the development of the self-consciousness of the working class. The Fuji struggle has been cited as one of the first instances in Japan in which a union struck for recognition from the company. The disturbance at the Train Manufacturing Company was deemed significant at the time because it was one of the first in which the main struggle was between two unions rather than between the union and the company.[63] It was, of course, only the first of many struggles within the labor movement over the correct political line. In the urban area where these struggles took place, however, the three incidents represent the end rather than the beginning of a pattern of uprisings.

These events were in some sense the culmination of the development of the branches of the Yūaikai in the large factories in Honjo in the early days of the organization. All three struggles involved unions with origins in the Yūaikai and affiliation with the Sōdōmei. In the Fuji strike, most of the leaders of the struggle had long been members of the Yūaikai. Even at Mitatsuchi Rubber, where the rapid turnover in employees was illustrated by the fact that only fifty-eight of the six hundred some employees had been at the company for ten years, some of the leaders of the strike had participated in the earlier Yūaikai branch. Further, many of the methods and channels of communication used in these struggles had been developed in the union branches. Speech meetings, a common instrument of the strikers, had been a regular feature of Yūaikai programs. The communist workers Watanabe and Yamamoto appeared at precisely the same types of meetings as Tanahashi and Asō had attended before them, and Aburadani and Suzuki before that.

We cannot know what direction the evolution of these unions would have taken if the earthquake of September 1, 1923, had not destroyed the factories themselves shortly after the conclusion of the last of the three disturbances. The Fuji factory was never rebuilt. It was some time before Mitatsuchi and the Train Manufacturing Company could restore their operations in Honjo to their original prosperity. There is no doubt that the earthquake disrupted the ties of the work force to the area. Hundreds of thousands fled the immediate destruction to find work in other cities of Japan; the laborers who flocked to Tokyo during the subsequent building boom were not the skilled workers who had left. The earthquake, then, provides some explanation for the fact that labor disturbances in Honjo no longer centered on the original branches of the Yūaikai chapter. In December 1923, members of the Vehicle Workers Union demanded better treatment from the Train Manufacturing Company.[64] With this exception, no further major labor struggles broke out at either Mitatsuchi or the Train Manufacturing Company.

The dramatic struggles that occurred in Honjo in the 1920s illustrate how the democratic ideals of the rights of ordinary individuals to oppose authority had penetrated the ranks of workers. These costly struggles held no promise, however, that resistance to authority would be easy or even effective. In practical terms, these incidents accomplished little; only at Mitatsuchi did the workers achieve their original aims. In fact, some workers ended up worse off; in each case a number of union members were fired and never rehired.

It seems likely, however, that the hundreds of workers involved in these struggles—some of whom no doubt continued to live in the neighborhood—learned a number of political lessons. Certainly they saw that strikes, although not always effective, were more likely to be effective with the organizational apparatus provided by a union. Union effectiveness was yet further enhanced when the local union was affiliated with a larger organization. Meeting rooms, public halls, printed materials, distinguished speakers, and experienced organizers flowed from central headquarters to the striking workers. The Sōdōmei in particular proved itself to be a faithful friend in struggle as well as at tea meetings. Moreover, the support from outside unions, although sometimes from idealistic academics and professionals, was by the 1920s often from other workers. Any worker who missed the political significance of class solidarity did not miss it for long, and the state pressed home the point by arresting outside supporters. The arrests that occurred in the disturbances in Honjo reflected the new government interpretation of Article 17, which permitted workers to organize themselves but which had little tolerance for agitators from outside the company.[65]

For the residents of the ward not directly involved in the struggles, the strikes presented a spectacle. The speech meetings, the demonstrations, and the clashes with police were visible to any passerby. These companies were major employers and many of the strikers no doubt lived near the factory, so local residents observing the spectacle knew that the livelihood of some of their neighbors was at stake. At the same time, the high walls that set large factories apart from the daily life of the neighborhood symbolized the aloofness of these enterprises from the communal life of the neighborhood. Strikes at Fuji Gas and the Train Manufacturing Company in no way disrupted the rotation among households for fire watch or the plans for the local shrine festival. Moreover, these factories produced for the nation and the world, not for local consumption. The struggles between employers and employees did not affect the daily lives of most local residents. Nearby shopkeepers and apprentices experienced no immediate shortage of textiles or rubber or railroad cars. Nearby residents did not know the managers and directors who were the objects of these strikes as either neighbors or local leaders.

Labor Disputes, Labor Unions, and the Neighborhood, 1923–1937

The Great Kantō Earthquake of 1923, which was as devastating to the industry of Honjo Ward as it was to its housing, made large factories less important in the life of the ward. Whereas in 1920 Honjo Ward had two factories with over a thousand workers and twenty-seven others employing over a hundred, in 1925 there were no factories having as many as a thousand workers and only fourteen factories employing more than a hundred. Even by 1933 there was only one factory employing over a thousand workers and only seventeen others employing over a hundred.[66] Some of the large companies—the Fuji Gas Spinning Company, for instance—simply chose not to rebuild their Honjo factory branch. Others reopened on a smaller scale than before; one soap factory that employed over a hundred in 1920 had only fifty-eight employees in 1925. The administrators of large factories were more than ever distant from the affairs of the ward. Even those owners who had earlier been active in public affairs disappeared from the scene.[67]

At the same time that large factories became less important in Honjo, they also became less important in the labor movement. By the mid-1920s, union organizing centered in small and medium enterprises. Historians concerned primarily with the role that labor ought to have played in Japanese history have interpreted the shift of labor activities from large Japanese firms to small and medium-sized firms in the 1920s as proof that the movement failed to influence the mainstream of Japanese society.[68]

If we set aside Western preconceptions as to how the labor movement ought to have functioned and look instead at how it actually operated in the neighborhoods where the workers lived, we find that, in the years after the earthquake, labor union activity in Honjo was more disruptive than ever before of the social and political ties in the neighborhood. Whereas most of the branches of the Honjo chapter of the Yūaikai began in large factories that were only one part of the total operation of a larger company, many of the strikes after the earthquake occurred in locally owned companies. There were even a number of disturbances in small factories, owned and managed by residents of the ward. The owners of small factories were often leaders of local organizations, at the very time when such organizations were articulating the neighborhood more explicitly than ever before. Thus, in striking, workers were confronting not only their employers but also the social order of their local neighborhood. Politicized laborers found themselves in direct confrontations with neighborhood organizations in 1934 when city officials called in members of the young men's associations to take the place of striking streetcar workers.

Aoki Naoji, the owner of the Aoki Dyeing Company, lived in Honjo Ward and was active in local affairs. Nevertheless, a union-led labor dispute occurred at his factory in 1926. Of the 170 employees, 140 belonged to the Kantō Amalgamated Labor Unions (Kantō gōdō rōdō kumiai). The workers presented a detailed list of demands on August 19. They asked for an increase in pay of ten *sen* for men and five *sen* for women, payment of raises twice per year, payment for days out of work because of job-related injuries, credit for such days toward perfect attendance, better food, and provision of severance pay. The company, which met all demands, settled the dispute within a week. More labor disputes occurred at this company in the 1930s. In April 1931, the same union demanded better treatment for the workers; another disturbance broke out in October of that year. A year later, the workers called for and were refused an increase in their bonus. In November 1933 and November 1934 the workers again presented demands.[69]

Members of the same union led a disturbance at the Tokyo Hat Company in 1929. When the company announced wage increases on May 31, the workers were dissatisfied with the system used to calculate the raises. They petitioned the company for equal raises for all workers, for other changes in the pay system (for instance, larger bonuses, a bonus for perfect attendance, and extra pay for overtime), and for the reinstatement of certain workers who had been fired. This struggle was not entirely successful, but the workers obtained twice-yearly raises, increased bonuses, and some extra compensation pay for the fired workers.[70]

The strike at the Great Japan Bicycle Company is a good illustration of the way a dispute between workers and their company could become the arena for a contest between opposing political forces. The strike itself was an unusually long one, lasting seventy-six days. All 241 workers at the factory participated. This strike had its roots in worker discontent with the wage system. The company paid a contracted amount to the section head, who then divided the pay among the workers. The workers objected to the way a certain section head, Kanai, was assessing their work. To deal with this problem, they organized a mutual benefit society and on March 26, 1928, they presented a list of ten demands to the company. In addition to changes in the pay system, they asked for the establishment of a dining hall and improvement of the eating utensils. They did not specifically mention Kanai.

The directors, managers, and representatives from the mutual benefit society met and drew up an agreement, which they announced on April 7. The company promised to make an official announcement on severance pay and to pay a portion of normal pay on national holidays. More important, although the pay system was not substantially changed, direct reference was made to a problem with the section head. The sixth item of the arbitration agreement said that the section head realized his past errors; he had reflected upon them and would henceforth lovingly lead the section. The workers, in turn, promised to obey him.[71]

It soon became apparent that the arbitration agreement had not solved the problem. The workers, feeling that Kanai was trying to break up their mutual benefit society, presented him with a resolution calling for his resignation. He responded by forcing some of the workers to resign. Because the dispute became violent, on April 27 the company fired five of the leaders of the mutual benefit society and two who were involved in the violence. The workers considered these dismissals unfair. The next day when the laborers reported to the factory, the fired workers reported with them. The assembled workers held a speech meeting. The company, declaring the factory temporarily closed, forced the workers to leave.

At this point, the members of the mutual benefit society, already in the midst of a full-fledged struggle, all joined the Tokyo Ironworkers Union, an affiliate of the Sōdōmei. Their organization then became the Honjo Number Two Branch. Opening ceremonies were held on April 29. On May 2, the workers formally petitioned the company to restore the seven fired workers, increase pay by 30 percent, give half pay for days missed from work because of military service, pay varying amounts for holidays, and refrain from making sacrificial victims of the leaders of the struggle. They demanded a reply by May 5. Meanwhile, on the same day, the company fired thirteen more workers and announced that the factory would remain temporarily closed and that wages would be paid only through May 8.

In the next stage of the struggle, the striking workers faced two problems. The first was to pin the company officials down to a definite date for negotiations. It seemed that some directors of the company had gone into hiding to avoid any consultation with the leaders of the strike. On May 17, groups of ten workers began calling on directors of the company, one at a time, in their homes. On May 22 twenty-three representatives met with Okazaki, the head of the company, at his home in Shiba and pressed for an answer to their demands. They did not meet with success. Their second problem was to prevent the striking workers from abandoning the struggle. The company strategy was to destroy the union and lure its members back to work. The management calculated that if one hundred workers returned, it would be worth their while to resume production. They announced several times that they would pay no wages after May 8. In addition, on May 21, they distributed a printed handout urging the strikers to return to work.

At a meeting on May 29, the leaders of the struggle resolved to combat the tactics of the company. They planned to circulate for signature a written covenant not to abandon the struggle and to distribute to the general public handbills censuring the political deviousness of the company head, Okazaki Kujirō. They resolved to take action if the company resumed production and to call upon other groups for aid. Circulation of the written covenant halted further defections.

During June, there were several attempts at negotiation between the strikers and the company, but the talks always broke down over the issue of restoring the fired workers to employment. The frustration of the workers over this impasse exploded in anger on June 26. Workers who had been lodging in the strike headquarters went to the factory and began throwing rocks at the windows. The police arrested seventeen of the workers. Negotiations reopened on June 29, but after four meetings, the representatives of the strikers, indignant because the company refused to consider restoration of the fired workers, again broke off the talks.

On July 7, representatives of the mediation section of the Metropolitan Police began consulting with both sides. On July 16, both sides affixed their seals to an agreement by which the strikers returned to work on July 20. The final agreement was by no means unfavorable to the workers. The company compromised on the question of the fired workers, agreeing to retain half of them and to give severance pay to those fired. The company also promised half pay for the days on strike and provided an additional sum for the relief of the workers' families. With respect to the issues that originally sparked the disturbance, the workers achieved a great deal. The company agreed to pay wages in a standard manner and to announce a policy on severance pay. The company also promised half pay for days missed because of military service and for the New Year's and Obon vacations.

Quite apart from its practical success, this strike is of historical significance for the way the strikers explicitly linked labor issues to popular participation in party politics. In May, when the struggle group circulated a printed bulletin addressed to the people of Tokyo on the unfair actions of the company, the publication was cosponsored not only by the Tokyo Ironworkers Union but also by the local chapter of the Social Democratic Party. This publication pointed out to the world at large that Okazaki Kujirō, president of the Great Japan Bicycle Company, had recently been elected to the Diet from Kanagawa prefecture as a Minseitō candidate. This publication and other handbills printed later by the Tokyo Ironworkers Union attacked Okazaki's political deceptiveness and the oppressive policies of the Minseitō. The union and the proletarian political party urged the residents of the neighborhood to join with the striking workers in an alliance against the capitalists, the landlords, and the members of the established political parties, and to do so not simply on behalf of the striking workers but for "the sake of the progress of state, society and the prosperity of all the people."[72] Both the strikers and the neighbors to whom they appealed had just three months earlier voted in their first national election, and they were confident of their place in the body politic.

After the earthquake, union activities were no longer confined to the large factories of the ward. Not every small-scale disturbance becomes inscribed in the historical record, but enough have been recorded to establish that union-led disturbances in small factories whose heads were resident in the ward was a common pattern in the late 1920s. Because the owners of the factories were closely connected with local organizations in the ward—organizations that were supposed to encompass all classes—and because small enterprises had usually operated as pseudofamily units, these disturbances were much more disruptive of the traditional vertical ties in the community than were the strikes at larger companies.

Twice in 1926 there were labor disturbances at the Saitō Watch factory in Mukōjima Susaki-chō, Honjo. In February, the twenty some workers at the plant organized to oppose the lowering of their wages; in October, they asked for a raise. Both times, the Kantō Metalworkers Union (Kantō kinzoku rōdō kumiai) supported the workers. Representatives from the labor union helped negotiate the agreement, which was signed on November 19. In contrast to the situations in which Suzuki Bunji had first served as a negotiator, the owner of the factory was not a remote figure living in a mansion in another ward. Saitō Sotarō was resident on the premises.[73]

Two other strikes that occurred in 1926 in factories owned by local residents were those at the Haneda Belt Company in Mukōjima Susaki-chō and at the Nimiya Glass Company in Yanagihara-chō. In November, twenty-five of the eighty employees of the belt factory went on strike for twenty-seven days demanding compensation for seven workers who had been fired. The striking workers were associated with the Tokyo Rubber Workers Union, an affiliate of the Hyōgikai, an association of unions that had split off from the Sōdōmei. At the glass factory, thirty-three of the forty-eight employees struck in protest against the firing of thirteen workers. The Tokyo Glassworkers Union, also an affiliate of the Hyōgikai, was involved in the struggle.[74]

Workers continued to fight for the right to join a union. In November 1927, eight of the twenty-six workers at the Ishibashi Cake Shop in Taihei-chō tried to join a union. The owner, who objected strongly to having a union, fired the eight workers and closed the factory. Representatives from the Kantō Amalgamated Labor Unions negotiated a settlement that provided severance pay for the fired workers. Again, a union mediated between workers and their employer, an employer who was not a stranger but whose residence adjoined their place of work.[75]

In many of these cases, the workers were on the defensive; the company had lowered their wages or denied them the right to a union or fired several workers. The strike demands were designed to recoup losses rather than to achieve positive gains. One incident notable for the relative success achieved by the workers in a small factory was that at the Chōgō Hat factory in Mukōjima Koume in June 1929. The workers presented demands and began a work slowdown on June 6. Their demands included a 30 percent increase in wages, a system of severance pay, a bonus for perfect attendance, twice yearly wage increases, and health insurance. The next day, the owner closed the factory and fired all the workers. After twenty days, the workers had to give up the struggle because they lacked strike funds to mitigate their families' hardships during this period with no pay. Nevertheless, the workers secured the rehiring of all but three or four of the workers, a percentage of normal pay for the strike period, severance pay for the fired workers, salary reductions for the factory head and the managers, and prize money for those with perfect attendance. Representatives from the Kantō Amalgamated Labor Unions assisted in negotiating this settlement. During the struggle, the workers took to the streets as peddlers to earn strike money and collect strike funds from the people of the immediate neighborhood. This sort of participation of the neighbors in a labor dispute was no doubt more embarrassing to a factory head such as Chōgō Gisuke, who lived on the premises, than to an owner who lived some distance from his factories or who was involved in many enterprises.[76]

Factory owners could be quite articulate about the resentment they felt against outsiders—the unions—destroying what they regarded as the special virtues of a family enterprise. Moriya Sadakichi was the owner of a scale-making factory in Honjo. When he learned in February 1927 that seventy workers at his factory had joined the Tokyo Ironworkers Union, he tried to force them to leave the union by temporarily closing his factory. He said that because his company had been a family enterprise for generations, he could not tolerate union activity. However heartfelt Moriya's sentiments, they were scarcely original. Factory owners had long justified independence from government regulation as well as from labor unions on the basis of their paternalism. Their rhetoric invoked the reciprocal relationships between a samurai and his lord and between a subject and his sovereign to explain the loyalty Japanese employees should feel toward their employers.[77]

Moriya's rhetoric did not intimidate his workers. When they went to his home to negotiate with him, he evaded them by locking the gate and turning out all the lights, even though it was only 8:30 P.M. Representatives of the Sōdōmei, affiliated with the Tokyo Ironworkers Union, attempted to mediate the conflict on February 26, but Moriya remained adamant in his refusal to allow the workers to join a union. Finally, on March 8, he agreed to recognize the right of the workers to join the union and the workers agreed to return to work on March 10. Moriya's eventual capitulation demonstrates the growing social acceptance of union activity. Moriya himself, however, no doubt believed sincerely that union activity was antithetical to the operation of a family enterprise.

The relative success of union activity in Honjo in the late 1920s reflected changes in both the labor movement and the state. The earlier skirmishes within the labor movement among reformers, anarchists, and communists had largely been won by the moderates. The left-wing unions, which broke away from the centrists to form the Hyōgikai, fell victim to state oppression in 1928. The state had shifted from opposition to all unions to encouragement of moderate unions as a means of preventing more radical ones. In 1926, the Diet repealed Article 17 and passed the Labor Disputes Conciliation Law. Although these measures fell short of formal recognition of the right to strike, the labor struggles in Honjo and elsewhere provide ample evidence that workers believed their demands were politically legitimate.[78]

In the early 1930s, however, both the depression and the Manchurian Incident created an atmosphere less favorable to labor. The labor union movement, which united workers against employers, constituted an implicit threat to the various neighborhood organizations whose aim was to unite neighbors of all classes. As the examples from Honjo make clear, union activity in small and medium-sized firms often brought workers into conflict with the leaders of their neighborhood. Leaders of the business community argued that legally recognized labor unions were a foreign institution unsuited to Japan, which made union members vulnerable to charges of insufficient patriotism.[79] The simultaneous growth of labor unions and neighborhood organizations thus created the possibility that the neighborhood associations, reservist units, or young men's associations could be called upon in the name of harmony and patriotism to oppose the disruptive foreign influence of the labor movement.

It was only when labor conflict threatened the daily routine of the urban population that this potential was realized. The people of Tokyo were almost entirely dependent upon streetcars and buses for transportation within the city. Consequently, a transportation strike assaulted them with a force roughly equal to an earthquake, typhoon, or major blizzard. As soon as the Tokyo Streetcar Workers Union (Tōkyō shiden jijikai) was formed in 1924, reservists began planning how to counter strikes.[80] The labor movement came into direct conflict with neighborhood organizations in 1930 and 1934 when the city mobilized members of the young men's associations of Tokyo to replace striking conductors and motormen.

A strike broke out in April 1930 when the Municipal Electric Bureau announced a retrenchment program that would cut bonuses by 10 percent and terminate the employment of a number of workers. Realizing that any interruption in service would provoke a public outcry, the city authorities determined to keep the buses and streetcars moving by transferring city clerical workers into transportation, hiring temporary labor, and accepting the services of fourteen hundred members of the Tokyo young men's associations. The strike was not a popular one. Editorials in the Japanese newspapers such as the *Tōkyō asahi,* the *Miyako,* and the *Nichinichi* accepted the city's financial crisis as genuine and argued that the workers were unreasonable in their demands. The general lack of sympathy toward the strike and the short duration of the struggle explain why no steps were taken to halt this use of the young men's associations. The action did provoke sharp criticism in the press.[81]

In 1934, the city once again called upon the young men's associations to counter a streetcar strike. On September 1 the Municipal Electric Bureau announced a readjustment plan that called for the dismissal of all employees, with generous severance pay. The city would then rehire the workers at 40 percent of their former wage. The union strenuously objected to this plan and the workers went on strike on September 5. By the second day of the strike, six hundred volunteers from several chapters of the young men's associations of Tokyo were aiding the Electric Bureau. By the next day, fourteen hundred volunteers were at work and Yamashita Matasaburō, the head of the Electric Bureau, was said to be depending upon this aid against the strikers.[82]

In this crisis, which affected nearly everyone in the city, political organizations of varying hues issued public statements. The Social Democratic Party announced full support for the strikers. The Restoration Youth Band (Ishin seinen tai), a reactionary group, urged the mayor to settle the incident as quickly as possible.[83] In this atmosphere, the members of the young men's associations could not help but realize that their actions constituted a weapon in a bitter and controversial struggle.

The strike was in its eighth day when the Ushigome chapter of the young men's association withdrew its services from the city. The head of the chapter said that the public did not appreciate the motive of the young men's association members, who had acted only out of concern for the inconvenience suffered by the city residents. The youth could not continue to serve, however, when no end could be seen to the struggle. Other chapters followed suit. The implicit distinction between emergency relief and participation in a labor dispute was articulated by Tazawa Yoshiharu, the head of the Japan League of Young Men's Associations. Tazawa said that young men's organizations should never be involved in labor disputes but that they were always available to maintain public order.[84]

Once their use became controversial, the young men's associations were liabilities rather than assets to the city. Yamashita circulated a letter to all chapters of the associations saying that the city no longer needed their help.[85] This incident demonstrated that the young men's associations were by no means compliant tools of the municipal government. The incident was also a measure of the extent to which the labor movement had established unions and strikes as legitimate instruments of power within Japanese society.

When Suzuki Bunji founded his friendly societies in 1912, Article 17 of the Police Act made union organizing and strikes illegal acts and the Factory Law of 1911 had not yet gone into effect. Suzuki began his work with the same spirit in which his friends and colleagues had established social welfare facilities and volunteer organizations such as the district welfare committees. Union organizers, reformist bureaucrats, and business leaders shared a vision of an orderly and prosperous Japan. Where they differed was in their conception of how that harmony should be achieved. By the 1930s, the means as well as the ends of the moderate labor movement had won acceptance.

The unions that developed out of the friendly societies provided workers with the means to shape their economic lives. Unions also educated workers on the relationship of their labor problems to the larger political problems of the society. The socialist political parties that developed after the passage of universal manhood suffrage in 1925 involved themselves in labor disputes in addition to giving workers a political voice in the metropolitan, prefectural, and national legislatures. In a word, union activities added the voice of labor to the many-voiced chorus that constituted Japanese political life.

If Japan is taken as a whole, the labor movement seems soft-spoken—a voice that was scarcely heard before it was silenced in 1940 when all unions were absorbed into the national mobilization for war. In Honjo, however, the union movement had a substantial impact. The Yūaikai organized a number of branches in Honjo, many of which took part in strikes. Only a minority of workers became anarchists or communists, but those who did came to Honjo to help in strikes. Labor schools perpetuated this educational force in the ward. After the earthquake, unions were both more moderate in their demands and more successful in their struggles. Although some have condemned this moderation as a reinforcement of Japanese capitalism rather than a challenge to it, the fact that labor could exist as a separate voice tells us that capitalist Japan was pluralistic.[86]

There is some merit to Stephen Large's characterization of the class consciousness of the moderate labor movement as "diffuse" and "nonspecific."[87] Whatever its failings as a self-conscious proletarian movement, however, the moderate labor movement was not simply a reinforcement of the social order. As the labor movement expanded after 1923 into small and medium-sized firms, it emphasized the divisions in the neighborhood, which other organizations—for instance, the neighborhood associations, the military reserve branches, and the young men's associations—were intended to bridge. In locally owned factories, conflicts over wages became conflicts with the elite of the neighborhood. The fact, however, that in 1934 city authorities were unable to sustain their attempt to use young men's associations to suppress a transportation strike demonstrates that unions were at the mercy of neither the state nor local community groups. Nor were young men's associations pliant weapons at the sole disposal of the mayor of Tokyo. The urban sense of community, which the government had fostered through local neighborhood organizations, did not preclude labor unions and strikes.

By the late 1920s, union activities were part of wider political struggles. Proletarian political parties supported strikes and attacked factory owners as members of established political parties. Labor activity, then, was part of the increasing involvement of the ordinary citizen in political life. The universal manhood suffrage elections—in which the proletarian political parties, with union support, elected representatives from Honjo to the city and prefectural assemblies and to the Diet—will be the subject of the next chapter.

— Chapter 6 —

Urban Voters

The Meiji constitution provided for popular participation in government through elections for the Lower House of the Diet. When the emperor promulgated the constitution in 1889, the election law permitted only a small fraction of the total population to participate in elections, but in 1925, the Diet enacted a universal manhood suffrage law. Passage of the law quadrupled the electorate to approximately twelve million voters.

Under more limited suffrage, two "established" political parties had developed in Japan. The older of these, the Seiyūkai, dated back to the turn of the century. The other, the Minseitō, had taken shape only in 1927, but it could claim descent—through its immediate predecessor, the Kenseikai—from the Dōshikai, founded in 1913. Since 1918, the office of prime minister had usually been held by the president of one or the other of the established political parties. The universal manhood suffrage elections offered to factory workers and shopkeepers as well as to bankers, industrialists, and bureaucrats, a choice among candidates of these two parties.

The universal manhood suffrage elections also offered voters something they had never had before, that is, an opportunity to vote for "proletarian" parties that advocated reform of the existing system in the interests of the working class. In the 1928 election, eighty-eight proletarian candidates stood for election, either from such parties or as independents holding kindred points of view.[1] Eight were elected. In 1936, twenty-two proletarian party candidates, eighteen of them from the Social Mass Party, won seats; in 1937, the Social Mass Party captured thirty-seven seats. The proletarian parties were particularly strong in Tokyo; six of the seven seats lost to the established parties were won by proletarian candidates. Nevertheless, the proletarian political parties posed no major threat to the established ones. In fact, on the national level, universal manhood suffrage initially increased the electoral strength of the established parties. In 1928, for the first time, both major parties elected candidates in every prefecture and together the two parties obtained 93 percent of seats in the Lower House.[2]

Universal manhood suffrage changed the relationship of ordinary citizens to the political process, however. Through elections, the adult males of Japan participated directly in local and national politics and their votes changed the composition of the elected representative bodies. Between 1925 and the outbreak of war with China in July 1937, there were five elections for representatives to the Diet (1928, 1930, 1932, 1936, and 1937). In addition, there were three elections for representatives to the Tokyo Prefectural Assembly (1928, 1932, and 1936) and three elections for representatives to the Tokyo City Assembly (1929, 1933, and 1937).[3] Turnout was reasonably high as citizens of all classes participated in the political life of the nation.

Despite the opportunity they provided for wide political participation, these elections have been largely ignored in the discourse on democracy in prewar Japan.[4] They occurred outside the chronological parameters usually set for discussions of Taishō democracy. The proletarian parties gained electoral strength vis-à-vis the established parties at a time when both the parties and the Diet within which they operated were losing ground in power struggles at the national level. After the assassination of Inukai Tsuyoshi on May 15, 1932, no representative of the political parties again held the office of prime minister until after 1945. Thus, in the Diet elections of 1936 and 1937, votes for any party, whether established or proletarian, did not translate directly into symbols of power such as cabinet positions. Moreover, all five universal manhood suffrage elections took place after the passage of the Peace Preservation Law, which many historians believe marked the end of Taishō democracy.

For the citizens of Tokyo, however, these elections were genuine contests in which individuals could choose among candidates of varying points of view. Candidates competed for the support of local organizations such as neighborhood associations, welfare facilities, young men's associations, reservists, and unions. Some established party incumbents met defeat, as socialists and independents carved out new constituencies. In these elections, urban citizens created electoral bases that provided political representation if not political power. Neither the disbanding of parties and unions in the war mobilization nor the banning of other organizations in the Occupation years could take this political experience away from the people of Tokyo.

Elections and Popular Participation

As a result of universal manhood suffrage, more men were qualified to vote than before 1925, and voters appeared at the polls on election day in proportions that have rarely been equaled in the postwar period. Voting constituted direct participation in the political affairs of the city, the prefecture, and the nation. Because campaign activities were far broader than the specific act of casting a ballot, elections affected the entire population and not merely the men over twenty-five who actually voted.

The Universal Manhood Suffrage Act, which removed all previous tax and property qualifications for voting and thus, with some restrictions, enfranchised all males over the age of twenty-five, increased the electorate in Tokyo as it did in the rest of the nation. Newspapers reported that 270,000 of the 369,190 voters in Tokyo in 1928 were voting for the first time. In the election district of which Honjo was one-half (the other half was adjoining Fukagawa Ward), the number of registered voters increased more than six times between the Diet election of 1924 and that of 1928. Whereas the degree of this change was no doubt slightly magnified because Honjo and Fukagawa experienced a temporary decline in population in 1924 right after the earthquake, the increase was still dramatic.[5]

Honjo was an urban area that was known for slums and flophouses, but this had only a small effect on political participation. The government drew up the voting lists on the basis of the household registers. Thus, in prewar Japan, ignorance of deadlines or political apathy did not translate as directly into disenfranchisement as they do in the United States where responsibility for voter registration rests with the citizen. The election law did contain restrictions that were disadvantageous to refugees from the earthquake area and others who were poor. The vote was denied to bankrupt persons who had not been rehabilitated, people who because of poverty required relief or assistance from public or private sources, and persons who had no place of residence. According to detailed figures available for the 1933 election of representatives to the Tokyo City Assembly, the registered voters in Honjo constituted 18.8 percent of the total population, one of the higher percentages in the city. This percentage was little different from the 20 percent for the entire nation.[6]

All of the voters of Japan, the newly enfranchised and the more experienced, appeared at the polls in very high proportions in the prewar period, especially in the first four universal suffrage elections. The rate of participation varied from 78.6 to 83.3 percent. Although the voter turnout for Diet elections was lower in Tokyo than for Japan as a whole, it was still always over 60 percent. Further, the influx of inexperienced voters after the passage of universal manhood suffrage lowered the voter turnout in the capital only slightly from 77 percent in 1924 to 75.8 percent in 1928.[7]

The variation in voter turnout from election to election followed the same pattern in Tokyo as in the rest of Japan. For the entire nation, the proportion of nonvoters in the elections for representatives to the Diet was 19.67 percent in 1928; it dropped to 16.66 percent in 1930 and then rose progressively to 18.32 percent in 1932, 21.3 percent in 1936, and 26.7 percent in 1937. The pattern was essentially the same for Tokyo prefecture, except that there was an even greater increase in nonvoters between 1936 and 1937. Honjo Ward varied from this pattern only slightly; there the voting rate was better in 1932 than in 1930.

Contrary to our expectations for an economically disadvantaged area, Honjo Ward usually had a higher voting rate than the entire city or prefecture. This was in part a result of the occupational characteristics of the population. The voting population of Honjo was largely composed of day laborers and shopkeepers who worked in the neighborhood and who were thus able to get to the polls during the designated hours between 7:00 A.M. and 6:00 P.M. In other sections of Tokyo where many "salary men" lived, the voters were unable to return home in time to vote. Shopkeepers and the owners of small factories were self-employed businessmen with an obvious stake in political affairs. According to contemporary accounts of the election of 1928, the newly enfranchised laborers of Honjo and Fukagawa were equally anxious to cast their votes. When the polls opened on the morning of the 1928 election, there were about 150 people jockeying for first position in line outside the Higashigawa Elementary School in Fukagawa. Each voter was dressed in his best attire; even so, some wore mended clothing, but all were scrubbed clean in honor of the event.[8] The urban working class had entered the political process with dignity and pride.

Election day culminated a month of campaign activities, extending from the dissolution of the Diet to the election, which the law required to be held within thirty days of the dissolution. Campaign activities, whatever their form, displayed the candidate himself, his name, and his policies. Under the new election law, house-to-house calls—the hallmark of election campaigns in the days of a limited electorate—were strictly prohibited. Now candidates advertised themselves in letters and postcards mailed to the voters' homes, in posters, and in handbills.

Universal manhood suffrage, which shifted the focus of campaign activities from the select few with substantial property to all adult men, greatly enhanced the impact of campaign activities on the general public. Campaign literature inundated homes. In 1928, in the Fourth District (Honjo and Fukagawa), each of the twelve candidates sent eighty thousand letters. Many voters had recently moved a short distance because of the land readjustment following the earthquake, and this complicated delivery of these letters; it may be imagined that postal workers enlisted many citizens to redirect them. Posters covered every available spot on walls, fences, telephone poles, and tree trunks. Sandwich boards and lanterns proclaimed the names of candidates. For a time in the 1932 campaign, the Seiyūkai displayed its slogans on two hundred buses of the Tokyo Bus Company. A few enterprising campaigners used projectors to display the name of the candidate in public places at night.[9]

At the specific request of some of the candidates, the Home Ministry approved campaign devices especially designed to involve children. Candidates arranged to have candy peddlers distribute small colored flags bearing the names of candidates. Lapel tags and blotters were given free to elementary schoolchildren and errand boys.[10]

One of the most popular activities was the staging of speaker meetings. Tokyo prefectural and municipal officials facilitated such meetings by making school buildings and city public halls available to candidates free of charge from 4:00 to 11:00 P.M.; candidates, however, had to pay for water, heat, and light themselves. In the 1936 election for representatives to the prefectural assembly, each candidate gave an average of fifteen speeches. Attendance at these meetings varied considerably, but at some meetings the crowds numbered over a thousand.[11]

In the election campaign of 1928, the leaders of both parties used modern technology to stage a larger number of meetings than the limits of human energy would normally permit. Both Tanaka Giichi, prime minister and head of the Seiyūkai Party, and Hamaguchi Yūkō, president of the Minseitō, recorded their campaign speeches on phonograph records. Ogawa Heikichi, the minister of railways, went one step further; he recorded his speeches on a talking movie film. He opened his address by expressing his pleasure at being able to make use of the latest fruits of scientific labors.[12]

The use of technology in political campaigns continued throughout the 1930s. In the 1930 election, Hamaguchi, who by then had become prime minister, followed Ogawa's lead and made a sound movie for use in the campaign. In the 1932 campaign, the Minseitō used recordings of the speeches of Wakatsuki Reijirō, former prime minister; Inoue Junnosuke, former finance minister; and Nagai Ryūtarō, chief secretary of the party. Machida Chūji, minister of commerce and president of the Minseitō, recorded a speech on Minseitō policy for the 1936 campaign. In the same election, phonograph records of Prime Minister Okada's speech were likewise popular at campaign meetings.[13]

The government was as active as the candidates in bombarding the public with information and advice. In 1928, the Home Ministry prepared posters instructing voters and giving the gist of the suffrage law; in 1930, the same ministry printed 240,000 leaflets urging citizens to exercise their right to vote.[14]

The Tokyo municipal authorities were diligent in getting out the vote. They took special measures to ensure that daily laborers would show up at the polls. During the campaign, the city extended closing hours at the municipal night shelters, where many day laborers lived, to 11 P.M. to allow the residents to attend political meetings. Directors of the night shelters instructed the workers on their duty to vote. The city also interceded with employers to give voters time off from work to vote. Before the election for representatives to the municipal assembly in 1937, the Tokyo Municipal Office enlisted seventy thousand students of girls' higher schools to distribute leaflets telling citizens to exercise their right to vote.[15]

The same law that expanded the suffrage for national elections brought the right to vote in local contests as well. Residents of Tokyo enjoyed the right to elect representatives to both the prefectural and municipal assemblies. The local campaigns were essentially calmer versions of those for national office. Name placards, usually three feet wide and ten feet high, adorned the neighborhoods as candidates held forth in speech meetings.

The Tokyo municipal assembly had a colorful history of bribery and corruption, and in 1929 a private foundation, the Tokyo Municipal Research Council (Tokyo shisei chōsa kai), led a movement to make the election for the municipal assembly a campaign for the reform of urban government. Much hope was placed in the candidacy of men of known ability who were considered to be above partisan considerations. Gotō Shinpei, formerly home minister and mayor of Tokyo, was persuaded to run in 1929, and his candidacy was greeted with enthusiasm, although in the end he had to withdraw from the race for health reasons. The election of better men was regarded as the only hope for the improvement of the city government, and the Tokyo Municipal Research Council, in addition to preparing handbills and holding demonstrations to urge voters to exercise their rights, endorsed certain men as "ideal candidates." The reformers, who included advocates of women's suffrage, designated the day before the election as Municipal Government Purification Day. The results of this election seemed promising at first: thirty-one of the forty-nine candidates endorsed by the Municipal Research Council won seats, and Gotō Shinpei greeted with enthusiasm the election of six proletarian candidates.[16]

The promise of reform was short-lived. Within a month of the election, there were reports that the two major parties were offering cash and high posts to independent assemblymen who would join their ranks. The next election for representatives to the municipal assembly was held in 1933, just as indictments were handed down to members of the assembly for involvement in four scandals regarding the Tokyo Gas Company, bribery in the 1929 municipal election, bribery in connection with the purchase of land in Chiba for a cemetery, and bribery in the election of the previous mayor, Nagata Hidejirō. The editors of several Japanese daily newspapers termed the results of the 1933 election "disappointing."[17]

The citizens of Tokyo responded to this seemingly incurable corruption with apathy rather than with revolt at the polls. Throughout the period in question, national elections always drew more voters to the polls in both Honjo and Tokyo than merely local ones did. For local elections, the turnout was between 60 and 70 percent; in the national elections it varied between 75 and 83 percent. Further, interest in local urban politics seems to have declined with each election. Some related this decline to the corruption of the municipal assembly, claiming that the municipal assembly members never defended the interests of citizens. Others thought the decline in citizen interest was because many people had come to the city merely to seek employment and thus considered themselves temporary residents of the city with no responsibility for city administration.[18]

Although enthusiasm for voting declined slightly during the period and although universal manhood suffrage was never able to purify the Tokyo City Assembly, it is clear that universal manhood suffrage succeeded in increasing the involvement of the citizenry, both voter and nonvoter, in the political life of the nation, the prefecture, and the city. Further, participation in elections was never separate from participation in the local community. Representatives to the prefectural and municipal assemblies were elected from the wards rather than from the city as a whole. The election district for Diet seats was composed of Honjo Ward and adjacent Fukagawa Ward. Whereas election activities never formally extended down to the level of the neighborhood associations, election struggles were always waged in the ward, where in the past the outcome of the vote had been determined by networks of personal associations among the propertied of the neighborhoods. In the cities, universal manhood suffrage created new relationships among the parties, the candidates, and the local voters.

The Established Political Parties
in 1928, 1930, and 1932

The existence of universal manhood suffrage did not suddenly change the political balance of power in Japan. In rural areas, where the majority of the Japanese population still lived, the newly enfranchised voters cast their ballots, as had the earlier limited electorate, for the candidates endorsed by the traditional leaders of the community. In small cities, as in the countryside, the broadening of the electorate merely drew support from poorer and less illustrious men for the same parties and candidates as in earlier elections.[19] Thus, the established political parties—the Seiyūkai and the Minseitō—continued to dominate the political life of the nation as they and their forerunners had done in the past.

In Tokyo, as well, the established political parties continued to be of importance. It was in the cities, however, that challenges to the domination of the older parties arose. Candidates of the proletarian parties were elected from Honjo to the Tokyo City Assembly, the prefectural assembly, and the Diet. Independent candidates gained seats that in the past had always belonged to the established parties. These gains of the proletarian political parties and independent candidates reflected the growing inability of the established parties to control the vote in the city, a failure that arose in part from the inability of the traditional methods of the parties to control the new electorate in a new decade.

In each of the elections of 1928, 1930, and 1932, one or the other of the major political parties controlled the cabinet. The elections of 1928 and 1932 took place under the direction of a Seiyūkai government; that of 1930, under the Minseitō. In 1932, in the aftermath of the assassination of Prime Minister Inukai on May 15, a nonparty national unity cabinet was established. (The two elections held under national unity cabinets will be discussed separately.)

Under party cabinets, the candidates of the party in power had two advantages. First, the party in power controlled the Home Ministry, which supervised elections; it was thus unlikely that candidates of that party would suffer police harassment or vote fraud. Second, the candidates of the party in power shared the prestige and publicity surrounding the prime minister and the cabinet. Active government intervention in election campaigns was a problem as old as the electoral system itself. In the 1892 election, the government resorted to physical attacks on liberal candidates and on their property. Even in more orderly elections, a government could use the police to prosecute the opposition candidates for real and imagined electoral law violations, to harass or even incarcerate opposition candidates, and to select election supervisors that were favorable to the government. Occasionally, the election supervisors came equipped with pockets full of progovernment votes that could be used to stuff the ballot box if necessary. On the basis of his study of the Diet elections from 1892 to 1937, Robert Scalapino concluded that no party in power ever lost an election.[20]

In the 1928 election, there were numerous charges of government pressure and Home Minister Suzuki Kisaburō gained considerable unpopularity for his blatant manipulation of the police. One indication of the extent of official interference is the imbalance of arrests for election law violations; by the day of the election, the Minseitō had experienced 1,701 arrests for 469 incidents and the various proletarian parties had suffered 301 arrests for 148 incidents. By contrast, the Seiyūkai, the party of the government, had experienced only 164 arrests for 63 incidents.[21]

The city of Tokyo was by no means spared these problems. Of the 499 violations of the election law registered with the Justice Ministry by the eve of the election, 72 (or 14 percent) were from Tokyo.[22] If the victories of candidates from the party in power were signs of election interference, the results from Honjo and Fukagawa suggest that government interference may have been even greater in the elections of 1930 and 1932. Whereas in 1928 two candidates from each of the two major political parties were elected, in 1930, under a Minseitō cabinet, three of the victors were Minseitō candidates and the fourth was Ōta Shinjirō, an independent who had run in 1928 as a Minseitō candidate. Two years later, in 1932, under a Seiyūkai cabinet, the three Minseitō Diet members ran again and lost; the victors were three Seiyūkai candidates and an independent Korean contender.[23]

In fact, direct interference in elections may well have been much less decisive than other, more subtle advantages of party control of the government. It is difficult to measure the impact on the general public of the prestige and publicity surrounding the prime minister and his cabinet, but it is undoubtedly true that the uncommitted voter of little education, respecting authority, voted for those who spoke with authority. One blatant example of the deliberate use of the prestige of the government was the speech made by Home Minister Suzuki Kisaburō on the eve of the 1928 election. Suzuki criticized the opposition party, the Minseitō, for advocating politics centered on the Diet. He termed this type of politics a violation of the national essence and the constitution; he was quick to make a comparison with the Seiyūkai, which from its inception "has been obedient to the principle of government centered on the emperor."[24] Thus, this particular speech took advantage not only of the prestige of the government but of the sacred sovereignty of the emperor as well, and brought them to bear on the Seiyūkai campaign efforts.

The party in power had the further advantage of sustained exposure to the public. The election campaign period was only one month long, but the prime minister and the cabinet were constantly before the public eye. Government policy seemed designed to keep them there. The activities sponsored by the Minseitō in the summer of 1929 as part of a nationwide thrift campaign bore a striking resemblance to election campaign activities. Minseitō ministers and members of parliament gave speeches at mass meetings, distributed leaflets, and showed films. Among those scheduled to speak on the radio and from various platforms were Prime Minister Hamaguchi, Finance Minister Inoue, Home Minister Adachi, and Education Minister Kobashi. Virtually every educational, religious, and social welfare organization in the empire was called upon to participate in the campaign. Prime Minister Hamaguchi's radio broadcast on retrenchment was said to have reached four million as people crowded into shops to listen to radios. Films made that evening—of the prime minister giving the speech, his grandchildren listening at home, and the crowds listening in the Ginza—were shown in local movie houses.[25]

Hamaguchi's radio broadcast draws attention to yet another advantage of the party in power, control of the radio. Radio broadcasting began in Japan in March 1925, the same year that the Diet enacted universal manhood suffrage. The Communication Ministry soon merged the three licensed companies into a national monopoly. In theory, radio had nothing to do with politics or elections; political argument and electioneering were categorically forbidden. Governments, however, could advertise policy, and they did; Hamaguchi's speech on retrenchment inaugurated the practice.[26]

The hierarchy of local, regional, and national associations of the Imperial Military Reserve Association and the Japan League of Young Men's Associations provided an effective means of disseminating information or ideas to all parts of the nation. Because the government supported these organizations, there was a good possibility that the organizations might therefore support the political party in power. The heads of both the Imperial Military Reserve Association and the Japan League of Young Men's Associations directed their members to refrain from any election activity undertaken as a body. The Labor Farmer Party (Rōdō nōmintō), one of the proletarian political parties, responded with skepticism; they said it was an open secret that the established parties were using the associations to gather votes.[27]

The line between government support and party abuse of the associations was difficult to draw. There does not seem to have been adverse comment when, early in February 1928, Prime Minister Tanaka attended the reservists' meeting in Osaka. When, however, the prime minister contributed twenty-seven thousand phonograph records of his election campaign speech to the branches of the young men's associations and the Imperial Military Reserve Association, there was a tremendous outburst of protest. General Ichinoe, the president of the reservists, and Maruyama Tsurukichi, director of the Japan League, criticized the action.[28]

When the Minseitō launched its thrift campaign in the summer of 1929, the Imperial Military Reserve Association and the young men's associations helped in the mobilization effort. One of the first steps of the campaign was to send circulars to the 15,000 branches of the Imperial Military Reserve Association and the 15,900 branches of the Young Men's Association to urge these groups to start their own independent movement for patriotic public service.[29] Inclusion of these local associations in the campaign was in some respects little different from their inclusion in celebrations of national holidays, but since thrift was one of the themes of the Minseitō in the election campaign of 1930, there is a suggestion here of mobilization for partisan as well as national purposes.

In the end, whatever the advantages of the party in power at the national level, the actual struggle for votes took place within the election district itself. As in rural areas, so in the downtown areas of Tokyo, the election strength of the major political parties did not rest on formal institutions such as neighborhood chapters. Generally, the only mediating unit between the voter and the national headquarters of the party was the prefectural branch. Qualifications for membership in political parties included the paying of dues and other requirements, which made it unlikely that any but those with special personal interests in politics would pay the price of party membership.[30] The only continuing representatives of party interests in local districts were the candidates for election to the Diet.

The prefectural branches of the parties chose the candidates for the Diet, subject to the approval of the national organization. Legally, any qualified voter who was thirty or more years of age could run if he signified his intention to the election authorities and deposited with them two thousand yen as security money. Any of those candidates, in turn, could choose to affiliate with either party. Under the system of multi-seat districts, one party could elect several candidates. Each district elected a set number (usually between three and five); technically, it was possible for all seats in a district to be won by the same party. It was thus in the interest of the party to make wise decisions not only about who ran as the party candidates for the Diet but also about how many candidates were in contention at any one time. A political party had nothing to gain by endorsing more candidates than there were seats in a district; indeed, if the votes for the party were split among too many candidates, a party was in danger of losing otherwise secure seats to more unified forces. The real problem of the party branches was to limit the number of candidates and balance them carefully. A very popular candidate might take so many votes that he would jeopardize the chances of other candidates from the same party. Parties preferred candidates who could provide their own election funds. In the 1930 election, Adachi Kenzō is reputed to have denied Minseitō approval to any candidate who could not raise thirty thousand yen on his own.[31]

The enlarged electorate complicated the decisions to be made. First, because of the proletarian political parties, there were more parties than before. Second, universal manhood suffrage inspired an unusually high number of candidates. Whereas in 1920 and 1924 there were only six candidates for three positions in the Fourth Election District, in 1928 sixteen men competed for four seats. The additional parties and candidates made it more difficult to predict just how many seats a given party could control. Moreover, the old party methods of winning elections would no longer work. The revised election law outlawed house-to-house calling, which would have been impractical in any case with an electorate that had suddenly increased fourfold. In every district of Japan, there were now too many voters to be bribed individually. The geographical mobility and diversity of occupations in the city made it impossible, as might have sufficed in a village, to use a few well-placed promises or bribes to control the whole electorate of an area. Thus, more than ever before, in the city the vagaries of the election campaign itself controlled large blocs of votes.

Candidates for the Diet were usually natives of the prefectures from which they ran. Most exceptions to this rule were in rapidly growing urban prefectures.[32] In Tokyo, as well, most of the Diet candidates endorsed by the major parties were men with strong local ties. They were not, however, all native born; in a district where many of the local professional and business leaders were first-generation residents of the city, birth in the city was far less important than achievement in the city as an adult. In 1928, of the ten major-party candidates in the Fourth District (Honjo and Fukagawa), only the two incumbents were natives of Tokyo.[33]

Each of the major parties ran one incumbent in the 1928 election, and both men were good examples of party candidates with strong ties to the Honjo-Fukagawa area. By the time of the 1928 election the Seiyūkai incumbent, Isobe Hisashi, had already served two terms in the Diet. After graduation from Tokyo University in 1899, he had a distinguished career in law and the Justice Ministry.[34] His position in Honjo was further enhanced because he was the adopted son of Isobe Shirō, a longtime resident of the ward, who had served in both the Lower House of the Diet and in the House of Peers.

Born in 1851, the son of a domain retainer in Toyama, Isobe Shirō was adopted into the family of another former samurai. After study in Tokyo, he pursued further education in law, government, and economics in France. From his return to Japan in 1879 until his resignation in 1892, he served in the Justice Ministry. Afterwards he practiced law privately. He served in the Diet in 1890 and from 1902 to 1908. He was active in the affairs of the city, serving as a member of the city assembly and as head of the Tokyo Lawyers Association (Tōkyō bengoshi kai).[35]

Through the lawyers association, Isobe Shirō participated in a number of movements that sought to assert democratic rights vis-à-vis the state and the ruling elite. He investigated the excessive use of police force in controlling the Hibiya riots of 1905, and the next year he delivered a resolution condemning police wrongdoing to the Home and Justice Ministries. Isobe was also active in the tenants movement, which sought to modify the system in which 9.1 percent of the landowners in Tokyo—most of them former daimyo or major industrialists—controlled 60 percent of the land.[36] At his death in the earthquake in 1923, the elder Isobe thus left to his adopted son a distinguished name, a strong political base, and a reputation for defending democracy.

Ōta Shinjirō, the Minseitō incumbent, represented a different strain of Tokyo's long urban history. He was a lumber wholesaler in Fukagawa. Born in Tokyo in 1873, he began serving in the Fukagawa Ward Assembly in 1900 and went on to the city assembly and the Diet.[37]

Not all of the candidates, however, had such strong ties to the district, and several of them were not native. This was true even in 1928, the first universal manhood suffrage election and thus the one most linked by custom and experience to the old system. The most important sign of local involvement, which almost all the party candidates had in common, was past experience as an elected representative from either Honjo or Fukagawa. Ōta Shinjirō and Isobe had served earlier terms in the Diet. Nakano Yūjirō, Fukayama Genbei, and Omata Masaichi had served in the prefectural assembly. Takizawa, Isobe, Omata, and Terata Iyaichirō had been representatives from Honjo to the city assembly.[38] Ōta, Kunieda Sutejirō, and Mori Kenji had represented Fukagawa in the city assembly.

The ten men who ran for the Diet as Seiyūkai and Minseitō candidates from Honjo and Fukagawa in 1928 provided most of the candidates for the Diet elections of 1930, 1932, and 1936. The seven additional men who became candidates represented an infusion of newcomers to the city into the political life of the district. None of them were born in Tokyo.[39] True to the established pattern, six of these candidates—Furushima Miyajirō, Mori Kendō, Ida Tomobei, Suginohara Eitarō, Ichimata Yasubei, and Miyamura Kiichi—had acquired credentials as local leaders in the Honjo-Fukagawa area by serving as representatives in the city assembly. Both Mori and Ida had strengthened their ties to their residential community by serving in the Honjo Ward Assembly, Mori serving from 1926 to 1930 and Ida beginning his term in 1930, several years before his first bid for the

Diet in 1936. Ichimata and Miyamura had both served in the Fukagawa Ward Assembly.[40]

The Seiyūkai and the Minseitō each won two seats in the Fourth
District in 1928, but both parties achieved this success almost in spite
of themselves. Five candidates from each party competed for four
seats. Both incumbents were reelected, one from each party. Although
the election was held under a Seiyūkai government, the highest vote
totals were won by Minseitō candidates, and the total Minseitō
vote (27,377) was considerably higher than the total Seiyūkai vote
(19,793) in this district. If the Minseitō had run fewer candidates and
divided their votes more evenly among the candidates, they could
easily have won another seat.[41] The Minseitō Party had reason, then,
to consider the Fourth District as something of a stronghold. In 1930,
with a Minseitō government in office, the party was confident of winning more seats than ever. To take advantage of these conditions, the
Minseitō imported a new political candidate into the district.

Thus far, all the established party candidates for the Diet were
members of the local community who attached themselves to one or
another of the major, nationwide parties. Manabe Gijū was a party
man, with no ties in either Honjo or Fukagawa, who happened to run
for office in this particular district. Born in Nagasaki to a former samurai family, he graduated from the normal school in his prefecture
before going to Tokyo to attend Meiji University. Although he came
to Tokyo in 1917, he did not appear in the affairs of the Fourth
District until 1930 when he was elected as a Minseitō candidate for
the Diet. Having achieved success in this district, he ran again in 1932,
1936, and 1937; the latter two attempts were successful. Instead of
status in the local elite, Manabe had long-standing ties with the powerful of the Minseitō. He joined the Kenseikai, a forerunner of the
Minseitō, in 1920. When he first ran for the Diet from this district in
1930, he was the private secretary of Koizumi Matajirō, minister of
communications in the Minseitō cabinet of Prime Minister Hamaguchi.[42]

Koizumi was a power to be reckoned with in the Minseitō; a
member of the cabinet, he had also served as secretary-general of the
party. He had risen to prominence in the party through his success in
local politics. Born in Kanagawa prefecture in 1865, he had no formal
education beyond elementary school. He served, however, as a member and president of the Yokosuka City Assembly, mayor of Yokosuka,

a member of the Kanagawa Prefectural Assembly, and as representative to the Diet from 1908. He was a proponent of labor legislation and had considerable labor support in his Yokosuka district.[43] His own experience, then, suggested that his protégé might be able to win election from an industrial district of Tokyo.

With the widened electorate, an outsider with time and money to spend on campaigning could attract a following on the basis of national connections and national issues more easily than under the more limited suffrage when each voter expected to be visited personally. Nevertheless, Manabe was not above using sensationalism to increase his campaign audience; he drew attention to himself in the press by vowing not to marry until he had been elected to the Diet. At the same time, Manabe did not ignore the importance of ties to local bases of power. He was strongly supported by the merchants of Honjo and Fukagawa, who promised to build a home for him in the Honjo-Fukagawa area if he won the election. When he succeeded in getting more votes than any other candidate, he was free to marry, and his marriage further strengthened his ties to the local elite; he married Fujiwara Kaneko, the daughter of a businessman.[44]

In subsequent elections, Manabe continued to court the vote of the small businessmen of the district. In his campaign statement in 1936, he declared that urban small businessmen were the most important elements in the backbone of the nation, and he termed it unbearable that this class had recently fallen into poverty. He blamed their impoverishment on the flourishing industrial guilds *(sangyō ku-miai)* and advocated limiting the expansion of these unions in order to protect the right of commerce. The industrial guilds, which were first set up during the Home Ministry's Local Improvement Movement after the Russo-Japanese War, were greatly expanded under the Saitō cabinet. The Ministry of Agriculture and Forestry initiated a five-year plan to expand the guilds and make them all-village units of mass mobilization.[45]

Manabe remained, however, the exception that proved the rule. In the Fourth District, most of those who actively represented the established political parties had vested economic interests in the district. Several of the candidates for the Diet were merchants, contractors, factory owners, or lawyers in Honjo and Fukagawa. Candidates for the prefectural and municipal assemblies and their campaign managers were similarly physicians, dentists, rice merchants, lumber merchants, factory owners, shopkeepers, or landlords. Although in other urban districts, company men, bureaucrats, writers, teachers, and newspapermen ran for office, few did so here.

In the elections themselves, the success of these candidates and the parties they represented depended on the support of the voters. The owners of factories, shops, and housing within the ward, who identified their own interests with those of the party, could use their economic position and personal ties to enlist support from those dependent upon them. Elections were invariably held on weekdays, which increased the influence of employer over employee. A newspaper editorial pointed out that some employers might give their workers time off to vote, on the understanding that their votes be cast for certain candidates, or some might prevent their employees from voting for other candidates. One of the proletarian parties, the Social Democratic Party, urged in its campaign literature that election day be made a holiday as part of the full realization of universal manhood suffrage.[46]

Local associations such as the neighborhood associations, the Imperial Military Reserve Association, the Young Men's Association, district welfare committees, and social work facilities could be used to buttress a candidate's block of votes. Several heads of neighborhood associations in Honjo were associated with the Seiyūkai. Hokujo Hikoshirō won election as a Seiyūkai candidate to the city assembly in 1929. Morise Binoshichi was a campaign manager for Sugino Zensaku's Seiyūkai candidacy for the prefectural assembly. Uchida Yasaemon ran as the Seiyūkai candidate in a special election for the prefectural assembly in 1925. Kobayashi Fuminosuke assisted in his campaign, while others considered supporting Yoshimura Takichi.[47]

Nevertheless, the neighborhood associations do not seem to have served as an arena to make potential candidates well known in the ward. Of the seventeen men who ran as Seiyūkai or Minseitō candidates in the Diet elections between 1928 and 1936, nine were from Honjo.[48] Of those nine only one, Isobe Hisashi, had served as head of a neighborhood association. Isobe was one of the candidates least in need of publicity, and it seems doubtful that he accepted the leadership of his neighborhood association to further his political career. More likely, his neighbors named him to this position in recognition of the services he and his father had performed for the neighborhood, the city, and the nation. Like all of the other heads of neighborhood associations active in major party politics, Isobe was a member of the Seiyūkai.

Some candidates listed participation in reservist or young men's associations as one of their qualifications for office. Takizawa Shichirō was one of these, and he derived some free publicity from this association. In March 1925, he gave a talk to the Honjo Ward Young Men's Association on his recent trip to the United States and Europe. Miyamura Kiichi was the manager of the Fukagawa reservist organization and a director of the Tokyo league of reservists.[49]

In these first three elections under universal manhood suffrage, there were warning signs that the established parties were losing their hold over the electorate of this district. In the elections of 1930 and 1932, neither the Seiyūkai nor the Minseitō exercised adequate control over the local members of the party. In 1930, an election in which public opinion favored the Minseitō, the Seiyūkai endorsed only two candidates, the two incumbents Isobe and Kunieda. Both lost; this is a case where if all Seiyūkai votes in the district had been cast for the same candidate, the Seiyūkai would have won a seat. It seems likely that the Seiyūkai had not anticipated that two incumbents could lose. To make matters worse, Mori Kenji ran as an unendorsed candidate. If his bloc of votes had been cast for either Isobe or Kunieda, that candidate would have won a seat. In 1932, a year when the Seiyūkai could expect to do well, the party endorsed only three candidates, all of whom won. Mori Kenji again ran without the party's endorsement, but this time his candidacy did no damage.

The Minseitō did no better at keeping the troops in line. In 1930, the Minseitō endorsed four candidates, even though one of their former members was running as an independent and would presumably take his constituency with him. The party paid virtually no penalty for this excessive optimism; three of the four were elected. The decision to endorse four candidates in 1932, a year when circumstances favored the Seiyūkai, was decidedly impractical. All four lost. The most likely explanation for these unwise decisions is that rivalry among factions at the ward, municipal, and prefectural levels outweighed the interests of the party as a whole.

Even when the parties nominated ideal candidates, men with both strong local ties and national reputations, the voters surprised them. Although the district was known as a stronghold for Isobe Hisashi of the Seiyūkai, and although Omata Masaichi of the Minseitō had a constituency *(jiban)* of many years standing, both experienced defeat under universal manhood suffrage. Isobe lost the election of 1930 as the Minseitō swept the ward, and Omata lost in 1932 as the Seiyūkai returned to power.[50]

The defeat of candidates with well-established electoral strong-holds was a sign not so much of the weakness of the parties as of the strength of the urban electorate. Because of geographical mobility and the diversity of occupations, much of the urban electorate was im-mune to either personal obligation or attempted vote-buying. Some urban voters were simply too sophisticated to be controlled. Well-informed about policies, they were unimpressed with the ex-ministers and peers who addressed campaign meetings.[51] Less decisive voters did not simply defer to the local elite. They cast their ballots for the candidates whose reputations and speeches impressed them most dur-ing the actual thirty-day campaign. In this sort of contest, a man such as Manabe Gijū, with strong national ties, could easily gain an advan-tage over Omata, despite the latter's strong local base. In fact, Manabe received a slightly larger number of votes than Omata in both 1930 and 1932.

Nevertheless, the established parties dominated the Fourth Dis-trict in the first two elections held under universal manhood suffrage. With two exceptions, they took all four seats in all three elections. One of the exceptions was Ōta Shinjirō, formerly of the Minseitō, who ran as an independent in 1930. Since he not only arose from within the ranks of the Minseitō but afterwards returned to the party, he can scarcely be regarded as a new force in the local political scene. Beginning in 1932, however, genuine independents and minor party candidates began to win seats away from the two established political parties.

The Proletarian Political Parties in 1928, 1930, and 1932

The passage of universal suffrage made possible the formation of a working-class party. The first proletarian political party, the Labor Farmer Party, was founded on March 5, 1926. Before the 1928 elec-tion, schisms within the Labor-Farmer Party created three more proletarian parties. These parties, in turn, divided and regrouped several times.

Because of their ideological stance, the proletarian political parties did not have the same relationship to the neighborhood as did the established parties. Whereas in the established political parties prominent residents of the neighborhood affiliated themselves with a party, in the proletarian parties individuals first associated with the labor, peasant, and party movements and only later identified with the neighborhood. Perhaps because they lacked the long-standing local ties of the Seiyūkai and the Minseitō, the proletarian political parties were particularly active in developing local chapters.

All the proletarian political party candidates from Honjo and Fukagawa, regardless of their particular party, had been active in leftist political movements and labor union activities, but only Karazawa Seihachi was by social origin a member of the working class. The other four proletarian candidates for the Diet in this district, far from being factory workers, were college graduates—Miyazaki Ryūsuke of Tokyo Imperial University and Asanuma Inejirō of Waseda. Kagawa Toyohiko and Majima Kan had both studied in the United States, Kagawa at Princeton and Majima at a medical school in the Chicago area. Karazawa, on the other hand, was born in Nagano prefecture and came to Tokyo to work in 1922. He left immediately after the earthquake but had returned to the capital by the end of 1923 and entered a labor school run by the Sōdōmei. He met Watanabe Masanosuke and became one of his close associates.

Karazawa was a member of the left wing of the Tokyo Ironworkers Union, and he and Watanabe were among those who split off from the Sōdōmei in May 1925 to form the Hyōgikai. Like Watanabe, Karazawa participated in the Japan Communist Party in its reorganized form of 1926. Karazawa lived in the headquarters of the Tokyo Amalgamated Labor Union, which served as the strike headquarters for a number of local labor disturbances. He was one of the speakers at a meeting in support of the strike at Toppan Printing in October 1925.[52] Karazawa was thus a resident of the ward of several years' standing and was well known among labor union members.

The Yūaikai and its successor the Sōdōmei brought bright young intellectuals into contact with the workers in the Honjo area. Whereas Karazawa was among the recruited, both Miyazaki and Asanuma were among the recruiters. Like Asō Hisashi and Tanahashi Kotora (mentioned above), Miyazaki was active in the New Men Society. On February 15, 1919, Miyazaki was at a universal suffrage rally in Hibiya Park when a worker approached him and asked how to become a member of the New Men Society. The worker was Watanabe Masanosuke, the son of a *tatami* maker in Chiba prefecture, who was working in a celluloid factory in Kameido, near Honjo. The result of this contact was that Miyazaki helped organize a union of celluloid workers. Watanabe went on to become a member of the Communist Party, to which he recruited Karazawa.[53]

Miyazaki could sincerely claim nearly a decade of acquaintance with this neighborhood, but he was known here—as throughout Japan—less for his own union organizing than for his father and his wife. His father, Miyazaki Torazō, was Sun Yat-sen's closest friend in Japan. The elder Miyazaki was born into a samurai family in Kumamoto in 1870. He first met Sun Yat-sen in Yokohama in 1897 and the friendship continued until Miyazaki Torazō's death in 1922. Torazō's various machinations on Sun's behalf were by nature secret, but his experiences made him an expert on China, and the Revolution of 1911 in China thrust him into the public eye. He published a series of feature articles in the Osaka *Mainichi* and gave a short talk at a mass meeting in Hibiya Park. Torazō was also much in the news when Sun visited Japan early in 1913. Miyazaki Ryūsuke inherited his father's position as a China expert. In May 1927 the Social Democratic Party dispatched Miyazaki to Shanghai, together with labor leader Matsuoka Komakichi. The two representatives met with Chiang Kaishek and reached an agreement for solidarity between the Kuomintang and the Social Democratic Party.[54]

It was, of course, an asset to any party to have a candidate who already possessed a national reputation. Miyazaki had achieved national notoriety in 1922 when the poetess Yanagihara Akiko, generally known by her literary name Byakuren, announced that she was leaving her wealthy industrialist husband to live with Miyazaki. On October 22, 1921, the *Asahi shinbun* devoted its entire social page to the Byakuren incident. The scandal was so great that Byakuren's brother resigned from the House of Peers and her family disowned her. The incident attracted national attention because the Yanagihara family was closely associated with the imperial court; Byakuren's aunt was the mother of the Taishō Emperor. Miyazaki's comrades in the New Men Society did not support his romantic adventure. Thanks to Miyazaki Torazō, several of the young men had been living together since April 1919 in the house that had belonged to the Chinese revolutionary Huang Hsing, but they moved out in 1920 to express their disapproval of Mizazaki's relationship with Byakuren.[55]

Miyazaki turned the scandal to good account by having his wife make a political appearance for him during the 1928 campaign. His friends and allies also turned out in force. Just as cabinet ministers lent their time (or at least their phonograph records) to candidates of their own party, so the famed leaders of the proletarian movement came to Honjo and Fukagawa. Abe Isō (a professor at Waseda University and the man known as the Father of Japanese Baseball), the novelist Kikuchi Kan, and Baba Tsunego (a noted journalist), all appeared at the Honjo Public Hall in support of Miyazaki Ryūsuke.[56]

In the 1928 election, Karazawa and Miyazaki were two of sixteen candidates in the Fourth District. If the votes for both candidates had been cast for one person, that person would have won the election. The two might seem to be linked by personal loyalties since Miyazaki brought Watanabe Masanosuke into the New Men Society, and Karazawa was a disciple of Watanabe, but the two workers had moved far to the left of their original teachers. Karazawa was one of eleven communists who ran as Labor-Farmer candidates in the 1928 election; editorials from the Comintern, far from advocating a common front among proletarian candidates, urged the communists to attack their enemies, the servile social democrats.[57] The voters of the Fourth District gave 3,581 votes to Miyazaki and 2,845 to Karazawa.

By the time another election for the Diet took place in 1930, Karazawa and Miyazaki had moved yet further apart. Karazawa was no longer within the boundaries of legality; he was arrested in the communist purge of March 1928, shortly after the election. Miyazaki, on the other hand, had become more conservative. In 1929, he left the Social Democratic Party and the next year formed his own National Democratic Party. In the 1930 election, he ran from the Fourth District as the candidate of that party but won fewer votes than in 1928.

The Social Democratic Party tried to maintain their position in the area by campaigning for Kagawa Toyohiko. Kagawa had both an established record as an activist in the labor and peasant movements and a history in Honjo; he continued to operate the Young Men's Christian settlement that he had set up in the ward after the earthquake. Already renowned as a Christian evangelist, he had received attention in the press in 1929 as an advisor to Mayor Horikiri on social problems. The weakness of his candidacy was his lack of interest in the political office. The party nominated him without his consent. He announced to the press that although he would accept the office if elected, he would not campaign. He said that his primary calling was as an evangelist, and he did not wish to run against Miyazaki. In addition, he had committed himself to campaign for Sugiyama Motojirō, who was running for the Diet from Osaka. True to his word, Kagawa left for Osaka and Kobe, and Majima Kan did all the campaigning for his candidacy. Kagawa later suggested that the Social Democratic Party had nominated him to gain exposure for the party in anticipation of the Honjo Ward Assembly elections scheduled for March 2.[58] Kagawa and Miyazaki together did not poll as many votes as Miyazaki had in 1928.

The proletarian candidate who came the closest to winning in 1930 was Asanuma Inejirō. Born in 1898 on Miyakejima, Asanuma was technically a native of Tokyo, although he was born far from the bustle of the capital. The chain of islands, which extends hundreds of miles to the south of the main island on which Tokyo is located, is nevertheless administered as part of Tokyo prefecture. Asanuma's claim to long-term ties with Honjo Ward was that he had attended the Third Prefectural Middle School, located there. Like Miyazaki, Asanuma had been active in leftist organizations since his student days during and after World War I. At Waseda University, he helped to found the Builders League, which studied English socialists, and the People's Society. He also worked for Russian famine relief and against programs of military research. After graduation, he was active in the peasant movement.[59]

Asanuma was one of the organizers of both the original proletarian party and the various permutations that followed, and he soon made the Fourth District his political home. In March 1929, he ran for the city assembly from Fukagawa. His political allies had also laid a political foundation in the district. Asanuma's political group broke off from the Labor Farmer Party and became the Japan Labor-Farmer Party (Nihon rōdō nōmintō); by the 1930 election, they were the Japan Masses Party, and by 1932, they had become the National Labor-Farmer Masses Party. Itō Sei, a driver for the Tokyo Streetcar Company who was active in the Tokyo Transportation Workers Union (Tōkyō kōtsu rōdōsha kumiai), was of the same political group and had established a base in Honjo. In 1928, he was the candidate of the Japan Labor-Farmer Party for the prefectural assembly, and in 1929 he ran as the Japan Masses Party candidate for the city assembly.[60]

In 1932, there were only two proletarian candidates for the Diet in the Fourth District. Asanuma ran again, with even greater success. Campaigning for himself this time, Majima Kan received more votes for the Social Democratic Party than Kagawa had done. Majima joined Kagawa in his social work in Kobe in 1918 and came to Honjo to work in Kagawa's settlement there. A physician, Majima ran the medical clinic of the settlement with the assistance of his sister Hisako. Majima was elected to the city assembly in 1929 as a candidate of the Social Democratic Party.[61]

As a member of the city assembly, Majima negotiated a number of labor disputes involving city employees. The Social Democratic Party had strengthened its relationship with labor by including workers among the candidates for office. Saitō Shojirō—once a worker at Tokyo Muslin, and a member of the Honjo branch of the Yūaikai as early as 1916—ran from Honjo for the prefectural assembly in 1928 as a Social Democrat.[62]

The election law limited all parties to a narrow range of activities: posters, mailings, and speech meetings. Lack of funds additionally constrained the proletarian parties. Those who campaigned for Kagawa in 1930 printed their campaign slogans on used pamphlets. Asanuma won public sympathy in one of his early campaigns when the newspapers reported that his father had sold the family cow to raise campaign funds.[63] As the poorly funded idealists out of power, the proletarian candidates were in neither a moral nor a financial position to purchase votes. Their parties did not enjoy the ties to the Home Ministry and the police that were the privilege of the party in power. The various proletarian parties further handicapped themselves by running candidates against each other. It is thus scarcely surprising that in these first three universal manhood suffrage elections, the proletarian parties never won a Diet seat in the Fourth District. They did send Majima Kan to the city assembly, however, and in addition, they acquired a great deal of public exposure and electoral experience.

Independent Candidates and Minor Parties

The breakdown of the networks that in the past had delivered votes with some reliability aided the growth of the proletarian parties. The same circumstances also permitted candidates with virtually no party affiliation, political experience, or local base, to enter the electoral arena and perform with some success. Under the more limited electorate, some candidates sought office as an entrée to the parties, and various splinters from the established parties maintained themselves as minor versions of their larger progenitors. One effect of universal manhood suffrage was to reduce the number of such independents and minor parties, but in the excitement of the 1928 election there were four such candidates in the Fourth District.

Terabe Raisuke ran from the Businessmen's Association (Jitsugyō dōshikai) of the industrialist Mutō Sanji. Kasuya Isobe was the candidate of the Reform Party, the amalgamation of several splinters from the established parties. As we might expect, Kasuya was little different from the candidates of the Seiyūkai and the Minseitō. He had served in the Honjo Ward Assembly and the city assembly. Morita Korokurō was a graduate of Tokyo Imperial University who had been an official of the Tokyo city government. Elected to the Diet twice from Aiichi prefecture, he had previously been affiliated with the Kenseikai. His earlier political success did not transfer effectively to Tokyo. Ōtani Beitarō, the owner of a small factory in Fukagawa, received the fewest votes of any candidate.[64] None of these men represented new political interests in the district or new electoral methods. The same can be said for the candidacies of Ōta Shinjirō (a veteran of the Minseitō) and Honda Ichirō (a writer from Fukagawa Ward) in the 1930 election.

The new phenomenon of the 1930s was the election of Pak Ch'un Kum, a Korean, as an independent in 1932. The Fourth District was a logical constituency for a Korean candidate, in that one-quarter of the Koreans in the city lived in Honjo Ward by the 1930s. Pak Ch'un Kum, in turn, was an early favorite to be the first Korean Diet member in Japan. In 1930, Koreans in the Tokyo area urged him to run, but he declined.[65]

Pak Ch'un Kum was not a Korean nationalist; he ran for the Japanese Diet, not as an opponent of Japan's occupation of Korea but as an advocate of Japanese-Korean cooperation. His campaign rhetoric included loyalty to the imperial throne and a fundamental settlement of the Manchurian Incident, presumably on terms favorable to the Japanese. He was a director of several companies and vice-president of the Sōaikai, a mutual aid society of Koreans in Japan. In 1928, in connection with the Sōaikai, he traveled to Manchuria with Hashimoto Hiyoshi to negotiate with the Chinese authorities about the persecution of Koreans in Manchuria.[66]

The Sōaikai linked Pak, who did not live in the Fourth District, to the Honjo area.[67] In 1921, Pak was one of the founders of the organization. After the earthquake, the Sōaikai cooperated with the government in setting up barracks for refugees on government land in Taihei-chō, Honjo. When the land was needed for a school, the work of the Sōaikai moved to another site in Honjo where a building was completed in April 1929.[68] Here the Sōaikai provided lodging, medical care, employment information, advice, mediation, and education.

The Home Ministry bureaucrat Maruyama Tsurukichi supported Pak's candidacy. Maruyama has already been mentioned in connection with the young men's associations. From July 1929 to April 1931, he was head of the Tokyo Metropolitan Police, after which he was appointed to the House of Peers. Maruyama had served in the colonial government in Korea and was an advisor to the Sōaikai. He was also a personal friend of Pak's and had acted as go-between in Pak's marriage to a Japanese woman. Pak, then, had personal wealth and powerful friends. With a former chief of the metropolitan police among his supporters, it is doubtful that he suffered any police harassment in his campaign activities. His wife provided emotional appeal to his candidacy, bursting into tears after uttering a few words on her husband's behalf.[69]

In 1932, Pak won nearly seven thousand votes, third place in the district, and a seat in the Diet. His victory clearly depended largely on non-Korean votes, for only 1,236 Koreans in the district had the right to vote.[70] He failed in his reelection campaign of 1936 but again won a Diet seat in 1937. His success illustrates, as does Manabe Gijū's, that in the days of universal manhood suffrage a personable candidate with a well-run, well-publicized, and well-financed campaign could gain a Diet seat without benefit of the local ties so assiduously cultivated by party candidates in the past.

The 1936 and 1937 Elections

In contrast to the first three universal manhood elections, the Diet elections of 1936 and 1937 took place under the direction of "transcendental cabinets" that placed themselves above the interests of either party. In these two elections, the powerful Home Ministry, which under party cabinets had used the police to party advantage, directed an "election purification" *(senkyo shukusei)* campaign. The campaign took two forms: strict enforcement of the election law, and educational events to inform the public and involve them in the election process.

The government launched its campaign prior to the prefectural elections of 1935.[71] In May 1935, it mandated election purification committees in every prefecture of Japan. The following month, it established a Central Election Purification League with former Prime Minister Saitō Makoto as head. During the electoral campaign for prefectural assemblies in the fall of 1935, the government used newspapers, pamphlets, cartoons, movies, and speech meetings to propagate its message.[72]

The government repeated these efforts for the Diet elections of 1936 and 1937, rivaling the political parties themselves in the ingenuity of its campaign. The authorities ordered elementary schoolchildren to wear election purification badges and to parade through the streets singing election purification songs. The Home Ministry planned to insert small cards bearing election purification slogans into the packages of cigarettes manufactured by the government tobacco monopoly.[73]

The municipal administration of Tokyo was vigorous in its support of election purification. It sponsored motion pictures in public halls and elementary schools and used neighborhood associations to organize citizen meetings. It even assembled troupes of instrumentalists and dancers *(chindonya)* to advertise the slogans of the campaign. As part of the annual kite-flying contest, the city distributed kites bearing election purification slogans such as "Tokyo sets the example for elections!" and "Exemplary clean elections first and above all from Tokyo!" The grand finale to the city's twelve-day purification campaign, held on January 25, 1936, included a fleet of one hundred automobiles, divided into ten separate processions, each of which drove through the streets of the city throughout the day distributing handbills and balloons while five airplanes dropped leaflets from the sky. Closer to the election day, the elementary school principals of Tokyo resolved to give every pupil a pencil inscribed "Election Reform."[74]

The instigators of this national campaign were Home Minister Gotō Fumio, and Maruyama Tsurukichi, Horikiri Zenjirō, and Tazawa Yoshiharu, all former Home Ministry bureaucrats, all men with long-standing interest in election reform in general and Tokyo in particular, and all "participation" bureaucrats. All three of Gotō's colleagues had administered Tokyo—Maruyama Tsurukichi as head of the Metropolitan Police Department, Horikiri Zenjirō as mayor, and Tazawa Yoshiharu as assistant mayor.[75] These men believed in universal manhood suffrage as an expression of the popular will, but they were determined to fight what they perceived to be party abuses of power.

In the Fourth District, the Seiyūkai and Minseitō were not in a strong position to defend their purity. During the 1936 campaign, the widow of former Minseitō Diet representative Omata Masaichi was imprisoned for vote-buying. Kunieda Sutejirō, a Seiyūkai representative to the Diet from this district in 1928 and 1932, was found guilty in 1933 in the Tokyo City Assembly scandals.[76]

Both the Minseitō and the Seiyūkai had a shortage of veteran politicians in this district. Of the three Seiyūkai men who had won seats in 1928, 1930, and 1932, Isobe Hisashi died in 1935, Kunieda disgraced himself in a city scandal, and only Nakano Yūjirō, the least experienced, remained to run for office in 1936. The Minseitō was only slightly better off. Of their four former representatives, Omata had died in 1933 and Furushima did exceptionally poorly in 1932 and did not run again in 1936, leaving Manabe and Ōta as Minseitō candidates in 1936.

Neither party had firm control over its local representatives. The Seiyūkai ran four candidates for four seats, while five men ran as Minseitō candidates, albeit two of them without party endorsement. The Minseitō did well anyway, winning three seats; but Mori Kendō, whom the party had not endorsed, won one of the seats, while Suginohara Eitarō, whom it had approved, finished fourteenth in a field of sixteen.

The candidate who won the highest number of votes in the district was from neither the Seiyūkai nor the Minseitō but from a new pro-

letarian party. The Social Masses Party resulted from the merger of
the National Labor-Farmer Masses Party and the Social Democratic
Party in the summer of 1932.[77] This merger joined nearly all the elements of the four proletarian parties of the 1928 election into one
party. In the Fourth District, the highly successful candidate of the
Social Masses Party was Asanuma Inejirō. He had twice before run
for the Diet, each time facing competition from other proletarian candidates. This time he was the only proletarian candidate, and he had
the further advantage of running as a public official, for in 1933 he
had won a seat in the municipal assembly.

The six remaining candidates were three independents and three
members of smaller parties. One of the independents was Pak Ch'un
Kum (discussed above). A second independent, Yamaguchi Kiyoshi,
received fewer votes than any other candidate. In foreign affairs, his
platform called for a national policy that would delicately handle relations with the United States, the Soviet Union, and China and that
would spread the Imperial Way in the world. Within the country, he
wanted to establish a new society that would guarantee the livelihood
of the people and eradicate the opposition between labor and capital.[78]

The third independent, Fukushima Usaburō, exemplified the opportunity the election purification elections offered to a nonpolitician
with personality, fame, and financial resources. An actor known on
the stage as Umeshima Noboru, Fukushima was a bonafide resident
of the Fourth District.[79] In his published statement of his political
views, Fukushima emphasized that he, an actor, was running for the
Diet precisely because he was not a professional politician. The professional politicians were corrupt and had failed Japan; the people,
disillusioned with corrupt politicians who cared only for their own
interests, were becoming disillusioned with politics as well. As a candidate, he stood for the involvement of the people in politics, the
purification of elections, and the achievement of a fair government
that worked for the welfare of all the citizens. All these ideals were
based, he said, on the principle of the preservation of imperial constitutional government.[80]

Fukushima thus stood for political participation outside the established parties, which he regarded as corrupt. Although his candidacy was not successful as a bid for office (he finished tenth of sixteen),
it added extra interest to the political process. The speakers at his
campaign meetings were his fellow actors and actresses—one of the

most popular actresses of her day, Mizutani Yaeko, for instance. Mizutani appealed to her audience on a personal and emotional rather than a political level. Mizutani told the audience that if Fukushima failed at the polls, he might cease to be an actor, and that would be inconvenient for her. Therefore, they should vote for Fukushima for her sake. Whatever the cogency of their arguments, however, the entertainment figures drew huge numbers of citizens to speech meetings. When a veteran kabuki actor appeared on Fukushima's behalf at a speech meeting at the Kayaba Primary School in Honjo, over one thousand people attended, far exceeding the average attendance for campaign meetings in Tokyo in this election of 128 per meeting.[81]

Two of the small political parties in the Fourth District in the 1936 election—the Kokumin Dōmei and the Shōwa Kai—were offshoots of the two established parties. The Kokumin Dōmei was founded in 1932 by Adachi Kenzō, who had resigned from the Minseitō, of which he had once been vice-president. Former members of the Seiyūkai, dropped from the party because of their cooperation with national unity cabinets, founded the Shōwa Kai in December 1935. Kasuya Isobei, who ran as a Kokumin Dōmei candidate, had (like many candidates of the established political parties) served in the Tokyo City Assembly. He had also served on a number of local committees on education and taxes, as the head of his neighborhood association, and in the Honjo Ward Assembly. Despite his considerable local involvement, he received fewer votes than Fukushima, the actor. Honda Ichirō, the candidate of the Shōwa Kai, was a writer from Fukagawa.[82] Both Kasuya and Honda had run for the Diet in earlier elections under other affiliations.

The one other political party, the Constitutional Health Party (Rikken yōseikai), was a right-wing organization founded in Tokyo in 1923. Katō Yoshitaka, who represented this party in the Fourth District, criticized the insincerity of the established political parties. On the other hand, he also rejected the approach of the proletarian political parties, arguing that the reform of Japan must be based on the spirit of the national polity rather than on the Western doctrine of conflict between classes. What Japan needed was a second great revolution such as the Meiji Restoration. Katō, an officer of the Constitutional Health Party, was a young man of thirty-three who lived in Meguro Ward, outside the Fourth District. The party had a number of branches in the Fourth District, but the number of votes received by Katō was lower than the number of members attributed to the party at the end of 1935.[83] The candidacies of Katō and the independent Yamaguchi show that the voters of Honjo and Fukagawa were offered the options of corporatism and restorationism. The low vote totals achieved by these candidates shows that the options were not attractive.

Although in the 1937 election in the Fourth District the established political parties were far more popular than the new right-wing parties, they no longer had the monopoly on Diet seats that they had enjoyed at the outset of universal manhood suffrage. The Seiyūkai ran a much more effective campaign than in 1936, supporting only two candidates, one of whom won. Takizawa Shichirō had a national reputation as an expert on the silk industry, and he also had a carefully established base in Honjo: he owned a factory in the ward, had served in the ward assembly, and was head of a young men's association.[84] The Minseitō, however, lost ground, retaining only one of their three seats, that of Manabe. Thus, the two parties together controlled only two of the four seats in the last election held under the prewar multiparty system. The other two seats were won by the independent Pak Ch'un Kum and by Abe Shigeo of the Social Masses Party.

Abe's victory in 1937 proved the firm base that the Social Masses Party had established in this district. When Asanuma ran in another district in 1937, Abe, who was virtually unknown outside the Honjo-Fukagawa area and the leftist movement, was able to win almost as many votes as Asanuma had in 1936. Like Asanuma, Abe had run in this district a number of times; he was a candidate for the Tokyo prefectural assembly in 1928; and he won election to the municipal assembly in 1933 and 1937.[85]

Universal manhood suffrage allowed the voters of Honjo and Fukagawa to break the hold on elected office that the established political parties—and through them the local elite—had maintained in this area. After the 1937 election, the Seiyūkai and the Minseitō together retained only two of the four seats in the district that they had once dominated election after election.

If we view these results from the perspective of the history of the political parties in Japan, then these results are simply one more failure of the parties in their struggle against their military and bureaucratic rivals. The Seiyūkai and the Minseitō, which had established a pattern of succession of the prime ministership from the head of one party to the head of the other, could no longer even hold onto their seats in the Diet. Whereas in the first three universal manhood suffrage elections the two parties together controlled over 90 percent of the seats in the Lower House, in 1936 they won only 81 percent of the seats and in 1937 only 76 percent. This diminished electoral support in 1936 and 1937 made it even less likely that the Seiyūkai and the Minseitō would regain control of the cabinet.

If we consider instead the experience of the voters who were newly enfranchised in 1928 and whose political and economic interests were often in conflict with the landlords, factory owners, and professionals who dominated the local Seiyūkai and Minseitō, then these results have a different meaning. Despite the weakening of parliamentary institutions at the national level, the voters continued to participate in electoral politics, and they succeeded in electing representatives of the Social Masses Party in both 1936 and 1937. Pak Ch'un Kum, the Korean independent who was elected in 1937, was scarcely a liberal; he was a strong supporter of the imperial state and he had powerful bureaucratic allies. His election nevertheless represented the existence of a significant bloc of votes free from domination by either of the two established parties. He and his bureaucratic allies represented a vision for Japan that, however weak its commitment to popular sovereignty and civil rights, was both inclusive and participatory.

For the three-quarters of the electorate in this district who were not enfranchised until 1925, the electoral politics of the early Shōwa years were more democratic than the Taishō era had been. They could vote, and they had more candidates with a wider range of political opinion to choose from than had been available to the voters of the more narrow electorate in 1920 and 1924. In the stiff competition for votes, politicians curried the favor of every variety of citizen, including the members of organized labor and the Korean residents in Japan.

Conclusion

In 1863, shortly before the Meiji Restoration, Abraham Lincoln called upon Americans to dedicate themselves to the preservation of liberty, equality, and "government of the people, by the people, for the people." In the Meiji Restoration, the Japanese endeavored to acquire for themselves the strength of the Western powers, but the constitutional order they established fell far short of Lincoln's ideals. Centered as it was on the imperial institution, it could accommodate neither the ideal of popular sovereignty nor the principle of cabinets responsible to an elected assembly, both of which are implicit in "government of the people, by the people." Nevertheless, in the era between 1905 and 1937, the Japanese political system allowed considerable development of what we might term "government with the people." The state also assumed new responsibilities for the people: for the health of its children, the safety of its workers, and the care of its poor.

In 1937, the ordinary citizens of Tokyo had far wider opportunities for legitimate political participation than they had had in September 1905 when crowds had marched through the streets of Tokyo carrying national flags draped in mourning and had set fire to police stations and official residences. In 1905, the factory workers, laborers, and shopkeepers who made up those crowds could neither vote nor run for office. By 1937, a number of measures had incorporated such ordinary residents more securely into the Japanese polity: the Education Ministry had increased the years of compulsory schooling from four to six; the passage of universal manhood suffrage in 1925 had given them the right to vote and run for office.

Moreover, in 1937, ordinary citizens had greater political knowledge and experience than they had had in 1905. Men who were old enough were the veterans of five national and several prefectural and municipal elections. The increased years of schooling meant the populace was better able to read magazines, newspapers, leaflets, and pamphlets that poured forth from official and commercial presses. Government exhortations to frugality and self-sacrifice could easily be overlooked in the abundance of propaganda distributed by entities as diverse as unions, political parties, Marxist or ultra-nationalist groups, not to mention commercial publishing houses.

In short, the potential for political involvement inherent in the expanded educational and electoral privileges was greatly enhanced because citizens enjoyed a high degree of participation in civic organizations. The entire city became a political space in which all could join in celebrations of national holidays and events in the life of the imperial family. The same streets and public buildings were the sites of election meetings and labor disputes.

A wide variety of associations allowed residents to gather on the basis of common age and gender and thus extended the political community beyond the ranks of qualified voters. The Imperial Military Reserve Association opened the privilege of membership in local patriotic support groups—originally the prerogative of a handful of wealthy patrons—to virtually all men in the neighborhood. Labor schools, unions, and socialist parties enlarged the intellectual horizons of the workers and drew them into national politics. Neighborhood associations, which incorporated all interested heads of households, provided an administrative link with the municipal government that paralleled political representation in the ward and municipal assemblies.

Moreover, citizen participation was widely inclusive. Local organizations sponsored special schools to provide tuition and school supplies to neighborhood children who would otherwise have remained illiterate. The system of district welfare committees brought even the poorest members of the community into contact with the local elite and the civilian bureaucracy. Both municipal and private, religious and secular settlement houses provided temporary shelter, day care, dining halls, and medical services. Even minorities such as Koreans and out-casts had their own organizations for self-improvement.

Paradoxically, in Tokyo in the early twentieth century, the prolif-eration of associations within society was significantly facilitated by the state, particularly the civilian bureaucracy. The credit for the in-creased breadth, depth, and inclusiveness of Japanese political partic-ipation belongs to the Home Ministry, which encompassed both the police and the social bureau. The Home Ministry was also responsible for local administration and thus played an integral role in both pre-fectural and municipal policies.

By contrast, the military had relatively little direct impact on urban residents. The Imperial Military Reserve Association often failed to absorb earlier military support groups founded on local initiative. Only a small percentage of those eligible for membership actually joined the reservist organization. The branches and squads functioned primarily as local groups with administrative guidance from the ward office, an extension of the Home Ministry.

The political parties certainly played some part in the expansion of citizen participation. It was, after all, a three-party coalition that enacted universal manhood suffrage in March 1925. Once suffrage was extended, the established parties used every possible technological innovation (such as projectors, phonographs, radio, and movies) to convey their campaign messages to the previously disenfranchised. In the first three universal manhood suffrage elections, the established parties each in turn made good use of the prestige and influence that came with control of the cabinet. The Seiyūkai was especially adept at forging ties with various local organizations.

The direct influence of the established political parties pales, how-ever, in comparison to that of the civilian bureaucracy, particularly the Home Ministry. The bureaucrats who administered Tokyo encour-aged citizen participation in many ways. Their number included ad-vocates of legalized labor unions, proponents of universal suffrage, directors of the Japan Young Men's Hall, sponsors of election puri-fication, and officials of philanthropic organizations for Koreans in Japan. Mayors, vice-mayors, and directors of the Metropolitan Police (such as Horikiri Zenjirō, Gotō Fumio, Tazawa Yoshiharu, Maeda Tamon, and Maruyama Tsurukichi) fostered participation in the young men's associations and the neighborhood associations, whose membership was open to all, regardless of class. They also encouraged ordinary citizens to participate in public affairs through labor unions and universal suffrage.

Functionaries of the Home Ministry were the chief tutors for political participation. They notified voters of their right to vote, informed them of the provisions of the election law, and allowed residents of municipal shelters to stay out late to attend political meetings. In the election purification campaigns of the 1930s, bureaucrats sent schoolchildren into the streets singing election songs and inserted voting reminders into cigarette cartons. In Tokyo, election purification slogans showed up on *chindonya*, kites, automobiles, balloons, and pencils.

The participation bureaucrats inherited the struggle of the Meiji oligarchs to win support for state economic and social policies. The various organizational pyramids sponsored by the Home Ministry were all attempts to extend the influence, if not the power, of the state into units of society below the lowest level of formal local government. The local government or self-government *(jichi)* system was intimately linked to the issue of citizen participation, for Yamagata Aritomo established it in the late 1880s to provide the local basis for the success of the national Diet, which first convened in 1890. Yamagata envisioned a system that would allow local responsibility, provide training for loyal, responsible citizens, and prepare local residents for service in the Diet. He hoped to keep the political parties out of the local government structure.[1]

In Tokyo, Yamagata's hopes were only partially realized. Veterans of the ward assemblies, the lowest level of the self-government system in the city, did win seats in the municipal and the prefectural assemblies, and many of the candidates for the Diet cut their political teeth in the municipal and prefectural assemblies. What was no doubt disappointing to Yamagata was the fact that the parties were involved at every level of this political tutorial system. Yamagata had no more desired the wheeling and dealing characteristic of the Tokyo municipal assembly than the authors of the American constitution had anticipated Tammany Hall.

Like Yamagata, the participation bureaucrats wanted a healthy, literate, patriotic population that would work hard in both war and peace and that would vote on the basis of conscience rather than party affiliation. But in the 1920s, they had to work within an institutional framework that was quite different from Yamagata's in the 1880s.

Once universal manhood suffrage was law, the state depended on the cooperation not simply of the local elite but of all adult males. The participation bureaucrats were engaged in keen competition to secure the allegiance of the newly enfranchised to the interests of the state. They were well aware that the parties enjoyed the advantage of over three decades of experience in exchanging favors for votes.

David Hammack has observed with respect to the distribution of power in the American city that historians who have focused on elites have discovered concentration of power, whereas those whose research concerns entrepreneurship, social policy, lower status groups, and local politics have found that power was dispersed. A wide dispersal of power was particularly characteristic of cities that were older, larger, and economically diverse.[2] Heretofore, scholars who have even touched upon either the participation bureaucrats or the institutions they fostered have been primarily interested in the Japanese state and its parliamentary opposition. It is not surprising, then, that research on the citizens of Tokyo, which was far older and larger than any American city, challenges some of our assumptions concerning state-sponsored voluntary organizations. The proliferation of state-sponsored local organizations was rather ineffectual in extending the power of the state into urban neighborhoods. It did, however, substantially enrich the social fabric of the city.

The common assumption that civilian bureaucrats organized the ordinary citizenry as handmaidens of the military is simply not borne out by the evidence. In their efforts to enlist urban society in the causes of the state, the participation bureaucrats were heirs to Yamagata's civil rather than his military responsibilities. The neighborhood associations, district welfare committees, and other citizen organizations began—in the 1920s and earlier—in response not to military initiatives or priorities but to urban problems. They developed with the cooperation of the urban local elite. In the 1930s, some of the participation bureaucrats (Gotō Fumio, for instance) served in the nonparty cabinets of the 1930s and cooperated with the military to form cabinet super-agencies, but their alliances with the military were forged only after the welfare facilities, neighborhood associations, and district welfare committees were already well established.

The conceptualization of the organizations sponsored by the Home Ministry as being either survivals from or revivals of the feudal past is inappropriate for an area that had experienced as much economic and social change as Tokyo had in the late nineteenth century. The bureaucrats themselves indeed fostered this illusion by invoking precedents from the Japanese past to legitimize modern, and sometimes foreign, innovations. Neighborhood associations and district welfare committees in fact bore little resemblance to the Tokugawa institutions the bureaucrats tried to associate them with. On the contrary, neighborhood associations took several of their essential characteristics from the sanitary associations, which were manifestations of the state prerogative to regulate society in the name of scientific expertise.

The neighborhood associations were thus a new institutional form, one that could obviate geographic and class differences to forge a local community. In some cases, the inclusion of all residents, regardless of class or geographic origin, may have broadened the base of support of local notables. At the same time, however, the associations severed community leadership from older forms of organization, based on hereditary family ties, which excluded newcomers from their ranks. In Honjo, where many of the heads of neighborhood associations were born in prefectures other than Tokyo, it was clearly possible to assume neighborhood leadership on the basis of one's own achievements rather than one's father's. These new organizations substituted only imperfectly for the security of family and village, but they did it without erecting barriers against newcomers or incurring onerous debts of moral indebtedness. They provided a useful degree of community to a highly mobile and diverse population, as the postwar versions of these organizations continue to do today.

It is far more fruitful to think of the Home Ministry bureaucrats as officials acting on behalf of an autonomous state rather than as defenders of a class alliance between the old feudal order and the new capitalists. The civilian bureaucrats fit Theda Skocpol's characterization of the likely leaders of an autonomous state: "organizationally coherent collectivities of state officials," "relatively insulated from ties to currently dominant socioeconomic interests." By 1900, the majority of civilian bureaucrats were graduates of the imperial universities who had passed rigorous qualifying examinations.[3] Once incorporated into the civilian bureaucracy, individuals engaged in constant research and study, supplemented by travel abroad, and this reinforced their self-image as an elite, qualified by their superior knowledge to determine society's needs.

Their education in politics and world history convinced the Home Ministry bureaucrats that there was an inexorable relationship between economic conditions and social order. From the late nineteenth century, scholars, statesmen, and journalists shared the assumption that capitalism and industrialization could reduce hardworking individuals to poverty, and that if the state did nothing about it, this poverty-stricken class would, by a process as inevitable as the laws of physics, turn to revolutionary doctrines. The bureaucrats drew this lesson from the destructive mob of the French Revolution, and its truth was already self-evident to them when the Soviets established their regime in Russia.[4]

Because they believed there was a necessary connection between economic conditions and political thought, the bureaucrats investigated the economic conditions of the urban poor and tried to improve them. The Tokyo social bureau investigated actual conditions in the city, urged the city assembly to fund projects ranging from maternity clinics to free night shelters, and enlisted volunteer support from responsible residents and private philanthropists. The municipal authorities worked closely with Christians, Buddhists, labor union organizers, and socialists, which suggests that they were more interested in providing social services than in restricting religious and political thought.

Participation bureaucrats cooperated with liberal intellectuals because bureaucrats and intellectuals shared what Peter Duus has called a "consensus model" of Japanese society, in which the state "resolved conflict by remedying the specific causes that provoked it or by generating a sense of shared interest or commitment within society." Like certain nineteenth-century graduates of the British public schools, they assumed positions of leadership in order to (as Meacham put it) "reconcile the conflicting interests of class for the good of the community as a whole."[5] It was to reconcile conflicting class interests that the participation bureaucrats cooperated with Suzuki Bunji and invited the advice of Kagawa Toyohiko and Majima Kan. Just as British reformers founded Toynbee Hall in the slums of East London in 1884, so in Japan, bureaucrats and reformers together generated shared interest and commitment through settlement houses, labor schools, and health clinics.

Despite strong state leadership in structuring political participation, citizens remained free to take part in a rich variety of voluntary organizations, including labor unions and political parties. An influential portion of the bureaucracy in fact supported legal labor unions. The new generation in the Home Ministry in the 1920s believed that, in capitalism, workers and employers would inevitably have conflicts of interest; and they believed that unions would enable workers to liberate themselves.[6] Indeed, labor unions provided workers with a horizontal framework of organization that made them less dependent upon the established economic and political hierarchies of their communities. Through unions, intellectuals introduced workers to ideas that challenged the social and economic order at both the local and the national level.

Thus, the participation bureaucrats worked willingly within a pluralist society. Although in wartime, the neighborhood associations and their subordinate units, the *tonarigumi,* constituted a compulsory hierarchical arrangement that suggests comparisons to the methods used in more recent decades by Peruvian leaders to organize urban squatters, any resemblance of Home Ministry programs prior to 1937 to corporatism is more apparent than real. To be sure, the Home Ministry created hierarchical organizations that conform to part of Philippe Schmitter's definition of corporatism; one could say of both the young men's associations and the neighborhood associations that they were "recognized or licensed (if not created) by the state" and that they enjoyed "deliberate representational monopoly within their respective categories." However, in contrast with Schmitter's further requirements that such hierarchies be singular, compulsory, functionally differentiated, and subject to state constraints on the choice of leadership, the Home Ministry set up multiple hierarchies with overlapping constituencies, voluntary membership, and local control of leadership. Although the participation bureaucrats shared the inclusionary aims of organic statists who wished to lessen society's vulnerability to organized class conflict, they did not employ their methods.[7]

Japanese civilian bureaucrats were directly influenced by contemporary developments in Europe and the United States. They shared many of the aims of American urban reformers. Frederic C. Howe, the Cleveland lawyer, social worker, politician, and writer, wrote in 1905 that one of the achievements of the American city was that in it the masses of the people received enlightenment and democratic opportunities from a host of institutions: night schools, art exhibitions, popular lectures and concerts, college settlements, parks, playgrounds, a cheap press, and labor organizations.[8] By 1937, Tokyo could boast all these institutions, thanks in large part to the municipal social bureau.

Like their American colleagues, the participation bureaucrats were supporters of parliamentary government. Precisely because of their desire for broad citizen participation, they had a strong interest in election politics at home and abroad. When Gotō Fumio was making a study tour of Europe and the United States from 1917 to 1919, he wrote a special report on the reform of the British election law. Convinced that wide citizen participation in politics was one reason England had won World War I, Gotō worked with Horikiri Zenjirō and others to promote support within the Home Ministry for universal suffrage.[9] Several of the participation bureaucrats themselves ran for political office. Tazawa Yoshiharu ran as an independent from Shizuoka in the 1924 election for the Lower House. In the postwar era, Gotō Fumio—who enjoyed an appointment to the prewar House of Peers—won election to the Upper House.

With their broad education and their travel abroad, the participation bureaucrats were aware that in the United States, party politics were not closely associated with good government. Whether in New York, Chicago, St. Louis, or Cleveland, idealists wanted nonpartisan government, by honest and well-qualified officials who would work on behalf of the people rather than line their own pockets. Howe railed against the boss, the machine, corruption, and the spoils system. He complained that in St. Louis the rich and influential used the Democratic Party and Boss Butler to control the administration of justice and that in Cincinnati "Boss Cox rules the servile city . . . as a mediaeval baron did his serfs." Howe's heroes were men such as Samuel M. Jones, who was elected mayor of Toledo as an independent. The most notorious of the city machines was Tammany Hall, the bastion of the Democratic Party in New York. In his successful campaign for mayor in 1933 on a Fusion ticket, Fiorello La Guardia promised to replace "the army of parasites fattening at the trough of the city treasury" with nonpartisan government by experts. He proposed a local welfare state "to replace the Tammany district leader who doled out a Christmas turkey, bucket of coal or some other form of charity."[10]

Both the history of urban party machines in the United States and the considerable talent that the major Japanese political parties had displayed under the limited franchise in exchanging favors for votes explain why, although Home Ministry bureaucrats were advocates of citizen participation in politics, they were not committed to the ideal that the two major political parties should control the cabinet. Many civilian bureaucrats, including the participation bureaucrats, believed that the two established political parties had promoted policies that were detrimental to the national interest. They resented how the parties had interfered with the prerogatives of the highly trained bureaucrats by securing party control over appointments to the police and to governorships of the prefectures.[11] Gotō Fumio and others, resentful of party infiltration into the bureaucracy, hoped that their state-sponsored organizations would provide avenues of public participation for Japanese citizens that were less divisive than the competition for spoils engaged in by the established political parties.

Like American reformers, the bureaucratic leaders of Tokyo wanted government for the benefit of the people with broad citizen participation under their own expert leadership. They possessed certain advantages over their American counterparts. As members of a select national civil service, respected for their expertise, they enjoyed considerable legitimacy and prestige. Although the Tokyo city council could equal any American city for scandals over vote-buying and graft, in Tokyo the masses were newly enfranchised and were not as yet under the direct control of the parties. Whereas in American cities there was broad political participation before cities grew large and the functions of urban government complex, in Japan universal suffrage came to a city that already had a population of over two million and that would soon annex nearly the entire metropolitan area.

The participation bureaucrats took measures to prevent the same problems American urban reformers were trying to correct. The neighborhood associations and district welfare committees provided a framework for the bureaucrats to circumvent the parties and work directly with local leaders in distributing the goods and favors that gave Tammany politicians in New York and precinct captains in Chicago such influence over votes. Tammany district leaders and Chicago precinct captains distributed food, coal, and sometimes cash to get their loyal voters through difficult economic times. In Tokyo, the system of district welfare committees was designed to keep access to charitable goods and the welfare system firmly under the direction of the Tokyo social bureau. In Chicago, precinct captains received complaints about streets, alleys, and other government services; in Tokyo, the head of the neighborhood association had direct links to the ward office, which made the mediation of the parties theoretically unnecessary.[12] There was a great deal of resonance between the election purification movement in Japan in the 1930s and La Guardia's campaign in New York in 1933. La Guardia and his supporters railed against Tammany Hall and its habit of treating public office as personal property. The election purification campaigns, their enlistment of schoolchildren, the young men's associations, and even the young women's associations, were methods of educating present and future voters on the responsible exercise of their privilege.

If we accept that one of the primary aims of the civilian bureaucrats was to increase political participation, then their programs succeeded. It is in no small measure thanks to the civilian bureaucracy that by the time the parties lost control over the cabinet, interest in political matters was so ingrained that the degree of public participation remained high. To be sure, after the institution of transcendental cabinets removed any direct link between the people as voters and the apparatus of the state, the voting rate did go down. Nevertheless, even at its lowest, the urban voting rate in the 1930s was far higher than the percentage of eligible men who joined the military reserves or the young men's associations.

The bureaucrats did not succeed, however, in completely destroying the local power base of the political parties. Despite their loss of power at the center, the political parties continued to mediate much of the popular participation. In Honjo and Fukagawa, with only two exceptions, the two major political parties controlled all the seats in the district up through the 1936 election. The one instance of bureaucratic policy damaging party interests in Honjo Ward is the case of Pak Ch'un-kum. His candidacy undoubtedly benefited from the declining power of the established parties at the national level and from the rhetoric of the election purification campaigns.

On balance, the participation bureaucrats facilitated party politics at the local level far more than they impeded it. The neighborhood associations, the young men's associations, and the district welfare committees increased communications between the established party candidates and less privileged members of their constituencies. They provided an organizational framework for contact across class, occupational, and enterprise lines. A candidate who placed members of his support group in these organizations or who recruited leaders of the community organization into his support group could forge ties with a wide range of interest groups within his district.

The bureaucrats could not eliminate the parties as a factor in urban politics, but neither did the party leadership completely take over the neighborhood associations or the district welfare committees. The parties and the local organizations existed in parallel, and ambitious local leaders could take advantage of either or both. The pluralism of the Japanese city has permitted alternatives to the major political parties: socialists and independents in the 1930s, and reform governments in the 1960s. Tocqueville observed that "Americans of all ages, all conditions, and all dispositions constantly form associations." He noted that they formed thousands of different kinds of associations and used them to do what in France would be done by the government and in England by a man of rank. He contrasted the American pattern to aristocratic communities:

> In aristocratic societies men do not need to combine in order to act, because they are strongly held together. Every wealthy and powerful citizen constitutes the head of a permanent and compulsory association, composed of all those who are dependent upon him or whom he makes subservient to the execution of his designs.[13]

Allinson's research on Kariya and Smethurst's research on Japanese villages suggest that in the small cities and villages of Japan the political parties, the military reserve units, and the young men's associations simply reinforced the local aristocrats. In the city, the organizations were genuinely plural and offered individuals real choices.

To be sure, neither the political parties nor the participation bureaucrats proved to be champions of liberalism. There is a rich literature on Japanese liberal and reformist thinkers, their visions of the Japanese polity, and the difficulties of sustaining that vision during the 1930s.[14] Neither the parties nor the participation bureaucrats provided reliable support for liberal ideals. Both supported restrictions on public expression. When extremists launched virulent attacks against Minobe Tatsukichi and his theories, which supported a liberal interpretation of the Japanese constitution, virtually no one came to his defense. There is ample documentation of the extensive powers of the Japanese state to censor and suppress individuals and ideas that it opposed.[15] In 1940, the elimination of the opposition political parties and the labor unions meant that any intellectual opposed to the state but still determined to participate in national life was left stranded in a political wilderness. He was left, in the words of Andrew Barshay, "all dressed up with no place to go except into the arms of the state, which was the sole repository of legitimate public service."[16]

When in the late 1930s many voices were silenced, it was because certain types of expertise and claims to legitimacy were privileged over others. That the military was primary among these privileged voices was partly because, after 1937, Japan was engaged in full-scale war in China and ever since the Manchurian Incident of 1931 Japan had been "hated by the Chinese, feared by the Soviets, and censored by the Anglo-Americans."[17] How and why Japan got into this position and why the country reacted the way it did are questions beyond the scope of this study.

The limits of liberalism in prewar Japan constituted a major flaw in its democracy. If democracy is to survive in a country, the legitimacy of democratic values must be widely accepted.[18] In Japan in the 1930s, the commitment to social welfare and broad political participation were not paralleled by an equally strong commitment to rights of free speech, free press, and free association. Only after facing the devastation of war and defeat have the Japanese become deeply committed to the liberal values now inscribed in the 1947 constitution.

Because the commitment to liberalism was limited, the political parties, the labor unions, and numerous voluntary organizations acquiesced in their own demise in the mobilization for war that occurred after 1938. The failure of liberalism enabled the elite to foreclose options on what citizens could say and do but it did not, however, destroy the twin legacies of broadly based popular political participation and state responsibility for social welfare that had been established by 1937. Government with the people readied the political soil for the government of and by the people that became possible after 1947. Government for the people continues in Japan today in the national health care system and in child welfare programs.[19]

Appendixes
Notes
Bibliography
Index

Appendix A

Mayors of Tokyo City and Their Ties to Tokyo Imperial University and the Home Ministry

	Dates as Mayor	Graduation from Tokyo	Home Ministry
Matsuda Hideo	10/98–6/03		
Ozaki Yukio	6/03–6/12		
Sakatani Yoshirō	7/12–3/15	x	
Okuda Gijin	6/15–8/17	x	
Tajiri Inejirō	4/18–11/20		
Gotō Shinpei	12/20–4/23		x
Nagata Hidejirō	5/23–9/24		x
Nakamura Korekimi	10/24–6/26	x	
Izawa Takio	7/26–10/26	x	x
Nishikubo Hiromichi	10/26–12/27	x	x
Ichiki Otohiko	1/28–2/29	x	
Horikiri Zenjirō	4/29–5/30	x	x
Nagata Hidejirō	5/30–1/33		x
Ushizuka Toratarō	5/33–5/37	x	x
Kobashi Ichita	6/37–4/39	x	x
Tsuboki Keikichi	4/39–2/40		
Okubo Tomejirō	4/39–7/42		x
Kishimoto Ayao	8/42–6/43		

Appendix B

Diet Candidates from the Fourth District, 1928–1937

Candidate	Party	Votes
1928		
Omata Masaichi	Minseitō	10,149
Ōta Shinjirō	Minseitō	9,949
Isobe Hisashi	Seiyūkai	4,465
Kunieda Sutejirō	Seiyūkai	4,204
Takizawa Shichirō	Seiyūkai	3,954
Nakano Yujirō	Seiyūkai	3,669
Miyazaki Ryūsuke	Shakai Minshūtō	3,581
Mori Kenji	Seiyūkai	3,501
Tsuya Ichijirō	Minseitō	3,363
Karazawa Seihachi	Rōnōtō	2,845
Fukayama Naobei	Minseitō	2,769
Morita Korokurō	Independent	1,420
Terata Iyaichirō	Minseitō	1,147
Terabe Raisuke	Jitsugyō Dōshikai	1,119
Kasuya Isobei	Kakushintō	813
Ōtani Beitarō	Independent	716
1930		
Manabe Gijū	Minseitō	11,134
Omata Masaichi	Minseitō	6,234
Furushima Miyajirō	Minseitō	6,000
Ōta Shinjirō	Independent	5,786
Kunieda Sutejirō	Seiyūkai	5,411
Isobe Hisashi	Seiyūkai	5,075
Mori Kendō	Minseitō	3,895
Honda Ichirō	Independent	3,585

210

Candidate	Party	Votes
Asanuma Inejirō	Taishū	3,298
Mori Kenji	Seiyūkai	2,837
Miyazaki Ryūsuke	Zenmin	2,122
Kagawa Toyohiko	Shakai Minshūtō	1,117
Okubo Shūjun	Chimu	246
1932		
Isobe Hisashi	Seiyūkai	11,813
Kunieda Sutejirō	Seiyūkai	10,460
Pak Ch'un-kum	Independent	6,966
Nakano Yūjirō	Seiyūkai	6,599
Manabe Gijū	Minseitō	6,573
Omata Masaichi	Minseitō	6,192
Mori Kendō	Minseitō	5,379
Mori Kenji	Seiyūkai	4,845
Asanuma Inejirō	Taishū	4,459
Furushima Miyajirō	Minseitō	3,564
Majima Kan	Shakai Minshūtō	1,638
1936		
Asanuma Inejirō	Shakai Taishūtō	13,805
Manabe Gijū	Minseitō	12,621
Mori Kendō	Minseitō	6,780
Ōta Shinjirō	Minseitō	6,660
Takizawa Shichirō	Seiyūkai	5,611
Pak Ch'un-kum	Independent	5,514
Honda Ichirō	Shōwakai	4,614
Nakano Yūjirō	Seiyūkai	4,087
Ida Tomobei	Seiyūkai	3,634
Fukushima Usaburō	Independent	3,379
Ichimata Yasubei	Seiyūkai	3,049
Kasuya Isobe	Kokumei	3,041
Miyamura Kiichi	Minseitō	2,548
Suginohara Eitarō	Minseitō	1,641
Katō Yoshitaka	Yōseikai	1,266
Yamaguchi Kiyoshi	Independent	761

Candidate	Party	Votes
1937		
Abe Shigeo	Shakai Taishūtō	12,096
Manabe Gijū	Minseitō	10,192
Takizawa Shichirō	Seiyūkai	8,352
Pak Ch'un-kum	Independent	7,915
Ōta Shinjirō	Minseitō	7,895
Honda Ichirō	Independent	7,015
Mori Kendō	Minseitō	5,915
Yamada Takeji	Minseitō	5,337
Nakano Yūjirō	Seiyūkai	3,797
Fukushima Usaburō	Independent	2,729
Nonomura Kanji	Yōseikai	2,194

Appendix C

Established Party Candidates for the Diet, 1928–1936

	Birthplace	*Date*	*Occupation*
Fukayama Naobei			
Furushima Miyajirō	Hiroshima		Contractor
Ichimata Yasubei	Tokushima	1890	Lawyer
Ida Tomobei	Saitama	1889	Manufacturer
Isobe Hisashi	Tokyo	1875	Lawyer
Kunieda Sutejirō	Gifu	1876	Company Director
Manabe Gijū	Nagasaki	1891	Author
Miyamura Kiichi	Chiba	1889	Coal Merchant
Mori Kendō	Kagoshima	1887	Lawyer
Mori Kenji	Toyama		Contractor
Nakano Yūjirō	Kyoto	1879	Lawyer
Omata Masaichi	Yamanashi	1879	Physician
Ōta Shinjirō	Tokyo	1873	Lumber Wholesaler
Suginohara Eitarō	Hiroshima	1886	Company Employee
Takizawa Shichirō	Nagano	1878	Factory Owner
Terata Iyaichirō			
Tsuya Ichijirō			

Notes

Abbreviations Used in Notes

JT&M	*Japan Times and Mail*
NS	*Nihon shinshiroku*
NSJN	*Nihon shakai jigyō nenkan*
SGSS	Tōkyō-fu senkyo shukusei jikkō bu. *Shūgiin giin sōsenkyo ni kansuru shirabe*
SSJ	*Shakai seisaku jihō*
TAS	*Tōkyō asahi shinbun*
THS	*Tōkyō hyakunen shi*

Introduction

1. For the definition of democracy used here, see Larry Diamond, Juan J. Linz, and Seymour Martin Lipset, *Democracy in Developing Countries,* vol. 3, *Asia,* p. xvi. For a slightly different definition of democracy and its application to Japan, see T. J. Pempel, "Prerequisites for Democracy," in *Democracy in Japan,* ed. Takeshi Ishida and Ellis S. Krauss, esp. pp. 18–19.

2. I take the term "unconditional democracy" from the title of Toshio Nishi's book. For a recent review of the literature on liberalism, see Germaine A. Hoston, "The State, Modernity, and the Fate of Liberalism in Prewar Japan," *Journal of Asian Studies* 51 (May 1992): 287–316.

3. Ishida and Krauss, *Democracy in Japan,* chaps. 1 and 14, esp. pp. 3, 328. The tendency to begin Japan's democratic history in 1945 is common among political scientists. A number of historians have stressed continuities in Japan's twentieth-century history, but with the notable exception of Sharon H. Nolte, *Liberalism in Modern Japan: Ishibashi Tanzan and His Teachers, 1905–1960,* these studies have been only tangentially concerned with the constructive development of democracy.

4. For a recent expression of the democracy out of atomic bombs view, see Barrington Moore Jr., "Japanese Peasant Protests and Revolts in Comparative Historical Perspective," *International Review of Social History* 33 (1988): 326–27.

5. Carol Gluck, *Japan's Modern Myths: Ideology in the Late Meiji Period,* p. 11.

6. These are the words of Yoshino Sakuzō, cited in Ryusaku Tsunoda, Wm. Theodore de Bary, and Donald Keene, *Sources of Japanese Tradition*

215

2:232. The quotation from de Tocqueville is from Alexis de Tocqueville, *Democracy in America* 2:125.

7. For a review of the literature on the state as an independent actor, see Theda Skocpol, "Bringing the State Back In: Strategies of Analysis in Current Research," in *Bringing the State Back In,* ed. Dietrich B. Evans, Dietrich Rueschemeyer, and Theda Skocpol, esp. pp. 11–12. On the limitations of liberal-pluralist and Marxist approaches to the state, see Alfred Stepan, *The State and Society: Peru in Comparative Perspective,* pp. 7–26.

8. Jon C. Teaford, *The Twentieth-Century American City: Problem, Promise, and Reality,* p. 16. Technical experts were particularly important in cities with an appointed manager, a system that began in Staunton, Virginia, in 1908 and that was by 1945 in effect in 350 American cities with a population of five thousand or more. Don Martindale, "Prefatory Remarks: The Theory of the City," in Max Weber, *The City,* pp. 44–45.

9. Lincoln Steffens, *The Shame of the Cities,* p. 7; Frederic C. Howe, *The City: The Hope of Democracy,* p. 90.

10. Yoshino Sakuzō from Tsunoda, de Bary, and Keene, *Sources* 2:218, 223, 224–26.

11. This particular scene was observed by Kawakami Hajime, later a professor at Kyoto Imperial University. Gail Lee Bernstein, *Japanese Marxist: A Portrait of Kawakami Hajime, 1879–1946,* p. 35.

12. Diamond, Linz, and Lipset, *Democracy in Developing Countries,* classify as semidemocratic "those countries where the effective power of elected officials is so limited, or political party competition is so restricted, or the freedom and fairness of elections so compromised that electoral outcomes, while competitive, still deviate significantly from popular preferences; and/or where civil and political liberties are so limited that some political orientations and interests are unable to organize and express themselves" (3:xvii). Edwin O. Reischauer used the title "What Went Wrong?" for his essay in *Dilemmas of Growth in Prewar Japan,* ed. James W. Morley.

13. Tocqueville, *Democracy in America* 2:115. Contemporary political scientists define participation broadly: "simply the efforts of ordinary people in any type of political system to influence the actions of their rulers, and sometimes to change their rulers." Such political participation may range in nature from "civil conversations and orderly voting to riotous rebellion." Joan M. Nelson, "Political Participation," in *Understanding Political Development,* ed. Myron Weiner and Samuel P. Huntington, pp. 104–5.

14. On India, see Jyotirindra Das Gupta, "India: Democratic Becoming and Combined Development," in *Democracy in Developing Countries,* ed. Diamond, Linz, and Lipset, 3:64; and Larry Diamond, "Introduction: Persistence, Erosion, Breakdown, and Renewal," in ibid. 3:50.

15. The seminal work on the prewar political parties is Robert A. Scalapino, *Democracy and the Party Movement in Prewar Japan: The Failure of the First Attempt.* Important studies that have substantially revised his original

formulation are Tetsuo Najita, *Hara Kei in the Politics of Compromise, 1905–1915;* Peter Duus, *Party Rivalry and Political Change in Taishō Japan;* Gordon Mark Berger, *Parties out of Power in Japan, 1931–1941;* Sharon Minichiello, *Retreat from Reform: Patterns of Political Behavior in Interwar Japan;* and Sheldon Garon, *The State and Labor in Modern Japan.*

16. On Tammany Hall, see Arthur Mann's introduction to William L. Riordan, *Plunkitt of Tammany Hall,* p. xv, and Arthur Mann, *La Guardia Comes to Power, 1933,* pp. 46–51. For personal observations on New York politics in the 1890s, see Frederic C. Howe, *The Confessions of a Reformer,* pp. 50–61.

17. Scalapino, *Democracy,* pp. 219 n. 295.

18. Richard J. Smethurst, *A Social Basis for Prewar Japanese Militarism: The Army and the Rural Community;* Gary Allinson, *Japanese Urbanism: Industry and Politics in Kariya, 1872–1972.*

19. See for instance Smethurst, *Social Basis,* pp. 88, 183, and Allinson, *Japanese Urbanism,* pp. 78–81. Smethurst has since revised his view of this era; in his recent book, *Agricultural Development and Tenancy Disputes in Japan, 1870–1940,* pp. 432–33, he concludes that suffrage was a significant part of the gradual process by which rural tenants became entrepreneurs, and he sees considerable change between 1870 and 1945, especially during the years from 1917 to 1941.

20. On the labor movement, some of the important studies are Robert A. Scalapino, *The Early Japanese Labor Movement: Labor and Politics in a Developing Society,* and two books by Stephen S. Large, *The Rise of Labor in Japan, 1912–19: The Yūaikai,* and *Organized Workers and Socialist Politics in Interwar Japan.* The felicitous phrase is from Garon, *State and Labor,* p. 3.

21. Andrew Gordon, *The Evolution of Labor Relations in Japan: Heavy Industry, 1853–1955,* and *Labor and Imperial Democracy in Prewar Japan.*

22. Gordon, *Imperial Democracy,* esp. p. 340; Michael Lewis, *Rioters and Citizens: Mass Protest in Imperial Japan.*

23. Weber, *The City,* p. 65.

24. See Theodore C. Bestor, *Neighborhood Tokyo,* pp. 8–9, 46–49, for a review of the scholarly literature on Tokyo as an urban village, a notion that both Bestor and I reject.

25. Gordon, *Imperial Democracy,* p. 82.

26. On state ideology, see Gluck, *Modern Myths;* on labor policy, see Garon, *State and Labor,* and W. Dean Kinzley, *Industrial Harmony in Modern Japan: The Invention of a Tradition;* on the higher police, see Elise K. Tipton, *The Japanese Police State: The Tokkō in Interwar Japan;* on economic planning, see Chalmers A. Johnson, *MITI and the Japanese Miracle: The Growth of Industrial Policy, 1925–1975;* on the media, see Gregory J. Kasza, *The State and the Mass Media in Japan, 1918–1945.*

27. Reischauer, "What Went Wrong?" p. 491; Garon, *State and Labor,* pp. 76–89.

28. For the riots, see Shumpei Okamoto, "The Emperor and the Crowd: The Historical Significance of the Hibiya Riot," in *Conflict in Modern Japanese History: The Neglected Tradition,* ed. Tetsuo Najita and J. Victor Koschmann, pp. 261–62; also Gordon, *Imperial Democracy,* pp. 26–27. Matsuo Takayoshi, *Taishō demokurashii no kenkyū,* pp. v, 6–7.

29. There are two recent anthropological studies of Tokyo that illustrate how local organizations, including neighborhood associations and volunteer welfare workers, continue to operate: Bestor, *Neighborhood Tokyo,* and Dorinne K. Kondo, *Crafting Selves: Power, Gender, and Discourses of Identity in a Japanese Workplace.*

30. Akira Iriye, "The Internationalization of History," *American Historical Review* 94 (February 1989): 1–10. This call was renewed with respect to American history by Ian Tyrrell, "American Exceptionalism in an Age of International History," *American Historical Review* 96 (October 1991): 1031–55.

31. Ellen Kay Trimberger, in *Revolution from Above: Military Bureaucrats and Development in Japan, Turkey, Egypt, and Peru,* pp. 111, 133, for instance, assumed on the basis of the scholarship available to her in English in the 1970s that no civic consciousness developed in Japan. She notes the role of the Home Ministry in creating local organizations, but she associates this with military rule in the 1930s rather than with any independent agenda of the civil bureaucracy.

Chapter 1

1. For a description of these ceremonies in a Tokyo elementary school in the 1890s, see Junichirō Tanizaki, *Childhood Years: A Memoir,* pp. 40–41. For the history of the development of such ceremonies during the Meiji era, see Gluck, *Modern Myths,* pp. 85–87.

2. Garon, *State and Labor,* pp. 56, 132; Michael Lewis, *Rioters and Citizens,* p. 244; Gordon, *Imperial Democracy,* p. 105; Kinzley, *Industrial Harmony,* p. 32.

3. Garon, *State and Labor,* and Kinzley, *Industrial Harmony,* our best accounts of social policy, are both primarily concerned with industrial labor rather than with broader urban problems.

4. Bob Tadashi Wakabayashi, "Aizawa Seishisai's *Shinron* and Western Learning, 1782–1825," p. 426.

5. Yasuhide Kawashima, "America Through Foreign Eyes: Reactions of the Delegates from Tokugawa, Japan, 1860," *Journal of Social History* 5 (1972): 505; Sidney Devere Brown and Akiko Hirota, eds., *The Diary of Kido Takayoshi,* vol. 2, *1871–1874,* p. 141; Kinzley, *Industrial Harmony,* p. 7.

6. Koji Taira, "Public Assistance in Japan: Development and Trends," *Journal of Asian Studies* 27 (November 1967): 101; Kinzley, *Industrial Harmony*, pp. 7–8. For the text of the law, see Kimura Takeo, *Nihon kindai shakai jigyō shi*, pp. 16–17.

7. Kyugoro Obata, *An Interpretation of the Life of Viscount Shibusawa*, pp. 143–49; K. O. Sakauye, "Social Movements in Tokyo," *Japan Magazine* 12 (April–May 1922): 111–12, 114.

8. Obata, *Interpretation*, pp. 143, 145; F. Ando, "The Tokyo Almshouse," *Japan Magazine* 6 (1915): 298–300.

9. Priscilla Ferguson Clement, *Welfare and the Poor in the Nineteenth-Century City: Philadelphia, 1800–1854*, pp. 82–117 (esp. 95).

10. *Japan Times*, January 27, 1912, and May 16, 1913. For other examples of official praise for the financially independent, see Sharon H. Nolte and Sally Ann Hastings, "The Meiji State's Policy Toward Women, 1890–1910," in *Recreating Japanese Women, 1600–1945*, ed. Gail Lee Bernstein, pp. 165–68.

11. Earl H. Kinmonth, "Fukuzawa Reconsidered: *Gakumon no susume* and Its Audience," *Journal of Asian Studies* 37 (August 1978): 681–82. For other examples of this attitude, see Kinzley, *Industrial Harmony*, p. 7.

12. Kimura, *Nihon kindai*, pp. 40, 44.

13. For details, see R. H. P. Mason, "The Debate on Poor Relief in the First Meiji Diet," *Journal of the Oriental Society of Australia* 3 (January 1965): 2–26.

14. On the Charity Organization Society in Great Britain, founded in 1869, see Standish Meacham, *Toynbee Hall and Social Reform, 1880–1914: The Search for Community*, p. 69, and Gertrude Himmelfarb, *Poverty and Compassion: The Moral Imagination of the Late Victorians*, pp. 185–206. On the adoption of these principles in Cleveland, see Frederic C. Howe, *Confessions of a Reformer*, pp. 76–79.

15. Kimura, *Nihon kindai*, p. 47. See also Kenneth B. Pyle, "Advantages of Followership: German Economics and Japanese Bureaucrats, 1890–1925," *Journal of Japanese Studies* 1 (1974): 127–64, and Oka Toshiro, "Kindai Nihon ni okeru shakai seisaku shisō no keisei to tenkai," *Shisō* 558 (1970): 69–88.

16. Pyle, "Advantages of Followership," pp. 140–41, 143, 146–48; Byron K. Marshall, *Capitalism and Nationalism in Prewar Japan: The Ideology of the Business Elite, 1868–1941*, p. 95.

17. Himmelfarb, *Poverty and Compassion*, p. 5.

18. Nishida Taketoshi, *Meiji-zenki no toshi kasō shakai*, pp. 8–9. The newspaper materials themselves are reprinted on pp. 55–63.

19. Yokoyama Gennosuke, *Nihon no kasō shakai*, pp. 33–34. For an example of this genre in English, see Iwagorō Matsubara, *In Darkest Tokyo: Sketches of Humble Life in the Capital of Japan*.

20. Zennosuke Tsuji, *Social Welfare Work by the Imperial Household of Japan*, p. 49.

21. Yoshida Kyūichi, *Shōwa shakai jigyōshi*, p. 19; Masao Takenaka, "Relation of Protestantism to Social Problems in Japan, 1900–1941," pp. 51–53; Suzuki Norihisa, "Christianity," in *Japanese Religion*, ed. Agency for Cultural Affairs, p. 85.

22. Yoshida Kyūichi et al., *Jinbutsu de tsuzuru kindai shakai jigyō no ayumi*, pp. 77–79, quotes the whole prospectus. On the donations, see J. H. Pettee, "Social Work: Eleemosynary Enterprises," in *The Christian Movement in Japan* 4 (1906): 123. For a fuller account of Noguchi's work, see Sally A. Hastings, "From Heroine to Patriotic Volunteer: Women and Social Work in Japan, 1900–1945," *Working Papers on Women in International Development*, no. 106 (November 1985): 5–6.

23. Hyman Kublin, *Asian Revolutionary: The Life of Sen Katayama*, pp. 96–98; Katayama Sen, *Jiden*, p. 300. On Greene's relationship to Banchō Church and its congregation, see Evarts Boutell Greene, *A New-Englander in Japan: Daniel Crosby Greene*, p. 254.

24. Takeo Yazaki, *Social Change and the City in Japan from Earliest Times Through the Industrial Revolution*, p. 190.

25. Kikuchi Hideo, *Edo Tōkyō chimei jiten*, pp. 113–14, 116, 121; Shigetō Sunao, *Tōkyō chōmei enkaku shi*, p. 251. For an account of life in this district in the early nineteenth century, see Katsu Kokichi, *Musui's Story*.

26. Edward Seidensticker, *Low City, High City: Tokyo from Edo to the Earthquake*, pp. 216–17.

27 27. Tōkyō-shi, *Tōkyō shi tōkei nenpyō* 15 (1918): 187.

28. This division is the organizing framework for Seidensticker's two volumes, *Low City, High City* and *Tokyo Rising: The City Since the Great Earthquake*. For an excellent discussion of the concepts in contemporary Tokyo, see Kondo, *Crafting Selves*, pp. 57–75.

29. Quotation is from Bestor, *Neighborhood Tokyo*, p. 7. On the Edokko, see Henry D. Smith II, "Tokyo as an Idea: An Exploration of Japanese Urban Thought Until 1945," *Journal of Japanese Studies* 4 (Winter 1978): 52–53, and "Tokyo and London: Comparative Conceptions of the City," in *Japan: A Comparative View*, ed. Albert M. Craig, p. 85.

30. Seidensticker, *Low City, High City*, pp. 214, 217.

31. Yoshida Kyūichi, *Nihon kindai bukkyō shakai shi kenkyū*, p. 544, and *Nihon shakai jigyō no rekishi*, p. 213; *Tōkyō hyakunen shi* 3:690 (hereafter referred to as *THS*).

32. Yoshida, *Nihon shakai jigyō no rekishi*, p. 213; Yamamuro Buhei, *Jindō no senshi Yamamuro Gunpei*, p. 59.

33. Yoshimichi Sugiura, "The Beginnings of St. Paul's School," *The Spirit of Missions* 74 (1909): 770; Kenneth Walter Cameron, ed., *American Episcopal Clergy: Registers of Ordinations in the Episcopal Church in the United States from 1785 Through 1904*; Masakazu Tai, "Thirty Years in the

Sei Ko Kwai," *The Spirit of Missions* 74 (1909): 773; Yoshimichi Sugiura, "A Japanese Pastor's Plea for His People," *The Spirit of Missions* 73 (1908): 521.

34. Yoshimichi Sugiura, "The Submerged Tenth in Japan," *The Spirit of Missions* 73 (1908): 105–8.

35. Yoshimichi Sugiura, "A Tokyo Rescue Mission," *The Spirit of Missions* 76 (1911): 663; Sugiura, "The Submerged Tenth," p. 106; Sugiura, "A Tokyo Rescue Mission," pp. 663–64.

36. Sugiura, "A Tokyo Rescue Mission," p. 664.

37. *Japan Times,* November 28, 1913; *Nihon shakai jigyō nenkan* (1920): 54 (hereafter referred to as *NSJN*).

38. Mr. Ito, head of the First Free Night Shelter, said in 1913 that the majority of the young men taking shelter there were from the country. *Japan Times,* July 23, 1913.

39. Ibid., August 17, 1912. The quotation is from Sugiura, "Pastor's Plea," p. 522. For the bishop's support, see Bishop McKim, "Our Evangelistic Work in the District of Tokyo," *The Spirit of Missions* 74 (1909): 780.

40. Sugiura, "Pastor's Plea," p. 521.

41. On the importance of this incident in inspiring social work, see Ashizawa Takeo, "Senzen no rōjin hogo o megutte," in *Shōwa shakai jigyōshi e no shōgen,* ed. Yoshida Kyūichi and Ichibangase Yasuko, pp. 401–2. A study of Kōtoku Shūsui has been done by F. G. Notehelfer, *Kōtoku Shūsui: Portrait of a Japanese Radical.*

42. Matsubara, *In Darkest Tokyo,* pp. 54, 40.

43. Garon, *State and Labor,* chapter 1; Gordon, *Labor Relations,* pp. 64–69.

44. *Japan Times,* February 9, 1911; *THS* 3:691.

45. Tōkyō-shi, *Tōkyō-shi tōkei nenpyō* 13 (1916): 440; *Japan Times,* November 15, 1911.

46. *Japan Times,* February 14, 1911; Ogawa Seiryō, "Sangyō shihon kakuritsu ki no kyūhin taisei," in *Nihon no kyūhin seido,* ed. Nihon shakai jigyō daigaku kyūhin seido kenkyūkai, pp. 145–46.

47. *Japan Times,* May 11, June 14, 21, 24, and July 2, 1911; Ogawa, "Sangyō shihon kakuritsu," p. 146 n.

48. Editorials from *Japan Times,* June 25, 1911.

49. Ibid., April 8, 1911.

50. Miyachi Masato, "Nichiro sengo no shakai to minshū," in *Kōza Nihon shi,* ed. Rekishigaku kenkyūkai and Nihonshi kenkyūkai, 6:156–58; Ogawa, "Sangyō shihon kakuritsu," p. 142.

51. For Hara Taneaki, see *Japan Year Book* (1908): 488. For the Salvation Army, see *Japan Times and Mail,* October 11, 1920 (hereafter referred to as *JT&M*), and Miyoshi Akira, "Yamamuro Gunpei to shakai jigyō," *Nihon rekishi* 254 (1969): 71. For St. Luke's Hospital, see *The Spirit of Missions* 80 (1915): 784, and *JT&M,* December 14, 1920.

52. *NSJN* (1920): 7, 8–9; *Japan Year Book* (1908): 488.

53. Ogawa, "Sangyō shihon kakuritsu," p. 142.

54. Miyachi, "Nichiro sengo no shakai," p. 158.

55. *Japan Times,* February 14, 1911.

56. These explanations of the failure of philanthropic work to develop in Japan prior to 1911 are listed by Tomeoka Kōsuke in an article entitled, "Saikin jizen jigyō no shinpō," published in *Jindō* in 1911. Dōshisha daigaku jinbun kagaku kenkyūjo, ed., *Tomeoka Kōsuke chosaku shū* 3:92–93.

57. *Japan Times,* February 16, 17, 1911.

58. Takenaka, "Relation of Protestantism," pp. 177–82; Joseph M. Kitagawa, *Religion in Japanese History,* p. 244.

59. See for instance Kun Sam Lee, *The Christian Confrontation with Shinto Nationalism,* pp. 127–28. In 1926, when the government gave awards to individuals who had contributed to the development of social work in Japan, twenty-two of the thirty-two recipients were Christians. Masao Takenaka, *Reconciliation and Renewal in Japan,* p. 28.

60. Kenneth B. Pyle, *The Making of Modern Japan,* p. 120; Peter Duus, *The Rise of Modern Japan,* p. 174.

61. Ogawa Seiryō, "Taishō demokurashii-ki no kyūhin taisei," in *Nihon no kyūhin seido,* ed. Nihon shakai jigyō daigaku kyūhin seido kenkyūkai, p. 156.

62. Shiota Shōbei, *Nihon rōdō undō no rekishi,* p. 65; Garon, *State and Labor,* p. 40.

63. John F. Embree, *Suye Mura: A Japanese Village,* pp. 170–72.

64. *THS* 4:960; Ogawa, "Taishō demokurashii-ki," p. 172.

65. James W. White, "Internal Migration in Prewar Japan," *Journal of Japanese Studies* 4.1 (1978): 89–91; Ezra F. Vogel, "Kinship Structure, Migration to the City, and Modernization," in *Aspects of Social Change in Modern Japan,* ed. R. P. Dore, pp. 93, 95.

66. Colonel Yamamuro, "Tokyo Paupers," *Japan Magazine* 5.5 (1914): 286.

67. Taikakai, *Naimushō shi* 1:338–39, 3:370.

68. Ogawa, "Sangyō shihon kakuritsu," p. 144 n; Kenneth B. Pyle, "The Technology of Japanese Nationalism: The Local Improvement Movement, 1900–1918," *Journal of Asian Studies* 33.1 (November 1973). For more on Inoue's thought, see Yoshida Kyūichi, *Shakai jigyō riron no rekishi,* pp. 129–32.

69. *NSJN* (1920): 16, 18, and (1922): 215–16.

70. Yamamuro, "Tokyo Paupers," p. 287; Yoshida, *Nihon shakai jigyō no rekishi,* pp. 242–44; Matsuo, *Taishō demokurashii,* p. 174.

71. *THS* 4:973–80; Seidensticker, *Low City, High City,* pp. 261–62.

72. Ogawa, "Taishō demokurashii ki," p. 168; *THS* 4:969; Yoshida, *Nihon shakai jigyō no rekishi,* pp. 242–44. See also Lewis, *Rioters and Citizens,* pp. 1–3, for other measures of economic deprivation, and pp. 11–15 on the inadequacy of government policy.

73. *THS* 4:985; Garon, *State and Labor,* pp. 39–40, 49; Lewis, *Rioters and Citizens,* pp. 29–30.

74. Taikakai, *Naimushō shi* 1:338–39.

Chapter 2

1. Hugh T. Patrick, "The Economic Muddle of the 1920's," in *Dilemmas of Growth in Prewar Japan,* ed. James W. Morley, pp. 214, 216.

2. Tōkyō shikai jimukyoku, *Tōkyō shikai shi* 5:105.

3. The following account of the debate is based on ibid. 5:236–38.

4. Tōkyō shiyakusho, *Toshi shakai gyōsei,* pp. 24–29, 33–34; Tōkyō shiyakusho, *Toshi gyōsei soshiki,* p. 217.

5. On Kubota, see Hata Ikuhiko, *Senzenki Nihon kanryōsei no seido, soshiki, jinji,* p. 428; *JT&M,* February 2, 12, 1920.

6. Tōkyō shiyakusho, *Toshi shakai gyōsei,* pp. 22–23, lists the heads of the social bureau from 1920 to 1927. Examples of heads of the social bureau who were both graduates of Imperial University and officials of the Home Ministry were Yasui Seiichirō, Hirose Tadamiki, and Mikuriya Kisan. Yamashita Saburō and Sawa Itsuyo were also graduates of Tokyo. On social bureaucrats, see Garon, *State and Labor,* pp. 76–89. On Yasui's reputation, see Tashiro Kunijirō, "Nihon shakai jigyō no tokushitsu," in *Shakai fukushi to shakai hendō,* ed. Tashiro Fujio, p. 27.

7. Garon, *State and Labor,* pp. 83–84 (Horikiri and Maeda are described as leading social bureaucrats, p. 271 n. 25).

8. Tashiro Kunijirō, "Nihon shakai jigyō," p. 32; Ashizawa Takeo, "Senzen no rōjin hogo o megutte," in Yoshida Kyūichi and Ichibangase Yasuko, *Shōwa shakai jigyōshi e no shōgen,* pp. 402–3.

9. *JT&M,* January 6, 1923, and December 3, 1929.

10. For Kusama Yasō's description of the urban poor, see his "Dai Tōkyō no saimingai to seikatsu no taiyō," in *Nihon chiri taikei* 3:370. For his place in the history of social work, see Yoshida Kyūichi, *Shakai jigyō riron no rekishi,* p. 152. An article by Kusama entitled "Hinmin seikatsu no jitsujō" appeared in the January 1920 issue of *Shakai to kyūsai.* Another early article, "Yōji hoiku to fūfu kyōdō no jitsujō," has been reprinted in *Nihon fujin mondai shiryō shūsei* 6:704–11. Kusama's books include *Furōsha to baishōfu no kenkyū* (1927), *Donzoko no hitotachi* (1929), *Jokyū to baishōfu* (1931), and *Suiko to yoriko no seikatsu* (1936).

11. *JT&M,* July 21, September 18, 1920. The city regulations are reprinted in *Nihon fujin mondai shiryō shūsei* 6:703–4.

12. On Hayashi, see Margit Nagy, "Middle-Class Working Women During the Inter-War Years," in *Recreating Japanese Women, 1600–1945,* ed. Gail Lee Bernstein. On Kajitsuka, see *Fujo shinbun,* June 19, 1921, p. 29.

13. Tōkyō-shi, *Tōkyō shinsai roku* 2:309–10.

14. *THS* 4:1118, 1172; Tōkyō shiyakusho, *Toshi shakai gyōsei,* p. 196.

15. Tōkyō-shi, *Tōkyō shinsai roku* 3:1552–53. By 1928, all but one of the nine municipal nurseries and health consultation centers, all but one of the labor exchanges, and all of the projected municipal dining halls were in operation. There were nine municipal pawnshops. On the other hand, only three of the ten projected cheap rooming houses had materialized. Tōkyō-shi, *Tōkyō-shi tōkei nenpyō* 26 (1930): 506–9.

16. Tōkyō shiyakusho, *Toshi shakai gyōsei*, pp. 93–94, 111, 118–19; Tōkyō shiyakusho, *Tōkyō shisei gaiyō* (1925): 251–52.

17. Tōkyō shiyakusho, *Toshi shakai gyōsei*, pp. 95, 105, 114, 122–23; Tōkyō shiyakusho, *Tōkyō shisei gaiyō* (1925): 247.

18. The analogy is Yokoyama Gennosuke's, in *Nihon no kasō shakai*, p. 48.

19. For official explanations, see Tōkyō shiyakusho, *Toshi shakai gyōsei*, p. 209, and Tōkyō shiyakusho, *Tōkyō shisei gaiyō* (1925): 265. On investigations, see Iwagorō, *In Darkest Tokyo*, pp. 48–49, and Yokoyama, *Nihon no kasō shakai*, pp. 47–49.

20. Nakama Teruhisa, ed., *Nihon chiri fūzoku taikei* 2:186; *JT&M*, July 21, 1929.

21. *THS* 4:1118.

22. This and the following paragraph are based on Yasoh Kusama, "Coping with Unemployment," *Contemporary Japan* 1 (1932): 294–96, and *JT&M*, September 15, October 28, 29, 1929, and February 27, 1932.

23. Kusama, "Coping with Unemployment," p. 300; *JT&M*, October 5, 1929.

24. Kusama, "Coping with Unemployment," p. 297; Ippei Fukuda, "Tokyo's Homes for the Homeless," *Contemporary Japan* 2 (1933): 494–96.

25. Hata, *Senzenki Nihon kanryōsei no seido, soshiki, jinji*, pp. 239–40.

26. On Tsugita, see ibid., pp. 153–54, and Garon, *State and Labor*, pp. 89–90, 95, 149 (p. 271 n. 25 lists him as a member of the class of 1900, which seems to be a typographical error for 1909). On Tsugita's connection to Yasui, see Yasui Seiichirō-shi kinenzo kensetsu, *Yasui Seiichirō den*, p. 287.

27. Yasui Seiichirō-shi kinenzo kensetsu, *Yasui Seiichirō den*, pp. 291–92. For a brief and chronologically shaky account in English, see William Axling, *Kagawa*, pp. 90–93. Axling's tale, written for an American audience, credits Kagawa with virtually every achievement of the social bureau.

28. Yasui Seiichirō-shi kinenzo kensetsu, *Yasui Seiichirō den*, pp. 298–300; *JT&M*, October 5, 11, 1929, and January 30, 1930.

29. Yasui Seiichirō-shi kinenzo kensetsu, *Yasui Seiichirō den*, pp. 292–94.

30. Kusama, "Coping with Unemployment," pp. 297–98; Fukuda, "Tokyo's Homes for the Homeless," p. 496.

31. Kusama, "Coping with Unemployment," p. 299.

32. Tōkyō-shi, *Tōkyō-shi tōkei nenpyō* 34 (1936): 406–8.

33. The provisions of the 1929 relief law are listed in *THS* 5:386–89.

34. Ibid., p. 390.

35. Tōkyō-shi, *Tōkyō-shi tōkei nenpyō* 34 (1936): 406–8.

36. Yoshimichi Sugiura, "Relief Work for Tokyo's Unfortunates," *The Spirit of Missions* 88 (1923): 322–25; P. A. Smith, " 'The Island' and Its Prophet," *The Spirit of Missions* 88 (1923): 611–16; Miyoshi Akira, *Yamamuro Gunpei*, p. 236; *NSJN* (1925): 21.

37. *JT&M*, November 24, December 15, 29, 1920. Unless otherwise noted, this account is based on Tsukamoto Shiuko, "Yoshimi Shizue," in *Shakai jigyō ni ikita joseitachi: sono shōgai to shigoto,* ed. Gomi Yuriko, p. 259, and Gladys D. Walser, "The Door of Hope," *Japan Evangelist* 30 (March 1923): 92–93. The quotation comes from *JT&M*, October 18, 1920.

38. Nara Tsunegorō, *Nihon YMCA shi*, p. 196; *NSJN* (1920): 58.

39. Tōkyō-shi Honjo kuyakusho, *Honjo-ku shi*, pp. 580–81; Home Office, Social Affairs Bureau, *The Great Earthquake of 1923 in Japan*, p. 59. *Honjo-ku shi* says that fire broke out in seventeen places. Tōkyō-to Sumida-ku, *Sumida-ku shi*, p. 1718, lists thirteen places, and Dai Nihon ōbenkai kōdansha, *Taishō daishinsai daikasai*, p. 20, lists twelve places, but the two lists do not correspond, suggesting more rather than fewer places of origin.

40. *THS* 4:1115, 1118; Home Office, *Great Earthquake*, pp. 55, 62. Many people died at other sites in Honjo Ward as well, such as in Yokokawabashi (773) and in Kinshi-chō Station (630).

41. Mikiso Hane, *Reflections on the Way to the Gallows: Rebel Women in Prewar Japan*, pp. 189, 191.

42. Quotation is from Seiji Noma, *Noma of Japan: The Nine Magazines of Kodansha, Being the Autobiography of a Japanese Publisher*, p. 228. For the panic and killing, see Imai Seiichi, *Taishō demokurashii*, pp. 379–94. One responsible estimate of the number of Koreans killed is 2,613 (the Home Ministry figure was 231). For recent discussion of estimates of the total number of Koreans killed, see Michael Weiner, *The Origins of the Korean Community in Japan, 1910–1923*, pp. 181–82.

43. Hane, *Reflections,* pp. 190–92. See also Gordon, *Imperial Democracy,* pp. 177–81.

44. *THS* 4:1103, 1117, 1211, 1214; Dai Nihon ōbenkai kōdansha, *Taishō daishinsai daikasai*, pp. 36, 293; Home Office, *Great Earthquake*, p. 525; Tōkyō shiyakusho, *Tōkyō shisei gaiyō* (1929): 453; Tōkyō-shi Honjo kuyakusho, *Honjo-ku shi*, p. 585; Tōkyō-shi, *Tōkyō-shi tōkei nenpyō* (1925): 113.

45. *THS* 4:1166; *Shakai seisaku jihō*, November 1923, p. 97 (hereafter referred to as *SSJ*); Tōkyō shiyakusho, *Tōkyō shisei gaiyō* (1925): 5. The November figure is higher than those in earlier newspaper reports of 48,000 in Honjo in mid-September and 58,120 on September 30. *JT&M*, September 24, October 2, 1923.

46. *NSJN* (1925): 15, 19; Naimushō shakaikyoku, *Taishō shinsai shi* 2:46, 587, 593, 639; Yoshimichi Sugiura, "Sending Him Off to Heaven," *Spirit of Missions* 91 (1926): 751; Alice Lewis Pearson, "Women's Christian Temperance Union," *Christian Movement in Japan, Korea, and Formosa* (1924): 314.

47. Naimushō, *Taishō shinsai shi* 2:124–25; *JT&M*, September 18, December 21, 1923.

48. *Foreign Missionary* 44 (1924): 4, and 45 (1925): 14.

49. Ibid. 44 (1924): 4–7, and 45 (1925): 14.

50. Ibid. 45 (1925): 10–16.

51. Henry Dewitt Smith II, *Japan's First Student Radicals*, pp. 142–43; *THS* 5:402–4. On Toynbee Hall, see Meacham, *Toynbee Hall*, pp. 35–50.

52. Smith, *Student Radicals*, pp. 143–44.

53. Yokoyama Haruichi, *Kagawa Toyohiko den*, pp. 199–204.

54. Ibid.; Nara, *YMCA shi*, p. 240.

55. *NSJN* (1925): 4, 7, 16; Yokoyama, *Kagawa*, pp. 128, 213, 246, 247, 269, 461, 463. Kidachi Yoshimichi, an associate of Kagawa's from Kobe, was in charge of the consumer union.

56. *Nihon rōdō nenkan* 6 (1925): 336–37, and 7 (1926): 270; Naimushō shakaikyoku, *Rōdō undō gaikyō* (1924): 242.

57. Yokoyama, *Kagawa*, pp. 454–56; Ōkōchi Kazuo and Matsuo Hiroshi, *Nihon rōdō kumiai monogatari* 2:146, 212, 214, 236, 278.

58. Naimushō, *Rōdō undō gaikyō* (1924): 242; *THS* 5:405.

59. *NSJN* (1926): 199; Tōkyō-fu, *Tōkyō-fu tōkei sho* (1931): 240.

60. Mitsui Kunitarō, *Aikoku fujinkai tokuhon*, pp. 98–100; *NSJN* (1925): 22; *JT&M*, September 8, 1924.

61. Edward W. Wagner, *The Korean Minority in Japan, 1904–1950*, pp. 2, 9; Naimushō keihokyoku, *Shakai undō no jōkyō* (1933): 1431; Weiner, *Origins*, pp. 76–77; Changsoo Lee and George De Vos, *Koreans in Japan: Ethnic Conflict and Accommodation*, pp. 47–49, 51–52.

62. Lee and De Vos, *Koreans in Japan*, p. 48. On National Foundation Day, see *JT&M*, February 10, 1928. The quotation is from Weiner, *Origins*, pp. 179–81.

63. *JT&M*, December 12, 1923, and August 27, September 11, 1924.

64. *NSJN* (1925): 7; Tōkyō-fu, *Tōkyō-fu tōkei sho* (1931): 913, 920, 930, and (1936): 238, 263.

65. Richard H. Mitchell, *The Korean Minority in Japan*, pp. 28–29; Wagner, *Korean Minority*, pp. 9–10.

66. Tōkyō-fu, *Tōkyō-fu tōkei sho* (1919): 107, (1931): 112, (1936): 100; Pak Kyong-sik, *Chōsenjin kyosei renko no kiroku*, p. 33.

67. Tōkyō-shi, *Tōkyō-shi tōkei nenpyō* 34 (1936): 405–9; Ogawa, "Sangyō shihon kakuritsu," p. 142; Taikakai, *Naimushō shi* 3:409.

68. *JT&M*, March 29, 1933; ibid., January 10, February 26, 1936 (reported seven hundred such beggars in the city); ibid., January 13, 1939.

69. Himmelfarb, *Poverty and Compassion*, p. 12.

70. Tōkyō-shi, *Tōkyō-shi tōkei nenpyō* 34 (1936): 406–7, 409; *THS* 5:15.

71. *NSJN* (1933): 82–83.

72. *JT&M*, January 26, February 1, 12, May 31, 1924; *Nihon kokusei jiten* 8:535.

73. Dai Nihon teikoku gikaishi kankōkai, *Dai Nihon teikoku gikaishi* 14:1083.

74. See for instance Miki Tamio, "Shakai mondai no tōjō Nisshin Nichiro sensō to haishō mondai," in *Kindai Nihon no tōgō to teikō*, ed. Kano Masanao and Yui Masaomi, 2:147–82. Quotation is from Melvin G. Holli, *Reform in Detroit: Hazen S. Pingree and Urban Politics*, p. xiii.

75. Jane Addams, *Democracy and Social Ethics*, p. 11; Jawaharlal Nehru, *An Autobiography*, p. 252.

Chapter 3

1. Since there is no exact English equivalent to *chō*, I shall use the Japanese word, but I shall use "neighborhood association" to translate *chōkai*. In this usage, I am in agreement with Henry Smith, "Tokyo as an Idea," p. 66. In translations of works by Japanese scholars into English, *chō* is sometimes translated as "town." See Yazaki, *Social Change*, p. 456, and Nakamura Hachirō, *Town Organizations in Prewar Tokyo*. Other scholars have put these English terms to different use. Soon after World War II, two articles appeared on "neighborhood associations": Ralph J. O. Braibanti, "Neighborhood Associations in Japan and Their Democratic Potentialities," *Far Eastern Quarterly* 7 (1948): 136–64, and John W. Masland, "Neighborhood Associations in Japan," *Far Eastern Survey* 15 (1946): 355–58. Both articles used "neighborhood association" to translate the Japanese term *tonarigumi*, a smaller unit than the *chō* (in fact a subdivision of it), which came into existence during the war years. In contrast to this, Ronald Dore's famed study of a Tokyo ward is in fact a study of a *chō*. He then uses "borough" to translate *ku*, which I and nearly everyone else call a "ward." R. P. Dore, *City Life in Japan: A Study of a Tokyo Ward*, n. 4.

2. Yazaki, *Social Change*, pp. 111, 184, 217, 222; Smith, "Tokyo as an Idea," pp. 51–52.

3. This section is based on Tōkyō shisei chōsakai, *Tōkyō-shi chōnaikai ni kansuru chōsa*, pp. 11–15; Tōkyō shiyakusho, *Tōkyō-shi chōnaikai no chōsa*, p. 120; and Tōkyō shiyakusho, *Tōkyō-shi chōkai jigyō gaiyō*, p. 112.

4. For instance, Oguri Tomigoro—head of the neighborhood association in Midori-chō 3-chome in Honjo in 1930—had come to Tokyo as a young married man to serve an apprenticeship. He opened a shop in Midori-chō in 1904. Yamamoto Shintarō, head of the neighborhood association in Kinshi-chō in Honjo in 1927, arrived in Tokyo from Fukui city in 1912 and

opened a rice shop in Kinshi-chō. Fukkō chōsa kyōkai, *Teito fukkō shi* 3:2917, 2920.

5. Tōkyō shiyakusho, *Tōkyō-shi chōnaikai no chōsa*, p. 24.

6. Tōkyō shiyakusho, *Shōwa gotairei hōshuku shi*, pp. 298–328; Tōkyō-shi Honjo kuyakusho, *Honjo-ku shi*, p. 208.

7. Two indications that this was so for Honjo Ward are the list of neighborhood associations thanked by the city for their efforts at the time of the earthquake, which is given in Tōkyō-shi, *Tōkyō shinsai roku* 4:836, and the list in Tokyo shisei chōsakai, *Tōkyō-shi chōnaikai*, pp. 357–59.

8. Tōkyō shiyakusho, *Tōkyō-shi chōnaikai no chōsa*, p. 24; Isomura Eiichi, *Ku no kenkyū*, p. 251.

9. Hayashi Tatsusaburō with George Elison, "Kyoto in the Muromachi Age," in *Japan in the Muromachi Age*, ed. John W. Hall and Toyoda Takeshi, pp. 28–30.

10. William B. Hauser, "Osaka: A Commercial City in Tokugawa Japan," *Urbanism Past and Present* 5 (1977–1978): 23–36, esp. p. 25; James L. McClain, *Kanazawa: A Seventeenth-Century Japanese Castle Town*, pp. 86–89; Smith, "Tokyo as an Idea," p. 50.

11. For this particular list, see Yazaki, *Social Change*, pp. 455–56.

12. Komori Ryūkichi, "Tōkyō ni okeru chōnaikai no hensen ni tsuite," *Nihon rekishi* 297 (1973): 83–84; D. Eleanor Westney, "The Emulation of Western Organizations in Meiji Japan: The Case of the Paris Prefecture of Police and the Keishi-cho," *Journal of Japanese Studies* 8 (1982): 307–41.

13. The results of the survey were published in Tōkyō shiyakusho, *Tōkyō-shi chōnaikai no chōsa*. J. Douglas Downard, "Tokyo: The Depression Years, 1927–1933," p. 200, n. 4, notes how interviews can generate spurious statistics on the antiquity of institutions. In September 1974, for example, Downard asked an official of the *chōnaikai* in his Tokyo neighborhood when the organization was founded: "His immediate response was that the chōnaikai was more than 100 years old." Downard adds, from his more informed perspective, "This area of Tokyo was only lightly settled prior to the 1920s, and there is no record of a chōnaikai in the vicinity until 1913."

14. Tōkyō-shi kikakukyoku, *Tōkyō-shi chōmei enkaku shi*, pp. 199–200.

15. Biographical information on Uchida is from *Taishō jinmei jiten*. On his membership in the ward assembly, see Tōkyō-shi Honjo kuyakusho, *Honjo-ku shi*, p. 41. For Uchida's leadership of the neighborhood association, see Tōkyō-shi Honjo kuyakusho, *Honjo kusei yōran*, 1926 and 1931; Tōkyō shiyakusho, *Tōkyō-shi chōkai jigyō gaiyō*; Tōkyō shiyakusho, *Tōkyō-shi chōkai yōran*, p. 105.

16. Nakamura Hachirō, *Town*, pp. 7–8; Nakagawa Gō, *Chōnaikai*, p. 146.

17. Tōkyō-shi Shitaya kuyakusho, *Shitaya-ku shi*, p. 1088; Komori Ryūkichi, "Tōkyō ni okeru," p. 84. For examples found after 1900, see Nakamura Hachirō, *Town*, pp. 18–19. Even in 1930, Koishikawa had twenty-seven

chōkai with names that varied from the usual pattern of the name of the *chō* with the suffix *chōkai*.

18. Sokyo Ono, *Shinto: The Kami Way*, pp. 46–48; Tōkyō shisei chōsakai, *Tōkyō-shi chōnaikai*, p. 92.

19. Tōkyō shiyakusho, *Tōkyō-shi chōnaikai no chōsa*, pp. 5–7; Nakamura Hachirō, *Town*, p. 13; Hirade Kojirō, *Tōkyō fuzoku shi* 1:120.

20. For Tokyo prefecture, see Tōkyō shisei chōsakai, *Tōkyō-shi chōnaikai*, and *THS* 1:721. For political organizations seeking out public health officials, see James R. Bartholomew, "Science, Bureaucracy, and Freedom in Meiji and Taishō Japan," in *Conflict in Modern Japanese History*, ed. Najita and Koschmann, p. 300. For political activists organizing as sanitation societies, see Irokawa Daikichi, *The Culture of the Meiji Period*, p. 147. For Japan's first laboratory for infectious diseases, see Bartholomew, "Science, Bureaucracy, and Freedom," p. 307.

21. Nakamura Hachirō, *Town*, pp. 16–17; Tōkyō shisei chōsakai, *Tōkyō-shi chōnaikai*, pp. 85–86. In a random sample, 92.3 percent of the neighborhood associations surveyed in 1925 had no sanitation union, 4.9 percent had a sanitation union as part of the neighborhood association, and only 2.8 percent had a separate sanitation union.

22. Tōkyō-shi Shitaya kuyakusho, *Shitaya-ku shi*, pp. 1088–89; Komori Ryūkichi, "Tōkyō ni okeru," p. 84. In Yanagihara 3-chome, the neighborhood had for many years had a tradition of rotating responsibility for neighborhood affairs among the leading families. The neighborhood associations in Tokuuemon-chō (founded 1920) and Matsui-chō 2-chome (founded 1924), both in Honjo, had also long maintained similar informal systems of rotation of responsibility and networks of communication. Tōkyō shiyakusho, *Tōkyō-shi chōnaikai no chōsa*, p. 1.

23. Hiratake Tatsu, "Tōkyō-shi no hōmen iin seido ni tsuite," *SSJ* (July 1921): 231–36; Tōkyō-shi Shitaya kuyakusho, *Shitaya-ku shi*, p. 1089.

24. See, for instance, the case of Matsui-chō 3-chome in Honjo. Tōkyō-shi, *Tōkyō shinsai roku* 4:216.

25. Ibid. 4:104, 217–18.

26. Quoted in Nakamura Hachirō, *Town*, pp. 22–23, 49 n.

27. *THS* 4:274.

28. Tōkyō shisei chōsakai, *Tōkyō-shi chōnaikai;* Tōkyō-shi Honjo kuyakusho, *Honjo kusei yōran*, 1926 and 1931; Tōkyō shiyakusho, *Tōkyō-shi chōkai jigyō gaiyō;* Tōkyō shiyakusho, *Tōkyō-shi chōnaikai no chōsa*. The main source of information on the occupation of neighborhood association heads is *Nihon shinshiroku* (hereafter referred to as *NS*).

29. That is, these individuals were listed as heads of factories located in Honjo in Nōshōmushō, *Kōjō tsūran*, or Tōkyō shiyakusho, *Tōkyō-shi kōjō yōran*, 1926 and 1929. I have used "landowner" to translate *jinushi* (owner of land), and "landlord" to translate *yanushi* (owner of buildings).

30. Based on information in *NS* (1935). For specific examples of factory owners, see chapter 5.

31. Yazaki, *Social Change*, p. 456.

32. Braibanti, "Neighborhood Associations," pp. 141–42.

33. For the text of this proclamation, see Akimoto Ritsuo, *Sensō to minshū: taiheiyō sensō shita no toshi seikatsu*, pp. 21–22.

34. The physicians society is mentioned in *Tōkyō asahi shinbun*, July 20, 1915 (hereafter referred to as *TAS*).

35. Tōkyō-shi Honjo kuyakusho, *Honjo-ku shi*, pp. 131–33, 146, 155.

36. *Japan Times*, August 6, July 9, 1912; Inoue Kiyoshi and Watanabe Tōru, *Kome sōdō no kenkyū* 3:284.

37. R. H. P. Mason, *Japan's First General Election, 1890*, p. 143; Bartholomew, "Science, Bureaucracy, and Freedom," p. 309; *Japan Times*, November 20, 1913.

38. *Japan Times*, April 9, July 22, 1913.

39. Ibid., February 23, March 10, 29, 1911.

40. Komori Ryūkichi, "Tōkyō ni okeru," p. 93.

41. Tōkyō-shi, *Tōkyō-shi chōkai yōran*, chart.

42. Tōkyō shikai jimukyoku, *Tōkyō shikai shi* 7:649–53.

43. Tōkyō shiyakusho, *Tōkyō shisei gaiyō* (1929): 404–7.

44. For Osaka, see Ogawa Seiryō, "Taishō demokurashii ki," pp. 185–86. For Okayama, see Kimura Takeo, *Nihon kindai shakai jigyōshi*, p. 90, and Taikakai, *Naimushō shi*, 2:469.

45. Ogawa Seiryō, "Taishō demokurashii ki," p. 186.

46. Ogawa Shigejirō, "Shakai jigyō no kisoteki shisetsu to shite no hōmen iin seido," *Kyūsai kenkyū* 9 (August and September 1921): 589.

47. Ibid., pp. 598–99.

48. Ibid., pp. 599–601, 670–71.

49. Naimushō shakaikyoku shakaibu, *Hōmen iin seido gaiyō*, p. 1.

50. *NSJN* (1925): 17; Naimushō, *Hōmen iin seido gaiyō*, p. 1; Ogawa Shigejirō, "Shakai jigyō," p. 589.

51. This account is based on Charles Richmond Henderson, *Modern Methods of Charity*, pp. 5–7.

52. Dorothy G. Becker, "Exit Lady Bountiful: The Volunteer and the Professional Social Worker," *Social Service Review* 38 (March 1964): 59–60, 66–69. In early American settlements, poor relief—following the pattern established by the English Poor Law of 1601—was distributed by overseers of the poor, who visited the homes of the needy. Clement, *Welfare and the Poor*, p. 39. On college women as charity visitors (presumably in Chicago), see Addams, *Democracy and Social Ethics*, pp. 13–70. On visiting as part of the work of the Charity Organization Society, see Himmelfarb, *Poverty and Compassion*, pp. 193–99.

53. W. Dean Kinzley, "Japan's Discovery of Poverty: Changing Views of Poverty and Social Welfare in the Nineteenth Century," *Journal of Asian History* 22.1 (1988): 1–24.

54. See for instance an article on the effectiveness of British home visitors in reducing urban infant death rates: Amaoka Naoyoshi, "Fujin no eisei shisatsu," *Shimin* 4.4 (May 28, 1909): 18–20. *Shimin* was published by the Hōtokukai, an organization closely associated with the Home Ministry.

55. Naimushō, *Hōmen iin seido gaiyō,* p. 1; Tashiro Fujio, *Shakai fukushi to shakai hendō,* pp. 76–78.

56. Tōkyō-shi Shiba kuyakusho, *Shiba-ku shi,* p. 775; Bunkyō kuyakusho, *Bunkyō-ku shi* 4:160–61.

57. Hiratake Tatsu, "Tōkyō-shi no hōmen iin," p. 231. Tokyo Municipal Office, *Tokyo* (1937): 33, says the term was four years.

58. Naimushō, *Hōmen iin seido gaiyō,* p. 19; Tōkyō-shi Shiba kuyakusho, *Shiba-ku shi,* p. 776.

59. Hiratake Tatsu, "Tōkyō-shi hōmen iin," pp. 231–32; Tōkyō-shi Kyōbashi kuyakusho, *Kyōbashi-ku shi* 2:985.

60. The distinction in degree of poverty was not peculiar to the Tokyo district welfare committees. Yamamuro Gunpei of the Salvation Army made a similar distinction in 1915: "The very poor of Tokyo may be divided into two kinds: those who need help in order to survive and those who can manage without relief." The Relief Law of 1929 likewise permitted two bases for eligibility for relief. The first type of eligibility was inability to work because of age, youth, or illness, and the second was for those who, although able-bodied, were afflicted by poverty. The Tokyo social bureau recognized a "semi-card class" as well, which was divided into those with no surplus, those with only a slight surplus, and those with some margin for survival. Yamamuro, "Tokyo Paupers," p. 285; Taikakai, *Naimushō shi* 3:405; Tōkyō-shi Kyōbashi kuyakusho, *Kyōbashi-ku shi* 2:986.

61. Hiratake Tatsu, "Tōkyō-shi hōmen iin," pp. 231–32.

62. Tōkyō-to Kōtō kuyakusho, *Kōtō-ku shi,* pp. 1018–19; Tōkyō-shi Akasaka kuyakusho, *Akasaka-ku shi,* p. 1224; Tōkyō-shi Nihonbashi kuyakusho, *Nihonbashi-ku shi* 2:886. Kōjimachi and Kanda each seem to have established a district after 1928 and before 1933.

63. Tōkyō-to Kōtō kuyakusho, *Kōtō-ku shi,* p. 1019; Tokyo Municipal Office, *The City of Tokyo: Municipal Administration and Government,* pp. 81–82.

64. Yoshida Kyūichi, *Nihon shakai jigyō no rekishi,* p. 302; Tōkyō-to Kōtō kuyakusho, *Kōtō-ku shi,* p. 1019.

65. Tōkyō-shi Kyōbashi kuyakusho, *Kyōbashi-ku shi* 2:986.

66. Taikakai, *Naimushō shi* 3:407–8; Hara Taiichi, "Kyūgohō no seitei o sokushin," in Yoshida Kyūichi and Ichibangase Yasuko, *Shōwa shakai ji-gyōshi e no shōgen,* pp. 54–58. The petition itself is reproduced in ibid., pp. 528–29.

67. Tōkyō-shi, *Tōkyō shinsai roku* 4:833; Tōkyō shiyakusho, *Shōwa go-tairei hōshuku shi,* p. 334.

68. Tōkyō-shi Shiba kuyakusho, *Shiba-ku shi,* pp. 776–78; Tōkyō-shi Shitaya kuyakusho, *Shitaya-ku shi,* p. 1121; Tōkyō-shi Kyōbashi kuyakusho, *Kyōbashi-ku shi* 2:990; Tōkyō-shi Nihonbashi kuyakusho, *Nihonbashi-ku shi* 2:886.

69. Tōkyō-shi Kyōbashi kuyakusho, *Kyōbashi-ku shi* 2:985. In 1936, control of the protection work of the committees was transferred from the mayor's office to the ward offices. Tōkyō-to Kōtō kuyakusho, *Kōtō-ku shi,* p. 1021.

70. Tokyo Municipal Office, *Tokyo,* p. 33.

71. For instance, Tanaka Ichirō of the Nihonbashi committee, who lived in Koishikawa.

72. Satō Aizō, who spearheaded the petition of the district welfare committee members to the emperor to implement the Relief Law, was a member of the Honjo Ward assembly. Tōkyō-shi Honjo kuyakusho, *Honjo-ku shi,* p. 43. Other examples were Mukoyama Shotarō of Kyōbashi and Mori Tomita of Shitaya. Tōkyō-shi Kyōbashi kuyakusho, *Kyōbashi-ku shi* 2:273, 991; Tōkyō-shi Shitaya kuyakusho, *Shitaya-ku shi,* pp. 312, 322, 1121.

73. Tōkyō shikai jimukyoku, *Tōkyō shikai shi* 7:607.

74. *TAS,* March 10, 1933; Miyoshi Toyotarō, "Tōkyō-shi no shakai gyōsei," *Toshi mondai* 18.1 (January 1934): 72.

75. The story is included in Noriko M. Lippit and Kyoko Selden, eds., *Stories by Contemporary Japanese Women Writers,* pp. 3–21.

76. On the relationship of the American political machine to the poor, see Howe, *Confessions of a Reformer,* pp. 56–61, and Mann, *La Guardia,* pp. 107, 145.

77. Alex Gottfried, *Boss Cermak of Chicago: A Study of Political Leadership,* pp. 19–20.

Chapter 4

1. Smethurst, *Social Basis,* pp. 16, 19–20.

2. Ibid., 1–2; *Japan Times,* November 6, 1910.

3. Smethurst, *Social Basis,* pp. 15–16.

4. Richard J. Smethurst, "The Creation of the Imperial Military Reserve Association in Japan," *Journal of Asian Studies* 30 (1971): 826.

5. Smethurst, *Social Basis,* pp. 8–9.

6. Tōkyō-shi Azabu kuyakusho, *Azabu-ku shi,* p. 718; Tōkyō-shi Hongō kuyakusho, *Hongō-ku shi,* p. 972; Tōkyō-shi Nihonbashi kuyakusho, *Nihonbashi-ku shi* 2:904; Tōkyō-shi Asakusa kuyakusho, *Asakusa-ku shi* 2:381; *Japan Times,* February 2, 1904.

7. Isomura Eiichi, *Ku no kenkyū,* p. 348; Tōkyō-shi Azabu kuyakusho, *Azabu-ku shi,* p. 718.

8. Tōkyō-shi Asakusa kuyakusho, *Asakusa-ku shi* 2:369; Smethurst, *Social Basis,* pp. 16–17. Preparation for the ward branches under the jurisdiction

of the Hongō Regiment (Hongō, Shitaya, Asakusa, Honjo, and Fukugawa) began in October 1910 or earlier. The term of the first head of the Honjo branch, Akimoto Genkan, is recorded as having begun in 1909. Tōkyō-fu, *Tōkyō-fu shi: Gyōsei hen* 5:557; Tōkyō-shi Honjo kuyakusho, *Honjo-ku shi*, p. 617. In other wards, the opening ceremonies for the branches were in 1911, on February 3 in Nihonbashi and on March 5 in Azabu.

9. Tōkyō-shi, *Tōkyō shinsai roku* 4:838. Honjo is an example that counters Smethurst's generalization (*Social Basis*, p. 67) that the urban reservist organizations did not reach to the *chō*, the "asphalt roots" of the city.

10. Smethurst, *Social Basis*, pp. 66–74.

11. Ibid., pp. 13, 18–19, 84–85. The number of factories in Tokyo is for October 1924, a little more than a year after the earthquake. Tōkyō-shi tōkeika, *Dai ikkai rōdō tōkei jitchi chōsa*, p. 5.

12. Tōkyō-shi Honjo kuyakusho, *Honjo-ku shi*, p. 617.

13. Ibid., p. 217.

14. Lewis, *Rioters and Citizens*, pp. 26, 159, 161–62, 223.

15. Tōkyō-shi, *Tōkyō shinsai roku* 4:262–66, 354, 838.

16. *JT&M*, September 18, 1924; Tōkyō shikai jimukyoku, *Tōkyō shikai shi* 6:934–35.

17. Ian Neary, *Political Protest and Social Control in Pre-War Japan: The Origins of Buraku Liberation*, pp. 87–88, 111 n. On Tanaka and rural folkways, see Gluck, *Modern Myths*, p. 181. For accounts that associate reservists with the massacres, see Imai Seiichi, *Taishō demokurashii*, pp. 379–94; Kan Tokusan, *Kantō daishinsai*, pp. 100–107; and Narita Ryūichi, "Toshi minshū sōjō to minponshugi," in *Kindai Nihon no tōgō to teikō*, ed. Yui Masaomi and Kano Masanao, 3:67.

18. Fukkō chōsa kyōkai, *Teito fukkō shi* 3:2902; *NS* (1930): 683; Tōkyō-shi Honjo kuyakusho, *Honjo kusei yōran* (1926); Tōkyō-shi, *Tōkyō shinsai roku* 4:344.

19. The text of the directive and its accompanying instructions are given in Kumagai Tatsujirō, *Dai Nihon seinendan shi*, Appendix, pp. 199–201, and Hirayama Kazuhiko, *Seinen shūdan shi kenkyū josetsu* 2:21–22. I have used "young men," rather than "youth," to translate *seinen* because the organizations were gender-specific, and the use of "youth" obscures the fact that there were separate organizations for young women.

20. For invocations of the Tokugawa past, see Tatsujirō Kumagai, *The Japan Young Men's Associations*, p. 4, and Tazawa Yoshiharu, *Sōhen*, p. 25. The organizational leadership of the 1930s was so fascinated by the Tokugawa origins of youth groups that it gathered eighty-three sets of records of *wakamonogumi* from all over Japan and published them as *Wakamono seido no kenkyū* (Research on the Wakamono system) in 1936. In English, see Richard E. Varner, "The Organized Peasant: The *Wakamonogumi* in the Edo Period," *Monumenta Nipponica* 32 (1977): 459–83.

21. Hirayama Kazuhiko, *Seinen shūdan* 2:12–15, gives a list of government actions concerning youth associations from 1906 to 1916. See also Kumagai, *Japan*, pp. 6–8; Pyle, "The Technology of Japanese Nationalism," pp. 62–63; and Gluck, *Modern Myths*, pp. 199–200.

22. Kumagai, *Dai Nihon seinendan shi*, pp. 113–14.

23. For a discussion of how leaders were chosen, see Varner, "Organized Peasant," pp. 467–68.

24. Taikakai, *Naimushō shi* 3:379.

25. Takeda Kiyoko, *Tennōsei shisō to kyōiku*, pp. 158, 172–73.

26. Ibid., pp. 173–74.

27. Taikakai, *Naimushō shi* 3:380–81; Tazawa Yoshiharu kinenkai, *Tazawa Yoshiharu*, p. 161.

28. Kumagai, *Dai Nihon seinendan shi*, p. 196; Tazawa Yoshiharu, *Sōhen*, pp. 21–22, 24–25.

29. Takeda Kiyoko, *Tennōsei*, pp. 147–51, 167, 170; Susan Beth Weiner, "Bureaucracy and Politics in the 1930's: The Career of Gotō Fumio," p. 157.

30. Kumagai, *Japan*, pp. 12, 25; *Dai Nihon seinendan shi*, p. 176; Hirayama Kazuhiko, *Seinen shūdan*, 2:83.

31. Kumagai, *Japan*, p. 25.

32. Takeda Kiyoko, *Tennōsei*, pp. 139–40. On Tazawa's tenure as executive director of the Kyōchōkai, see Kinzley, *Industrial Harmony*, pp. 68–69, 98–100.

33. Tōkyō shiyakusho, *Toshi shakai gyōsei*, p. 22; Hirayama Kazuhiko, *Seinen shūdan* 2:95.

34. A list of all the officials of the Japan League of Young Men's Associations and the Japan Young Men's Hall is included in Kumagai, *Dai Nihon seinendan shi*, Appendix, pp. 179–93. On the careers of Ikeda Hiro, Gotō Shinpei, and Maruyama Tsurukichi, see Hata, *Senzenki Nihon kanryōsei no seido, soshiki, jinji*, pp. 32, 102, and 221. On Ikezono, see *Who's Who in Japan* (1938). Gotō Shinpei donated his retirement pay as mayor (a hundred thousand yen) to the Young Men's Associations. *JT&M*, January 7, 1938.

35. Tōkyō-shi Ushigome kuyakusho, *Ushigome-ku shi*, pp. 458–59.

36. *Jiji shinpō*, May 5, 1917, quoted in *THS* 4:600; Tōkyō-shi Shiba kuyakusho, *Shiba-ku shi*, pp. 747–48; Michael Lewis, *Rioters and Citizens*, p. 24; Kumagai, *Dai Nihon seinendan shi*, p. 137.

37. Tōkyō-shi Honjo kuyakusho, *Honjo-ku shi*, pp. 190–91.

38. Dai Nihon rengō seinendan chōsabu, *Zenkoku seinendan kihon chōsa*, p. 246; Tōkyō-shi Honjo kuyakusho, *Honjo-ku shi*, pp. 191–94; Tōkyō-shi Kyōbashi kuyakusho, *Kyōbashi-ku shi* 2:918; Tōkyō-shi Nihonbashi kuyakusho, *Nihonbashi-ku shi* 2:423–24; Tōkyō-shi Ushigome kuyakusho, *Ushigome-ku shi*, p. 453.

39. Kumagai, *Dai Nihon seinendan shi*, pp. 173, 180.

40. Tōkyō-shi Shiba kuyakusho, *Shiba-ku shi*, p. 748; Tōkyō-shi Shitaya kuyakusho, *Shitaya-ku shi*, p. 916; Tōkyō-shi Nihonbashi kuyakusho, *Nihon-bashi-ku shi* 2:422–23; Tōkyō-shi Honjo kuyakusho, *Honjo-ku shi*, p. 162. *Tōkyō shinsai roku* 4:234–35 lists heads of the young men's association branches of Honjo for 1923. It is possible, through the *Honjo-ku shi* to identify all of the heads of school groups as principals.

41. *NSJN* (1921): 38.

42. Ibid. (1921): 138, and (1925): 97, 100; Ōya Soichi, "Tōkyō-shi seinendan no kaibō," *Chūō kōron*, June 1930, p. 131.

43. Kumagai, *Japan*, p. 14; Smethurst, *Social Basis*, pp. 75–76.

44. Tazawa Yoshiharu, "Danshi seinendan," in Iwanami Kōza, *Kyōiku kagaku*, quoted in *THS* 4:602–3.

45. Kumagai, *Dai Nihon seinendan shi*, pp. 405, 409; Appendix, pp. 14, 18–19, 24; Noma, *Noma of Japan*, p. 242.

46. Ōya, "Tōkyō-shi seinendan no kaibō," pp. 131–33; Tōkyō-shi Ushigome kuyakusho, *Ushigome-ku shi*, p. 453.

47. Kumagai, *Dai Nihon seinendan shi*, Appendix, pp. 300, 332.

48. Ibid., pp. 17, 19, 24, 25, 40.

49. *THS* 4:603; Tōkyō-shi Ushigome kuyakusho, *Ushigome-ku shi*, p. 454; Tōkyō shiyakusho, *Shōwa gotairei hōshuku shi*, p. 328.

50. Tōkyō-shi Shiba kuyakusho, *Shiba-ku shi*, p. 749; *JT&M*, April 17, 1924. Tōkyō-shi Ushigome kuyakusho, *Ushigome-ku shi*, p. 455, mentions a January 1928 meeting at the Hibiya bandstand building. Isomura, *Ku no kenkyū*, p. 348.

51. Tazawa Yoshiharu, "Danshi seinendan," in Iwanami Kōza, *Kyōiku kagaku*, quoted in *THS* 4:603.

52. Tōkyō-shi Ushigome kuyakusho, *Ushigome-ku shi*, p. 454.

53. Ibid., p. 453.

54. *Zenkoku seinendan kihon chōsa*, pp. 212–15.

55. For the common wisdom, see Ishida Takeshi, *Japanese Political Culture: Change and Continuity*, pp. 10, 16, 98–99.

56. *JT&M*, September 19, 1929; Kumagai, *Dai Nihon seinendan shi*, Appendix, p. 27.

57. *JT&M*, October 7, 1920, February 10, 1928, and January 27, 1938.

58. Tsunoda, de Bary, and Keene, *Sources of Japanese Tradition* 2:199.

59. Itō Takashi, "The Role of Right-Wing Organizations in Japan," in *Pearl Harbor as History: Japanese-American Relations, 1931–1941*, ed. Dorothy Borg and Shumpei Okamoto, pp. 400, 718–19 n. 15.

60. Ogata Sadako, "The Role of Liberal Nongovernmental Organizations in Japan," in *Pearl Harbor as History*, ed. Borg and Okamoto, pp. 471–72.

61. Smethurst, *Social Basis*, p. 176.

62. Richard J. Smethurst, "The Military Reserve Association and the Minobe Crisis of 1935," in *Crisis Politics in Prewar Japan: Institutional and*

Ideological Problems of the 1930s, ed. George M. Wilson, pp. 1–23; Frank O. Miller, *Minobe Tatsukichi: Interpreter of Constitutionalism in Japan*, pp. 217–20.

63. Smethurst, "Military Reserve Association," p. 5. On the relationship of the Minobe crisis to ongoing academic disputes, see Miller, *Minobe*, pp. 199–207. On the lasting effects of the crisis on freedom of expression, see Kasza, *State and Mass Media*, pp. 129–37.

64. Smethurst, "Military Reserve Association," pp. 3, 6; (Tōkyō-shi Azabu kuyakusho, *Azabu-ku shi*, does not list Okudaira as an officer of the ward branch and does not mention the Minobe crisis); Miller, *Minobe*, p. 237.

65. Kumagai, *Dai Nihon seinendan shi*, pp. 339–41.

66. Ibid., pp. 340–42.

67. Ibid., pp. 370–72; *JT&M*, December 11, 1937, and February 12, 1938.

68. *JT&M*, November 8, 1937, and January 14, 1938.

69. Tōkyō-shi Kōjimachi kuyakusho, *Kōjimachi-ku shi*, p. 889; Tōkyō-shi Shitaya kuyakusho, *Shitaya-ku shi*, p. 916; Tōkyō-shi Akasaka kuyakusho, *Akasaka-ku shi*, p. 734; Ōya Soichi, "Tōkyō-shi seinendan no kaibō," p. 132.

70. In Akasaka, none of the five heads of reservist units headed any of the ten young men's associations; in Ushigome, there was no overlap between the leaders of the twelve reservist associations and those of the eighteen *chō*-based young men's associations; and in Shiba only two of the heads of the thirty-seven reservist units were also head of one of the forty-six young men's associations. Tōkyō-shi Akasaka kuyakusho, *Akasaka-ku shi*, pp. 609, 734; Tōkyō-shi Ushigome kuyakusho, *Ushigome-ku shi*, pp. 448, 451–52; Tōkyō-shi Shiba kuyakusho, *Shiba-ku shi*, pp. 751–54, 924.

71. A list of sixteen heads of young men's associations in Honjo is given in Tōkyō-shi, *Tōkyō shinsai roku* 4:234–35. On Fukushima, see Fukkō chōsa kyōkai, *Teito fukkō shi* 3:2917.

72. On Gotō's reputation for spreading reactionary thought, see Ōya Soichi, "Tōkyō-shi seinendan no kaibō," p. 132. On Gotō's local service and family control over young men's associations, see Tōkyō-shi Kyōbashi kuyakusho, *Kyōbashi-ku shi* 2:260–61, 276, 919–20. On his candidacy for the Diet, see Kōmei senkyo renmei, *Shūgiin giin senkyo no jisseki*, pp. 300, 319. By the early 1930s, Gotō seems to have been succeeded by his son as head of the household. *Taishū jinji roku* (1934).

73. The socialist pamphleteers are from *JT&M*, September 16, 1921. On the tenant union leader who recommended activists in military reserve associations as potential leaders for tenant unions, see Ann Waswo, "In Search of Equity: Japanese Tenant Unions in the 1920s," in *Conflict in Modern Japanese History*, ed. Najita and Koschmann, p. 388.

74. On Kita Ikki, see Ben-ami Shillony, *Revolt in Japan: The Young Officers and the February 26, 1936, Incident*, p. 73. On Nagai Ryūtarō, see

Minichiello, *Retreat from Reform*, p. 96. On Kamei Kanichirō, see William Miles Fletcher III, *The Search for a New Order: Intellectuals and Fascism in Prewar Japan*, p. 98.

Chapter 5

1. Takeshi Ishida, for instance, writes of Japan in the 1920s and 1930s: "Even in urban areas, however, a basic unit similar to the hamlet was established. This was the workshop, in which workers could feel a sense of solidarity and in-group consciousness similar to that in a hamlet." "Conflict and Its Accommodation: *Omote-Ura* and *Uchi-Soto* Relations," in Ellis S. Krauss, Thomas P. Rohlen, and Patricia G. Steinhoff, eds., *Conflict in Japan*, p. 24.

2. *THS* 3:525; Nōshōmushō, *Kōjō tsūran*. The exact figures were 426 factories and 18,670 workers.

3. Nōshōmushō, *Kōjō tsūran;* Joseph Alphonse Laker, "Entrepreneurship and the Development of the Japanese Beer Industry, 1872–1937," p. 127. There is a photograph of this company in S. K. Wada, *Japan's Industries and Who's Who*, p. 172.

4. Edward Seidensticker, *Kafū the Scribbler: The Life and Writings of Nagai Kafū, 1879–1959*, pp. 221, 215, 212.

5. Hiroshi Hazama, "Historical Changes in the Life Style of Industrial Workers," in *Japanese Industrialization and Its Social Consequences*, ed. Hugh Patrick, p. 26; Gordon, *Labor Relations*, pp. 26, 41.

6. Based on information from Nōshōmushō, *Kōjō tsūran.*

7. For the Fuji Gas Spinning Company, see Wada, *Japan's Industries*, p. 34; *Japan Times*, July 10, 1913. For the Seikō Watch factory, see Wada, *Japan's Industries*, p. 572. For the Great Japan Beer Company, see Laker, "Entrepreneurship," p. 191.

8. Sawada Ken and Ogimoto Seizo, *Fuji bōseki kabushiki gaisha gojūnenshi*, p. 145; Gordon, *Labor Relations*, p. 41.

9. *Who's Who in Japan;* Wada, *Japan's Industries*, p. 583.

10. *Gendai jinmei jiten; NS* (1906).

11. Nōshōmushō, *Kōjō tsūran*, pp. 220, 547; Tōkyō-shi Honjo kuyakusho, *Honjo-ku shi*, pp. 42–45; Tōkyō shikai jimukyoku, *Tōkyō shikai shi* 4:1186.

12. *JT&M*, March 29, 1920; *TAS*, March 4, 1909.

13. *Japan Times*, March 20, 1912, and July 24, 1913; *JT&M*, July 19, 1920. Some Japanese scholars have suggested that the factories of this era were so unsanitary as to constitute small slums. Sugihara Kaoru and Tamai Kingo, *Taishō Osaka suramu: Mō hitotsu no Nihon kindaishi*, p. 23.

14. *Chūō kōron*, September 4, 1899, quoted in Laker, "Entrepreneurship," p. 164 (see also p. 166).

15. Tokyo Municipal Office, *Annual Statistics of the City of Tokyo;* Hazama, "Historical Changes," pp. 24, 27; Gordon, *Labor Relations*, pp. 24–25.

16. Nōshōmushō, *Kōjō tsūran,* p. 579; Tōkyō shikai jimukyoku, *Tōkyō shikai shi* 4:1188.

17. *Kanpō,* no. 1925 (January 6, 1919), p. 3, lists investors. *NS* (1930) shows that two of the investors, Ishii Fujirō and Asaoka Eizō, had shops in Honjo.

18. *Japan Times,* February 15, 1912. When fire broke out in an electro-plating smithy in Honjo, eight male employees, ranging in age from sixteen to fifty-six, were asleep on the second floor.

19. Hazama, "Historical Changes," pp. 28–29.

20. *Japan Times,* February 10, 1911, and February 15, 28, December 29, 1912.

21. Aoki Kōji, *Nihon rōdō undō shi nenpyō.* Two incidents reported in the *Japan Times* (March 1 and 20, 1912) are not on Aoki's list. All of the examples below are taken from Aoki, *Nihon rōdō undō shi nenpyō,* pp. 109, 129, 133, 135–36, 150, 172.

22. *TAS,* March 8, 1901; *Japan Times,* March 1, 1912; Aoki, *Nihon rōdō undō shi nenpyō,* p. 129.

23. Large, *The Yūaikai,* pp. 13, 16, 30. Other Social Policy Society members associated with the Yūaikai were Takano Iwasaburō and Soeda Jui-chi. Garon, *State and Labor,* p. 33.

24. Large, *The Yūaikai,* pp. 47–48.

25. Ōkōchi Kazuo and Watanabe Tōru, *Sōdōmei gojūnenshi* 1:126; Large, *The Yūaikai,* p. 54. *Rōdō,* 1918, p. 32; May 1919, p. 48; and June 1919, p. 33.

26. For instance, when Suzuki Kenjirō of Mitatsuchi Rubber Company died, Nozaki Tadashi of the same branch attended the funeral. When Andō Einosuke, also of Mitatsuchi, died, twenty officers went to the calling hours. *Rōdō,* August 1919, p. 43, and September 1919, p. 38.

27. Ibid., February 1919, p. 41, and June 1919, p. 27.

28. Large, *The Yūaikai,* pp. 35, 38–39.

29. Ibid., p. 33. Aburadani served as acting head of the Yūaikai when Suzuki went to the United States from September 1916 to January 1917, mediated a labor dispute in January 1917, and participated in the celebration of the fifth anniversary of the Yūaikai in April 1917. Ōkōchi and Matsuo, *Nihon rōdō* 2:76–77, 80, 82.

30. Aburadani spoke at a party held on February 10, 1917, in the Sapporo Beer Garden in Honjo and at a speech meeting on May 19, 1917, at a school. Both Aburadani and Suzuki spoke at the autumn speech meeting of the Honjo chapter on November 24, 1917, and at the New Year's party of the Honjo chapter in 1918. *Rōdō oyobi sangyō,* February 1918, pp. 64, 72; July 1918, p. 46; and December 1918, p. 45. Kitazawa Shinjirō (1887–1980) graduated from Waseda in 1910 and returned to teach there in 1914 after study in the United States. From 1957–1967, he was president of Tokyo University of Economics. *Konsaisu jinmei jiten.*

31. Ōkōchi and Watanabe, *Sōdōmei gojūnenshi* 1:1217, 1220; Ōkōchi and Matsuo, *Nihon rōdō* 2:80–81; Matsuo, *Taishō demokurashii*, pp. 179–80.

32. *TAS*, July 30 and August 1, 1917; *Rōdō oyobi sangyō* 3 (January 1916): 7, and 4 (July 1916): 63.

33. *TAS*, August 1, 2, 3, 1917; Ōkōchi and Watanabe, *Sōdōmei gojūnenshi* 1:984.

34. Gordon, *Labor Relations*, pp. 72–74.

35. For an account of citizen movements among the middle-class residents of Tokyo, see Narita Ryūichi, "Taishō demokurashii ki no toshi jūmin undō: Tōkyō-shi ni okeru," *Chihō shi no kenkyū* 30.5 (October 1980): 33–42.

36. Large, *The Yūaikai*, pp. 107–52.

37. Shiota, *Nihon rōdō undō no rekishi*, p. 297; Fujii Tei, "Waga kuni saikin no rōdō undō no gaisei," *SSJ* 1 (1920): 41.

38. Gordon, *Labor Relations*, p. 82; Large, *The Yūaikai*, p. 142.

39. Smith, *Student Radicals*, pp. 42–45, 252, 292, 298; Large, *The Yūaikai*, pp. 147, 151; Matsuo, *Taishō demokurashii*, p. 204; Ōkōchi and Matsuo, *Nihon rōdō* 2:115–16. On Asō, see also *Konsaisu jinmei jiten* (1976). For a brief sketch of Sano Manabu, see George M. Beckmann and Genji Okubo, *The Japanese Communist Party, 1922–1945*, p. 381.

40. Large, *The Yūaikai*, pp. 133–39.

41. Ōkōchi and Matsuo, *Nihon rōdō* 2:193–95.

42. *Rōdō oyobi sangyō*, December 1918, p. 37; January 1919, p. 44; February 1919, p. 41; April 1919, p. 38; May 1919, p. 46; August 1919, p. 42; and October 1919, p. 51.

43. Ibid., April 1918, p. 79, and August 1918, p. 45.

44. Aoki, *Nihon rōdō undō shi nenpyō*, esp. pp. 221–22, 235, 268, 281; *Nihon rōdō nenkan* (1919): 21. See also Gordon, *Labor Relations*, p. 250.

45. Unless otherwise noted, this account is based on *TAS*, July 15, 16, 17, 1920; Ōkōchi and Matsuo, *Nihon rōdō* 2:201–2; *Rōdō*, September 1920, p. 19. For Tamura's and Akaishi's earlier association with the Yūaikai, see *Rōdō oyobi sangyō*, January 1917, p. 69; October 1918, p. 37; and September 1919, p. 41.

46. Large, *The Yūaikai*, p. 156; Large, *Organized Workers*, pp. 24, 40; Ōkōchi and Matsuo, *Nihon rōdō* 2:117.

47. Ōkōchi and Matsuo, *Nihon rōdō* 2:201; Garon, *State and Labor*, p. 109; Kinzley, *Industrial Harmony*, pp. 67–69.

48. *SSJ*, January 1923, p. 2.

49. *Rōdō*, May 1920, p. 22; February 1921, p. 17; July 1921, pp. 16, 22. For the earlier involvement of Ono Sakichi (1917), Suzuki Kenjirō (1918), Ishikawa Gonnosuke (1918), and Miyahara Takeo (1919) in the Yūaikai, see Ōkōchi and Watanabe, *Sōdōmei gojūnenshi* 1:1032, 1077, 1099, and *Rōdō oyobi sangyō* 6 (1917): 199; September 1918, p. 48; and November 1918, p. 45. Tanaka Takako was the wife of the liberal philosopher Tanaka

Odō. Educated at Stanford and the University of Chicago, she served as an advisor to the Japanese government on women workers at the first International Labor Organization in Washington in 1919. Nolte, *Liberalism,* pp. 119–23.

50. Unless otherwise noted, this account is based on *SSJ,* January 1923, p. 2, and February 1923, p. 82; *TAS,* November 7, 8, 10, 11, 12, 14, 15, 1922.

51. Kyōchōkai, *Nihon shakai rōdō undō shiryō shū,* reel no. 57. Yokoishi was an officer of the Sōdōmei. Ōkōchi and Matsuo, *Nihon rōdō* 2:264.

52. Naimushō, *Rōdō undō gaikyō* (1922): 135. For further information on these rivalries, see Large, *Organized Workers,* pp. 41–45, 49, 94, and Ōkōchi and Matsuo, *Nihon rōdō* 2:220–22.

53. *SSJ,* November 1922, p. 135, and December 1922, p. 4.

54. Naimushō, *Rōdō undō gaikyō* (1922): 134, 146. Watanabe Manzō of the clock makers union was a founding member of the Japan Socialist Alliance (Nihon shakaishugi dōmei), formed at the end of 1920. Ōkōchi and Matsuo, *Nihon rōdō* 2:205–6. For another example of police interference when workers expressed solidarity across factory lines, see Gordon, *Imperial Democracy,* p. 170.

55. Naimushō, *Rōdō undō gaikyō* (1923): 173–74; *SSJ,* April 1923, p. 105.

56. Kyōchōkai, *Nihon shakai rōdō undō shiryō shū,* reel no. 57; Naimushō, *Rōdō undō gaikyō* (1923): 174, 176–77. Andō had been a member of the Honjo branch of the Yūaikai since 1916. *Rōdō oyobi sangyō* 3 (January and March 1916): 84, 252, and 4 (July 1916): 65.

57. Naimushō, *Rōdō undō gaikyō* (1923): 174–75. On the Ōjima Labor Hall, and the ties it provided to Okamoto Torikichi, Hirasawa Keishichi, and other labor leaders, see Gordon, *Imperial Democracy,* pp. 148–51.

58. Gordon, *Imperial Democracy,* pp. 178–79; *TAS,* May 29, 1923.

59. Naimushō, *Rōdō undō gaikyō* (1923): 181; *TAS,* June 22, 1923.

60. Naimushō, *Rōdō undō gaikyō* (1923): 182. For a biographical sketch of Watanabe Masanosuke (1899–1928), see Beckmann and Okubo, *Japanese Communist Party,* pp. 387–88. On Uchida Tōshichi, see Gordon, *Labor Relations,* pp. 85–86, 96–97.

61. Ōkōchi and Matsuo, *Nihon rōdō* 2:225; *TAS,* June 13, 1923; Naimushō, *Rōdō undō gaikyō* (1923): 182; *TAS,* June 18, 1923; *SSJ,* August 1923, p. 144.

62. Naimushō, *Rōdō undō gaikyō* (1923): 181–82.

63. George O. Totten III, "Collective Bargaining and Works Councils as Innovations in Industrial Relations in Japan During the 1920s," in *Aspects of Social Change in Modern Japan,* ed. R. P. Dore, p. 209; Naimushō, *Rōdō undō gaikyō* (1923): 183.

64. Sawada and Ogimoto, *Fuji bōseki,* p. 222; *SSJ,* March 1924, p. 126. The representative of the workers was Kohinata Tetsugorō, who had been in the Seibokukai faction in the disturbances earlier in the year.

65. Garon, *State and Labor*, p. 51.

66. Tōkyō-shiyakusho, *Tōkyō-shi kōjō yōran* (1926) (this figure may be off by one or two factories; the only available copy of this survey had a few pages missing); Tōkyō tōkeika, *Dai yonkai Tōkyō-shi rōdō tōkei jitchi chōsa*, p. 22.

67. Sawada and Ogimoto, *Fuji bōseki*, p. 222; Tōkyō-shiyakusho, *Tōkyō-shi kōjō yōran* (1926): 349. Both Aoki Naoji and Kurihara Kohachi are listed at Honjo addresses in *NS* (1930), but neither ever appeared as a local leader after 1923.

68. Matsuzawa Hiroaki, *Nihon shakaishugi no shisō*, p. 112.

69. Hōsei daigaku, Ōhara shakai mondai kenkyūjo, *Rōdō undō shiryō dai ichi shū: Kantō gōdō sōgi chōsa kiroku*, p. 62. Keishichō rōdō kakari, *Rōdō sōgi junpō* (1931) nos. 11, 29; (1932) no. 30; (1933) no. 31; (1934) no. 32, in Kyōchōkai, *Nihon shakai rōdō undō shiryō shū*, reel no. 75.

70. Hōsei daigaku, *Kantō gōdō*, pp. 20–21.

71. Unless otherwise noted, information on this incident comes from Shakaikyoku rōdōbu, *Rōdō undō nenpō* (1928): 496–509.

72. Gordon, *Imperial Democracy*, pp. 224–25.

73. Shakaikyoku rōdōbu, *Rōdō undō nenpō* (1926): 327; Kyōchōkai, *Nihon shakai rōdō undō shiryō shū*, reel no. 82, no. 23. Saitō's address in *NS* (1930): 341 was the same as that of the factory.

74. Shakai kyoku rōdō bu, *Rōdō undō nenpō* (1926): 340, 342.

75. Hōsei daigaku, *Kantō gōdō*, p. 48. The address of the owner, Ishibashi Keisuke, is from *NS* (1930): 84.

76. Hōsei daigaku, *Kantō gōdō*, pp. 21–22. The owner's address is from *NS* (1930): 488.

77. For the development of these ideas in the Meiji era and their continued defense in the 1930s, see Marshall, *Capitalism and Nationalism*, pp. 62–69, 85–90. Unless otherwise noted, information on this incident is from *TAS*, February 24, 25, 27, and March 10, 1925.

78. See, for instance, Gordon, *Imperial Democracy*, p. 224, for a discussion of how this legislation provided recognition for labor disputes. For an opposite view, that the essence of state policy was its failure to recognize unions, see Matsuzawa, *Nihon shakaishugi no shisō*, p. 111.

79. Marshall, *Capitalism and Nationalism*, p. 87.

80. Naimushō, *Rōdō undō gaikyō* (1924): 446. At the annual meeting of the Jijikai in October, Sasaki of the Honjo branch presented a resolution to oppose the plans of reservist groups to interfere in any strike. Smethurst, *Social Basis*, p. 146, cites three instances in which factory reservist branches interfered in strikes: at a steel plant in Muroran, at the Yawata Ironworks, and during an Osaka trolley strike.

81. *JT&M*, April 19, 22, 24, 25, 1930. The protest of the incident was Ōya, "Tōkyō-shi seinendan no kaibō."

82. *JT&M*, September 6, 7, 1934.

83. Ibid., September 5, 8, 1934.

84. *JT&M* and *TAS,* September 12, 1934.

85. *JT&M,* September 13, 1934.

86. Large, *Organized Workers,* p. 4.

87. Ibid., p. 90.

Chapter 6

1. George Oakley Totten III, *The Social Democratic Movement in Prewar Japan,* pp. 414–16, lists a total of eighty-eight candidates. He based his list primarily on *Nihon rōdō nenkan* 10 (1929): 320–23. Kōno Mitsu and Akamatsu Katsumaro, *Nihon musan seitōshi,* p. 345, list ninety candidates. The two additional candidates were one independent and one other from the Japan Farmer Party. Toyama Shigeki and Adachi Yoshiko, *Kindai Nihon seijishi hikkei,* p. 210, list only eighty-two proletarian candidates. They omit three local party candidates (Imai, Kawashima, and Otaguro) and three candidates from the Japan Farmer Party (Suga, Hirahara, and Saeki).

2. Robert A. Scalapino, "Elections and Political Modernization in Prewar Japan," in *Political Development in Modern Japan,* ed. Robert E. Ward, p. 277.

3. These dates refer to Honjo Ward. The prefectural elections held in the rest of the nation in 1927 were postponed until 1928 in certain wards of Tokyo because of lingering disorganization from the earthquake.

4. In English, one important exception is R. L. Sims, "National Elections and Electioneering in Akita Ken, 1930–1942," in *Modern Japan: Aspects of History, Literature, and Society,* ed. W. G. Beasley.

5. *JT&M,* February 22, 1928. The exact figures for Honjo and Fukagawa (12,430 registered in 1924 and 78,016 in 1928) are from Toyama and Adachi, *Kindai Nihon,* pp. 203, 208.

6. Tōkyō-shi tōkeika, *Tōkyō-shi no jōkyō: Shikai giin senkyo gaikyō.* Chapter 2 of the 1925 election law appears in David John Lu, *Sources of Japanese History* 2:115. The entire text of the law is included in Harold S. Quigley, *Japanese Government and Politics: An Introductory Study,* pp. 378–410.

7. *JT&M,* February 22, 1928. For election turnout, see Bradley M. Richardson, *The Political Culture of Japan,* p. 9.

8. *JT&M,* March 18, 1933; Imai Seiichi, "Kanshō to danatsu no naka de dai ikkai fusen," in *Shōwa shunkan,* ed. Asahi Janaru, 1:26.

9. *JT&M,* January 28, February 16, 1928, and February 7, 1932.

10. Ibid., January 28, 1928.

11. Ibid., January 24, February 18, 21, 1928; Tōkyō shiyakusho, *Fukai giin sōsenkyo ni kansuru chōsa.*

12. *JT&M,* February 1, 2, 1928; *Nihon kokusei jiten* 8:565.

13. *JT&M,* January 25, 1930; January 23, 1932; January 30, February 2, 1936.

14. Ibid., January 8, 13, 1928, and January 25, 1930.

15. Ibid., January 30, 1928, and March 12, 1937.

16. Ibid., March 2, 4, 6, 8, 14, 19, 1929. See also Ichikawa Fusae, *Ichikawa Fusae jiden*, pp. 201–6.

17. *JT&M*, March 24, 1929, and March 15, 1933. Some of the dailies expressing disappointment in the election were the *Tōkyō asahi*, the *Yomiuri*, and the *Miyako*. *JT&M*, March 19, 21, 1933.

18. *JT&M*, March 8, 12, 1937.

19. These patterns have been noted by Berger, *Parties out of Power*, p. 14, and Allinson, *Japanese Urbanism*, p. 80.

20. Scalapino, *Democracy*, p. 160; Berger, *Parties out of Power*, p. 19; Scalapino, "Elections," p. 283.

21. Scalapino, "Elections," p. 276; Berger, *Parties out of Power*, p. 51; Imai, "Dai ikkai fusen," p. 30.

22. *JT&M*, February 21, 1928. Total offenses included 206 cases of buying and selling votes and 858 cases of accepting meals.

23. Asahi shinbunsha, *Daisankai fusen sōsenkyo taikan*, p. 37.

24. A translation of the speech is given in Berger, *Parties out of Power*, pp. 47–48.

25. *JT&M*, August 17, 28, 30, 1929.

26. Kasza, *State and Mass Media*, pp. 72, 83–84, 91, 93, 95.

27. *JT&M*, February 2, 1928.

28. Ibid., February 4, 18, 1928.

29. Ibid., August 2, 1929.

30. Arthur E. Tiedemann, "The Hamaguchi Cabinet: First Phase July 1929–February 1930: A Study in Japanese Parliamentary Government," p. 49; Scalapino, "Elections," p. 271.

31. Tiedemann, "Hamaguchi Cabinet," pp. 176–80, 192.

32. Three-quarters of the candidates elected in 1930 were natives of the prefectures from which they ran. Ibid., pp. 220–21. Allinson's study of Kariya shows that it was essential there for a successful candidate to be a native son. *Japanese Urbanism*, pp. 69–87.

33. A list of all the candidates from the district is provided in Fujisawa Rikitarō, *Sōsenkyo tokuhon*, p. 119. The four born in Tokyo were Omata Masaichi, Ōta Shinjirō, Isobe Hisashi, and Kunieda Sutejirō. Biographical information on all four of these men is included in Kokkai shūgiin sangiin, *Gikai seido shichijūnenshi* 8:54, 90, 109, 175.

34. Kokkai shūgiin sangiin, *Gikai seido shichijūnenshi* 8:54. Isobe Hisashi was already living in Kamezawa-chō, Honjo, as early as 1906. *NS* (1906).

35. *Taishō jinmei jiten*, p. 131; *Daijinmei jiten* 1:215; Kokkai shūgiin sangiin, *Gikai seido shichijūnenshi* 8:53.

36. Narita, "Toshi minshū sōjō," pp. 41–42, 46–52.

37. Kokkai shūgiin sangiin, *Gikai seido shichijūnenshi* 8:109; Tōkyō-fu senkyo shukusei jikkō bu, *Shūgiin giin sōsenkyo ni kansuru shirabe*, pp. 76–77 (cited hereafter as *SGSS*).

38. Tōkyō-shi Honjo kuyakusho, *Honjo kusei yōran* (1926): 62–63.

39. See appendix C.

40. Tōkyō-shi Honjo kuyakusho, *Honjo-ku shi*, pp. 46–47; *SGSS*, pp. 85, 89.

41. See appendix B.

42. *JT&M*, February 1, 1930. Unless otherwise noted, biographical information on Manabe is from *SGSS*, pp. 72–73.

43. Tiedemann, "Hamaguchi Cabinet," p. 73 n; Garon, *State and Labor*, pp. 159, 161.

44. *JT&M*, February 1, 23, 1930.

45. *SGSS*, p. 73; Berger, *Parties out of Power*, pp. 69–70.

46. *JT&M*, January 31, 1928; Kenneth Colegrove, "Labor Parties in Japan," *American Political Science Review* 23 (May 1929): 347–48 n. The five prewar universal manhood suffrage elections were held on Monday, February 20, 1928; Thursday, February 20, 1930; Saturday, February 20, 1932; Thursday, February 20, 1936; and Friday, April 30, 1937.

47. *JT&M*, March 19, 1929; Tōkyō shiyakusho, *Fukai giin sōsenkyo ni kansuru chōsa*, p. 41; *TAS*, February 15, 24, 1925.

48. Seven others were from Fukagawa. The last was Manabe, who was not really from either ward, although he always used a Fukagawa address.

49. *TAS*, March 11, 1925; *SGSS*, p. 89.

50. For the reputed electoral strength of the two candidates, see *TAS*, February 1, 1930.

51. *JT&M*, January 29, February 16, 26, 1932.

52. Kyōchōkai, *Nihon shakai rōdō undō shiryō shū*, reel no. 79. Unless otherwise noted, biographical information on Karazawa is from Beckmann and Okubo, *Japanese Communist Party*, p. 367.

53. Smith, *Student Radicals*, pp. 47–51, 79.

54. Marius B. Jansen, *The Japanese and Sun Yat-sen*, pp. 54–58, 134–35, 158, 160; Totten, *Social Democratic Movement*, p. 255; Ōkōchi and Matsuo, *Nihon rōdō* 3:121.

55. Miyazaki Ryūsuke, "Yanagihara Byakuren to no hanseki," *Bungei shunjū* 45 (June 1967): 224–27; Smith, *Student Radicals*, pp. 59–60.

56. *JT&M*, February 18, 1928.

57. Beckmann and Okubo, *Japanese Communist Party*, pp. 150–51.

58. *JT&M*, January 29, 1930; Kagawa Toyohiko zenshū kankōkai, *Kagawa Toyohiko zenshū* 24:108–9.

59. Unless otherwise noted, biographical information on Asanuma is from *Konsaisu jinmei jiten*.

60. *Nihon rōdō nenkan* 10 (1929): 300, 330, and 11 (1930): 327; Shakai rōdō kyōkai, *Rōdō jinji meikan*, p. 1347.

61. *Japan Biographical Encyclopedia and Who's Who*, p. 777; Yokoyama, *Kagawa Toyohiko den*, p. 213; *Nihon rōdō nenkan* 11 (1930): 327.

62. *Nihon rōdō nenkan* 10 (1929): 330; Ōkōchi and Watanabe, *Sōdōmei gojūnenshi* 1:282; *Rōdō oyobi sangyō* 4 (July 1916): 63.

63. Kagawa Toyohiko zenshū kankōkai, *Kagawa Toyohiko zenshū* 22:109; Asanuma tsuitō shuppan henshū iinkai, *Bakushin: Ningen kikansha Numásan no kiroku,* p. 70.

64. *SGSS,* p. 87; Kokkai shūgiin sangiin, *Gikai seido shichijūnen shi* 8:391.

65. *JT&M,* February 2, 1930.

66. Ibid., February 3, 1930, and January 27, February 28, 1932; Asahi shinbunsha, *Daisan fusen,* p. 106.

67. *The Japan-Manchuria Year Book* (1934) gives Pak's address as 571 Kitasenzokumachi, Ōmori Ward.

68. Tsuboe Senji, *Chōsen minzoku dokuritsu undō hishi,* pp. 271–72.

69. *JT&M,* January 27, February 20, 1932.

70. The Korean votes seem to have figured in his success. In 1942, when a second Korean ran in the district, attendance at Pak's campaign meetings dropped considerably in comparison to 1936. Edward J. Drea, *The 1942 Japanese General Election: Political Mobilization in Wartime Japan,* pp. 100–101.

71. The voters of Tokyo did not participate in this election. When the government held the first prefectural elections under universal manhood suffrage in 1927, the authorities judged Tokyo and Yokohama to be insufficiently recovered from the earthquake of 1923 to participate, and so this area had ever since remained on a local election schedule of its own.

72. Awaya Kentarō, *Shōwa no seitō,* p. 262.

73. *JT&M,* January 26, 31, 1936. In 1937, the authorities again used posters, pamphlets, and phonograph records to urge citizens to cast their votes honestly and conscientiously. *JT&M,* April 10, 1937. Apparently, the government did not make quite the same conspicuous efforts in 1937 as in 1936, but Soma Masao ("Senkyo shukusei undō no shisō to yakuwari," *Toshi mondai* 50.8 [August 1959]: 59) and Suzaki Shin'ichi ("Senkyo shukusei undō no tenkai to sono yakuwari," *Rekishi hyōron* 310.2 [February 1976]: 54) agree that the campaign operated approximately the same in both elections.

74. *JT&M,* January 9, 12, 15, 20, 26, 1936; *TAS,* February 9, 1936.

75. The list of Home Ministry bureaucrats is taken from Berger, *Parties out of Power,* p. 72.

76. *TAS,* February 1, 1936; *Nihon kokusei jiten* 9:481.

77. Totten, *Social Democratic Movement,* p. 89.

78. *SGSS,* p. 93.

79. *NS* (1935): 505 gives his address as Mukōjima 3–9.

80. *SGSS,* pp. 84–85.

81. *JT&M,* January 30, February 21, 1936. For figures on attendance per meeting, see Drea, *General Election,* p. 100.

82. Berger, *Parties out of Power,* pp. 43, 56; *SGSS,* p. 87; Tōkyō-shi Honjo kuyakusho, *Honjo kusei yōran* (1926 and 1931); *SGSS,* p. 14.

83. Naimushō keihokyoku, *Shakai undō no jōkyō* 5 (1933): 762, and 7 (1935): 766; *SGSS,* pp. 14, 91–92.

84. *SGSS,* p. 78; Tōkyō shiyakusho, *Tōkyō-shi kōjō yōran* (1929): 247; Kokkai shūgiin sangiin, *Gikai seido shichijūnenshi* 8:297.

85. *Tokkō geppō,* September 1930, p. 49; Tōkyō shikai jimukyoku, *Tōkyō shikai shi* 8:958 and 9:1233–34.

Conclusion

1. Neil L. Waters, "The Second Transition: Early to Mid-Meiji in Kanagawa Prefecture," *Journal of Asian Studies* 49 (May 1990): 307.

2. David Hammack, "Problems of Power in the Historical Study of Cities, 1800–1960," *American Historical Review* 83 (April 1978): 333–34.

3. Skocpol, "Bringing the State Back In," 9; Bernard S. Silberman, "The Bureaucratic State in Japan: The Problem of Authority and Legitimacy," in *Conflict in Modern Japanese History,* ed. Najita and Koschmann, pp. 236–37; Robert M. Spaulding Jr., "The Bureaucracy as a Political Force, 1920–45," in Morley, *Dilemmas of Growth,* p. 41.

4. On the liberals and their concern with the French Revolution, see Peter Duus, "Liberal Intellectuals and Social Conflict in Taishō Japan," in Najita and Koschmann, *Conflict in Modern Japanese History,* p. 416.

5. Duus, "Liberal Intellectuals," p. 427; Meacham, *Toynbee Hall,* p. 2.

6. Garon, *State and Labor,* p. 98.

7. For the definition of corporatism, see Philippe C. Schmitter, "Still the Century of Corporatism?" in *The New Corporatism: Social-Political Structures in the Iberian World,* ed. Frederick P. Pike and Thomas Stritch, pp. 93–94. For organic statists in Peru, see Stepan, *State and Society,* esp. pp. 158, 164, 166.

8. Howe, *The City,* p. 25.

9. Weiner, "Bureaucracy and Politics," pp. 27–29, 32.

10. Howe, *The City,* p. 80; Mann, *La Guardia,* pp. 104, 107.

11. On party penetration of the bureaucracy, see Najita, *Hara Kei,* pp. 35–45.

12. On precinct captains in Chicago, see Gottfried, *Boss Cermak of Chicago,* p. 22.

13. Tocqueville, *Democracy in America* 2:114, 115.

14. Hoston, "The State."

15. Kasza, *State and Mass Media;* Richard H. Mitchell, *Thought Control in Prewar Japan* and *Censorship in Imperial Japan.*

16. Andrew E. Barshay, *State and Intellectual in Imperial Japan: The Public Man in Crisis,* p. 25.

17. James B. Crowley, "A New Asian Order: Some Notes on Prewar Japanese Nationalism," in *Japan in Crisis: Essays on Taishō Democracy,* ed. Bernard S. Silberman and H. D. Harootunian, p. 272.

18. Larry Diamond, "Introduction," in *Democracy in Developing Countries,* vol. 3, *Asia,* p. 49.

19. On child welfare, see Martha N. Ozawa, "Child Welfare Programs in Japan," *Social Service Review* 65.1 (March 1991): 1–21.

Bibliography

Addams, Jane. *Democracy and Social Ethics.* New York: Macmillan, 1907; reprinted Cambridge: Harvard University Press, 1964.

Akimoto Ritsuo. *Sensō to minshū: Taiheiyō sensō shita no toshi seikatsu* (War and people: Urban life during the Pacific War). Gakuyō shobō, 1974.

Allinson, Gary. *Japanese Urbanism: Industry and Politics in Kariya, 1872–1972.* Berkeley and Los Angeles: University of California Press, 1975.

Amaoka Naoyoshi. "Fujin no eisei shisatsu" (Women health inspectors). *Shimin* 4.4 (May 28, 1909): 18–20.

Ando, F. "The Tokyo Almshouse." *Japan Magazine* 6 (1915): 298–300.

Aoki Kōji. *Nihon rōdō undō shi nenpyō* (Chronology of the Japanese labor movement). Shinseisha, 1968.

Asahi shinbunsha. *Daisankai fusen sōsenkyo taikan* (General view of the third universal manhood suffrage election). 1932.

Asanuma tsuitō shuppan henshū iinkai. *Bakushin: Ningen kikansha Numasan no kiroku* (A record of the life of Asanuma Inejirō). Nihon Shakaitō, 1961.

Ashizawa Takeo. "Senzen no rōjin hogo o megutte" (Care of the elderly in the prewar era). In *Shōwa shakai jigyōshi e no shōgen* (Eyewitness accounts of the history of Shōwa social work), edited by Yoshida Kyūichi and Ichibangase Yasuko. Domesu, 1982.

Awaya Kentarō. *Shōwa no seitō* (Shōwa political parties). Shōwa no rekishi, no. 6. Shogakkan, 1983.

Axling, William. *Kagawa.* New York: Harper and Brothers, 1932; revised edition, 1946.

Barshay, Andrew E. *State and Intellectual in Imperial Japan: The Public Man in Crisis.* Berkeley and Los Angeles: University of California Press, 1988.

Bartholomew, James R. "Science, Bureaucracy, and Freedom in Meiji and Taishō Japan." In *Conflict in Modern Japanese History: The Neglected Tradition,* edited by Tetsuo Najita and J. Victor Koschmann. Princeton: Princeton University Press, 1982.

Becker, Dorothy G. "Exit Lady Bountiful: The Volunteer and the Professional Social Worker." *Social Service Review* 38 (March 1964): 57–72.

Beckmann, George M., and Okubo, Genji. *The Japanese Communist Party, 1922–1945.* Stanford: Stanford University Press, 1969.

Berger, Gordon Mark. *Parties out of Power in Japan, 1931–1941.* Princeton: Princeton University Press, 1977.

Bernstein, Gail Lee. *Japanese Marxist: A Portrait of Kawakami Hajime, 1879–1946.* Cambridge: Harvard University Press, 1976.

Bestor, Theodore C. *Neighborhood Tokyo.* Stanford: Stanford University Press, 1989.

Braibanti, Ralph J. O. "Neighborhood Associations in Japan and Their Democratic Potentialities." *Far Eastern Quarterly* 7 (1948): 136–64.

Brown, Sidney Devere, and Akiko Hirota, eds. *The Diary of Kido Takayoshi.* Vol. 2, *1871–1874.* Tokyo: University of Tokyo Press, 1985.

Bunkyō kuyakusho. *Bunkyō-ku shi* (Bunkyō Ward history). 5 vols. 1969.

Cameron, Kenneth Walter, ed. *American Episcopal Clergy: Registers of Ordinations in the Episcopal Church in the United States from 1785 Through 1904.* Hartford, Conn.: Transcendental Books, 1970.

Chūbachi, Masayoshi, and Koji Taira. "Poverty in Modern Japan: Perceptions and Realities." In *Japanese Industrialization and Its Social Consequences,* edited by Hugh Patrick. Berkeley and Los Angeles: University of California Press, 1976.

Clement, Priscilla Ferguson. *Welfare and the Poor in the Nineteenth-Century City: Philadelphia, 1800–1854.* Rutherford, N.J.: Farleigh Dickinson Press, 1985.

Colegrove, Kenneth. "Labor Parties in Japan." *American Political Science Review* 23 (May 1929): 329–63.

Crowley, James B. "A New Asian Order: Some Notes on Prewar Japanese Nationalism." In *Japan in Crisis: Essays on Taishō Democracy,* edited by Bernard S. Silberman and H. D. Harootunian. Princeton: Princeton University Press, 1974.

Daijinmei jiten (Biographical dictionary). 1953–1956.

Dai Nihon teikoku gikaishi kankōkai. *Dai Nihon teikoku gikaishi* (History of Japan's Imperial Diet). 18 vols. 1926–1930.

Dai Nihon ōbenkai kōdansha. *Taishō daishinsai daikasai* (The Taishō great earthquake and great fire). 1923.

Dai Nihon rengō seinendan chōsabu. *Zenkoku seinendan kihon chōsa* (Nationwide investigation of young men's associations). 1934.

Das Gupta, Jyotirindra. "India: Democratic Becoming and Combined Development." In *Democracy in Developing Countries.* Vol. 3, *Asia,* edited by Larry Diamond, Juan J. Linz, and Seymour Martin Lipset. Boulder, Colo.: Lynne Rienner Publishers, 1989.

Diamond, Larry, Juan J. Linz, and Seymour Martin Lipset, eds., *Democracy in Developing Countries.* Vol. 3, *Asia.* Boulder, Colo.: Lynne Rienner Publishers, 1989.

Dore, R. P. *City Life in Japan: A Study of a Tokyo Ward.* Berkeley and Los Angeles: University of California Press, 1958.

Downard, J. Douglas. "Tokyo: The Depression Years, 1927–1933." Ph.D. diss., Indiana University, 1976.

Drea, Edward J. *The 1942 Japanese General Election: Political Mobilization in Wartime Japan*. Lawrence, Kans.: Center for East Asian Studies, University of Kansas, 1979.

Duus, Peter. *Party Rivalry and Political Change in Taishō Japan*. Cambridge: Harvard University Press, 1968.

————. "Liberal Intellectuals and Social Conflict in Taishō Japan." In *Conflict in Modern Japanese History: The Neglected Tradition*, edited by Tetsuo Najita and J. Victor Koschmann. Princeton: Princeton University Press, 1982.

————. *The Rise of Modern Japan*. Boston: Houghton Mifflin, 1976.

Embree, John F. *Suye Mura: A Japanese Village*. Chicago: University of Chicago Press, 1969.

Fletcher, William Miles, III. *The Search for a New Order: Intellectuals and Fascism in Prewar Japan*. Chapel Hill: University of North Carolina Press, 1982.

Foreign Missionary. 1924, 1925.

Fujii Tei. "Waga kuni saikin no rōdō undō no gaisei" (Outline of the recent Japanese labor movement). *Shakai seisaku jihō* (Social policy review) 1 (1920): 37–43.

Fujisawa Rikitarō. *Sōsenkyo tokuhon* (Election reader). Iwanami shoten, 1928.

Fujo shinbun (Women's news). 1921.

Fukkō chōsa kyōkai. *Teito fukkō shi* (History of the restoration of the capital). 3 vols. 1930.

Fukuda, Ippei. "Tokyo's Homes for the Homeless." *Contemporary Japan* 2 (1933): 490–96.

Garon, Sheldon. *The State and Labor in Modern Japan*. Berkeley and Los Angeles: University of California Press, 1987.

Gendai jinmei jiten. Tōkyō jinji chōsabu, 1952.

Gluck, Carol. *Japan's Modern Myths: Ideology in the Late Meiji Period*. Princeton: Princeton University Press, 1985.

Gordon, Andrew. *The Evolution of Labor Relations in Japan: Heavy Industry, 1853–1955*. Cambridge: Council on East Asian Studies, Harvard University, 1985.

————. *Labor and Imperial Democracy in Prewar Japan*. Berkeley and Los Angeles: University of California Press, 1991.

Gottfried, Alex. *Boss Cermak of Chicago: A Study of Political Leadership*. Seattle: University of Washington Press, 1962.

Greene, Evarts Boutell. *A New-Englander in Japan: Daniel Crosby Greene*. Boston: Houghton Mifflin, 1927.

Hane, Mikiso. *Reflections on the Way to the Gallows: Rebel Women in Prewar Japan*. Berkeley and Los Angeles: University of California Press, 1988.

Hammack, David. "Problems of Power in the Historical Study of Cities, 1800–1960." *American Historical Review* 83 (1978): 323–49.

Hara Taiichi. "Kyūgoho no seitei o sokushin" (Hastening the institution of the relief law). In *Shōwa shakai jigyōshi e no shōgen* (Eye-witness accounts of the history of Shōwa social work), edited by Yoshida Kyūichi and Ichibangase Yasuko. Domesu, 1982.

Hastings, Sally A. "From Heroine to Patriotic Volunteer: Women and Social Work in Japan, 1900–1945." *Working Papers on Women in International Development,* no. 106 (1985).

Hata Ikuhiko. *Senzenki Nihon kanryōsei no seido, soshiki, jinji* (System, organization, and personnel in the prewar Japanese bureaucracy). Tōkyō daigaku shuppankai, 1981.

Hauser, William B. "Osaka: A Commercial City in Tokugawa Japan." *Urbanism Past and Present* 5 (Winter 1977–1978): 23–36.

Hayashiya Tatsusaburō, with George Elison. "Kyoto in the Muromachi Age." In *Japan in the Muromachi Age,* edited by John W. Hall and Toyoda Takeshi. Berkeley and Los Angeles: University of California Press, 1977.

Hazama, Hiroshi. "Historical Changes in the Life Style of Industrial Workers." In *Japanese Industrialization and Its Social Consequences,* edited by Hugh Patrick. Berkeley and Los Angeles: University of California Press, 1976.

Henderson, Charles Richmond. *Modern Methods of Charity.* New York: Macmillan, 1904.

Himmelfarb, Gertrude. *Poverty and Compassion: The Moral Imagination of the Late Victorians.* New York: Alfred A. Knopf, 1991.

Hirade Kojirō. *Tōkyō fūzoku shi* (History of Tokyo). 3 vols. Fuzanbō, 1904; Hara shobō, 1968.

Hiratake Tatsu. "Tōkyō-shi no hōmen iin seido ni tsuite" (The district welfare committees of Tokyo City). *Shakai seisaku jihō* (July 1921), pp. 231–36.

Hirayama Kazuhiko. *Seinen shūdan shi kenkyū josetsu* (Collection of research on youth groups). 2 vols. Shinsensha, 1978.

Holli, Melvin G. *Reform in Detroit: Hazen S. Pingree and Urban Politics.* New York: Oxford University Press, 1969.

Home Office, Social Affairs Bureau. *The Great Earthquake of 1923 in Japan.* 1926.

Hōsei daigaku, ōhara shakai mondai kenkyūjo. *Rōdō undō shiryō daiichi shū: Kantō gōdō sōgi chōsa kiroku* (First collection of labor documents: Records of the conflicts of Kantō gōdō). n.d.

Hoston, Germaine A. "The State, Modernity, and the Fate of Liberalism in Prewar Japan." *Journal of Asian Studies* 51 (May 1992): 287–316.

Howe, Frederic C. *The City: The Hope of Democracy.* New York: Charles Scribner's Sons, 1912.

———. *The Confessions of a Reformer.* New York: Charles Scribner's Sons, 1925.

Ichikawa Fusae. *Ichikawa Fusae jiden* (The autobiography of Ichikawa Fusae). Shinjuku shobō, 1974.

Imai Seiichi. *Taishō demokurashii* (Taishō democracy). Chūō kōronsha, 1972.

————. "Kanshō to danatsu no naka de dai ikkai fusen" (Interference and oppression in the first universal suffrage election). In *Shōwa shunkan* (Shōwa images), edited by Asahi Janaru. Asahi shinbunsha, 1974.

Inoue Kiyoshi and Watanabe Tōru. *Kome sōdō no kenkyū* (Research on the rice riots). 5 vols. Yūhikaku, 1959–1962.

Iriye, Akira. "The Internationalization of History." *American Historical Review* 94 (February 1989): 1–10.

Irokawa Daikichi. *The Culture of the Meiji Period,* edited and translated by Marius B. Jansen. Princeton: Princeton University Press, 1985.

Ishida, Takeshi. *Japanese Political Culture: Change and Continuity.* New Brunswick: Transaction Books, 1983.

————. "Conflict and Its Accommodation: *Omote-Ura* and *Uchi-Soto* Relations." In *Conflict in Japan,* edited by Ellis S. Krauss et al. Honolulu: University of Hawaii Press, 1984.

Ishida, Takeshi, and Ellis S. Krauss, eds. *Democracy in Japan.* Pittsburgh: University of Pittsburgh Press, 1989.

Isomura Eiichi. *Ku no kenkyū* (Research on wards). Shisei jinsha, 1936.

Itō Takashi. "The Role of Right-Wing Organizations in Japan." In *Pearl Harbor as History: Japanese-American Relations, 1931–1941,* edited by Dorothy Borg and Shumpei Okamoto. New York: Columbia University Press, 1973.

Jansen, Marius B. *The Japanese and Sun Yat-sen.* Stanford: Stanford University Press, 1970.

Japan Biographical Encyclopedia and Who's Who. Tokyo: Rengo Press, 1958.

The Japan-Manchuria Year Book. 1934.

Japan Times. 1904, 1910–1913.

Japan Times and Mail (JT&M). 1920–1921, 1923–1924, 1928–1930, 1932–1934, 1936–1939.

Japan Year Book. 1908.

Johnson, Chalmers A. *MITI and the Japanese Miracle: The Growth of Industrial Policy, 1925–1975.* Stanford: Stanford University Press, 1982.

Joseishi kojiten (Small dictionary of women's history).

Kagawa Toyohiko zenshū kankōkai. *Kagawa Toyohiko zenshū* (The collected works of Kagawa Toyohiko). Kirisuto shinbunsha, 1962–1964.

Kang Toku-san. *Kantō daishinsai.* Chūō kōronsha, 1975.

Kanpō (Gazette).

Kasza, Gregory J. *The State and the Mass Media in Japan, 1918–1945.* Berkeley and Los Angeles: University of California Press, 1988.

Katayama Sen. *Jiden* (Autobiography). Hakubunkan, 1922.

Katō, Shuichi. "Taishō Democracy as the Pre-Stage for Japanese Militarism."
In *Japan in Crisis: Essays on Taishō Democracy*, edited by Bernard S.
Silberman and H. D. Harootunian. Princeton: Princeton University
Press, 1974.

Katsu Kokichi. *Musui's Story*, translated by Teruko Craig. Tucson: University
of Arizona Press, 1988.

Kawashima, Yasuhide. "America Through Foreign Eyes: Reactions of the
Delegates from Tokugawa, Japan, 1860." *Journal of Social History* 5
(1972): 491–511.

Kikuchi Hideo. *Edo Tōkyō chimei jiten* (Dictionary of place names in Edo and
Tokyo). Sekkasha, 1963.

Kimura Takeo. *Nihon kindai shakai jigyōshi* (History of social work in modern Japan). Kyoto: Minerva shobō, 1964.

Kinmonth, Earl H. "Fukuzawa Reconsidered: *Gakumon no susume* and Its
Audience." *Journal of Asian Studies* 37 (August 1978): 677–96.

Kinzley, W. Dean. "Japan's Discovery of Poverty: Changing Views of Poverty
and Social Welfare in the Nineteenth Century." *Journal of Asian History*
22.1 (1988): 1–24.

———. *Industrial Harmony in Modern Japan: The Invention of a Tradition*. London: Routledge, 1991.

Kitagawa, Joseph M. *Religion in Japanese History*. New York: Columbia University Press, 1966.

Kokkai shūgiin sangiin. *Gikai seido shichijūnenshi* (Seventy years of the Diet).
12 vols. Ōkurashō, 1960–1963.

Kōmei senkyo renmei. *Shūgiin giin senkyo no jisseki* (Results of elections for
the Lower House of the Diet). 1967.

Komori Ryūkichi. "Tōkyō ni okeru chōnaikai no hensen ni tsuite" (Changes
in neighborhood associations in Tokyo). *Nihon rekishi* 297 (February
1973): 81–96.

Kondo, Dorinne K. *Crafting Selves: Power, Gender, and Discourses of Identity
in a Japanese Workplace*. Chicago: University of Chicago Press, 1990.

Kōno Mitsu and Akamatsu Katsumaro. *Nihon musan seitōshi* (Japanese proletarian political parties). Hakuyosha, 1931.

Konsaisu jinmei jiten (Concise biographical dictionary). Tokyo: Sanseido,
1976.

Kublin, Hyman. *Asian Revolutionary: The Life of Sen Katayama*. Princeton:
Princeton University Press, 1964.

Kumagai, Tatsujirō. *The Japan Young Men's Associations*. Tokyo, Foreign
Affairs Association of Japan, 1938.

———. *Dai Nihon seinendan shi* (History of the young men's associations
of Japan). Nihon seinenkan, 1942.

Kusama, Yasoh. "Coping with Unemployment." *Contemporary Japan* 1
(1932): 294–96.

Kusama Yasō. "Dai Tōkyō no saimingai to seikatsu no taiyō" (An account of life in the slums of Tokyo). In *Nihon chiri taikei.* 17 vols. Kaizōsha, 1930.

Kyōchōkai. *Nihon shakai rōdō undō shiryō shū* (Collection of historical materials on the Japanese social labor movement). 118 reels. Yushodo, n.d.

Laker, Joseph Alphonse. "Entrepreneurship and the Development of the Japanese Beer Industry, 1872–1937." Ph.D. diss., Indiana University, 1975.

Large, Stephen S. *The Rise of Labor in Japan: The Yūaikai, 1912–19.* Tokyo: Sophia University, 1972.

————. *Organized Workers and Socialist Politics in Interwar Japan.* Cambridge: Cambridge University Press, 1981.

Lee, Changsoo, and George De Vos. *Koreans in Japan: Ethnic Conflict and Accommodation.* Berkeley and Los Angeles: University of California Press, 1981.

Lee, Kun Sam. *The Christian Confrontation with Shinto Nationalism.* Philadelphia: Presbyterian and Reformed Publishing, 1966.

Lewis, Michael. *Rioters and Citizens: Mass Protest in Imperial Japan.* Berkeley and Los Angeles: University of California Press, 1990.

Lippit, Noriko Mizuta, and Kyoko Iriye Selden, eds. and trans. *Stories by Contemporary Japanese Women Writers.* Armonk, N.Y.: M. E. Sharp, 1982.

Lu, David John. *Sources of Japanese History.* 2 vols. New York: McGraw-Hill, 1974.

Mann, Arthur. Introduction to *Plunkitt of Tammany Hall,* by William L. Riordan. New York: E. P. Dutton, 1963.

————. *La Guardia Comes to Power.* Philadelphia: J. B. Lippincott, 1933.

Marshall, Byron K. *Capitalism and Nationalism in Prewar Japan: The Ideology of the Business Elite, 1868–1941.* Stanford: Stanford University Press, 1967.

Masland, John W. "Neighborhood Associations in Japan." *Far Eastern Survey* 15 (1946): 355–58.

Mason, R. H. P. "The Debate on Poor Relief in the First Meiji Diet." *Journal of the Oriental Society of Australia* 3 (January 1965): 2–26.

————. *Japan's First General Election, 1890.* London: Cambridge University Press, 1969.

Matsubara, Iwagorō. *In Darkest Tokyo: Sketches of Humble Life in the Capital of Japan.* Yokohama, 1897.

Matsuo Takayoshi. *Taishō demokurashii no kenkyū.* Aoki shoten, 1966.

————. *Taishō demokurashii* (Taishō democracy). Iwanami shoten, 1974.

Matsuzawa Hiroaki. *Nihon shakaishugi no shisō.* Chikuma shobō, 1973.

McClain, James L. *Kanazawa: A Seventeenth-Century Japanese Castle Town.* New Haven: Yale University Press, 1982.

McKim, Bishop. "Our Evangelistic Work in the District of Tokyo." *The Spirit of Missions* 74 (1909): 779–81.

Meacham, Standish. *Toynbee Hall and Social Reform, 1880–1914: The Search for Community.* New Haven: Yale University Press, 1987.

Miki Tamio. "Shakai mondai no tōjō Nisshin-Nichiro sensō to haishō mondai." In vol. 2, *Kindai Nihon no tōgō to teikō,* edited by Yui Masaomi and Kano Masanao. Nihon hyōronsha, 1982.

Miller, Frank O. *Minobe Tatsukichi: Interpreter of Constitutionalism in Japan.* Berkeley and Los Angeles: University of California Press, 1965.

Minichiello, Sharon. *Retreat from Reform: Patterns of Political Behavior in Interwar Japan.* Honolulu: University of Hawaii Press, 1984.

Mitchell, Richard H. *The Korean Minority in Japan.* Berkeley and Los Angeles: University of California Press, 1967.

―――. *Thought Control in Prewar Japan.* Ithaca: Cornell University Press, 1976.

―――. *Censorship in Imperial Japan.* Princeton: Princeton University Press, 1983.

Mitsui Kunitarō. *Aikoku fujinkai tokuhon* (A reader on the Patriotic Women's Society). 1935.

Miyachi Masato. "Nichiro sengo no shakai to minshū" (Society and the masses after the Russo-Japanese War). In *Kōza Nihon shi,* edited by Rekishigaku kenkyūkai and Nihonshi kenkyūkai. 10 vols. Tōkyō daigaku shuppankai, 1970.

Miyamoto Yuriko. "The Family of Koiwai." In *Stories by Contemporary Japanese Women Writers,* edited by Noriko Mizuta Lippit and Kyoko Iriye Selden. Armonk, N.Y.: M. E. Sharp, 1982.

Miyazaki Ryūsuke. "Yanagihara Byakuren to no hanseki" (A half century with Yanagihara Byakuren). *Bungei shunjū* 45 (June 1967): 220–30.

Miyoshi Akira. "Yamamuro Gunpei to shakai jigyō" (Yamamuro Gunpei and social work). *Nihon rekishi* 254 (1969): 62–72.

―――. *Yamamuro Gunpei.* Yoshikawa kobunkan, 1971.

Miyoshi Toyotarō. "Tōkyō-shi no shakai gyōsei" (The social administration of Tokyo City). *Toshi mondai* 18.1 (January 1934): 71–76.

Moore, Barrington, Jr. "Japanese Peasant Protests and Revolts in Comparative Historical Perspective." *International Review of Social History* 33 (1988): 312–27.

Nagy, Margit. "Middle-Class Working Women During the Inter-War Years." In *Recreating Japanese Women, 1600–1945,* edited by Gail Lee Bernstein. Berkeley and Los Angeles: University of California Press, 1991.

Naimushō keihokyoku. *Shakai undō no jōkyō* (Condition of the social movement). 1927–1942.

Naimushō shakaikyoku. *Rōdō undō gaikyō* (An outline of the labor movement). 1922–1924.

————. *Taishō shinsai shi* (History of the Taishō earthquake). 3 vols. 1926.

Naimushō shakaikyoku shakaibu. *Hōmen iin seido gaiyō* (Outline of the district welfare committee system). 1933.

Najita, Tetsuo. *Hara Kei in the Politics of Compromise, 1905–1915.* Cambridge: Harvard University Press, 1967.

Nakagawa Gō. *Chōnaikai* (Neighborhood associations). Chūō kōronsha, 1980.

Nakamura Hachirō. *Town Organizations in Prewar Tokyo.* United Nations University, 1980.

Nara Tsunegorō. *Nihon YMCA shi* (History of the Japan YMCA). Nihon YMCA Dōmei, 1959.

Narita Ryūichi. "Taishō demokurashii ki no toshi jūmin undō: Tōkyō-shi ni okeru." *Chihō shi no kenkyū* 30.5 (October 1980): 33–42.

————. "Toshi minshū sōjō to minponshugi." In vol 3, *Kindai Nihon no tōgō to teikō,* edited by Yui Masaomi and Kano Masanao. Nihon hyōronsha, 1982.

Neary, Ian. *Political Protest and Social Control in Pre-War Japan: The Origins of Buraku Liberation.* Atlantic Highlands, N.J.: Humanities Press, 1989.

Nehru, Jawaharlal. *An Autobiography.* London: John Lane, 1936; Delhi: Oxford University Press, 1989.

Nelson, Joan M. "Political Participation." In *Understanding Political Development,* edited by Myron Weiner and Samuel P. Huntington. Boston: Little, Brown, 1987.

Nihon chiri fūzoku taikei. Edited by Nakama Teruhisa. 19 vols. Shinkōsha, 1931–1932.

Nihon fujin mondai shiryō shūsei (Collected documents on Japanese women's history). 10 vols. Domesu, 1980.

Nihon kokusei jiten (Japanese government dictionary). 10 vols. Nihon kokusei jiten kankōkai, 1953–1958.

Nihon rōdō nenkan (Japan labor yearbook). 1919, 1925, 1926, 1929, 1930.

Nihon shakai jigyō nenkan (NSJN) (Japan social work yearbook). 1920, 1922, 1925.

Nihon shinshiroku (NS). 1906, 1930, 1935.

Nishi, Toshio. *Unconditional Democracy: Education and Politics in Occupied Japan, 1945–1952.* Stanford: Hoover Institution Press, 1982.

Nishida Taketoshi. *Meiji-zenki no toshi kasō shakai* (Lower-class urban society in the early Meiji era). Vol. 2 of *Seikatsu koten sosho* (Series on daily life). Koseikan, 1970.

Nolte, Sharon H. *Liberalism in Modern Japan: Ishibashi Tanzan and His Teachers, 1905–1960.* Berkeley and Los Angeles: University of California Press, 1987.

Nolte, Sharon H., and Sally Ann Hastings. "The Meiji State's Policy Toward Women, 1890–1910." In *Recreating Japanese Women, 1600–1945,* edited by Gail Lee Bernstein. Berkeley and Los Angeles: University of California Press, 1991.

Noma, Seiji. *Noma of Japan: The Nine Magazines of Kodansha, Being the Autobiography of a Japanese Publisher.* New York: The Vanguard Press, 1934.

Nōshōmushō. *Kōjō tsūran* (Survey of Japanese factories). 1921.

Notehelfer, F. G. *Kōtoku Shūsui: Portrait of a Japanese Radical.* Cambridge: Cambridge University Press, 1971.

Obata, Kyugoro. *An Interpretation of the Life of Viscount Shibusawa.* Tokyo insatsu kabushikigaisha, 1937.

Ogata Sadako. "The Role of Liberal Nongovernmental Organizations in Japan." In *Pearl Harbor as History: Japanese-American Relations, 1931–1941,* edited by Dorothy Borg and Shumpei Okamoto. New York: Columbia University Press, 1973.

Ogawa Seiryō. "Sangyō shihon kakuritsu ki no kyūhin taisei" (Poverty relief in the era of the establishment of industrial capitalism). In *Nihon no kyūhin seido* (The Japanese system of poor relief), edited by Nihon shakai jigyō daigaku kyūhin seido kenkyūkai. Keisō shobō, 1960.

————. "Taishō demokurashii ki no kyūhin taisei" (The system of poor relief in the era of Taishō democracy). In *Nihon no kyūhin seido* (The Japanese system of poor relief), edited by Nihon shakai jigyō daigaku kyūhin seido kenkyūkai. Keisō shobō, 1960.

Ogawa Shigejirō. "Shakai jigyō no kisoteki shisetsu to shite no hōmen iin seido" (The district welfare committees as basic instruments of social work). *Kyūsai kenkyū* 9 (August and September 1921): 589–601, 669–91.

Okamoto, Shumpei. "The Emperor and the Crowd: The Historical Significance of the Hibiya Riot." In *Conflict in Modern Japanese History: The Neglected Tradition,* edited by Tetsuo Najita and J. Victor Koschmann. Princeton: Princeton University Press, 1982.

Oka Toshirō. "Kindai Nihon ni okeru shakai seisaku shisō no keisei to tenkai" (The origins and changes of social policy thought in modern Japan). *Shisō* 558 (1970): 69–88.

Ōkōchi Kazuo and Matsuo Hiroshi. *Nihon rōdō kumiai monogatari* (Story of Japanese labor unions). 5 vols. Chikuma shobō, 1965.

Ōkōchi Kazuo and Watanabe Tōru. *Sōdōmei gojūnenshi* (Fifty years of the Sōdōmei). 3 vols. Sōdōmei gojūnenshi iinkai, 1964.

Ono, Sokyo. *Shinto: The Kami Way.* Tokyo: Bridgeway Press, 1962.

Ōya Soichi. "Tōkyō-shi seinendan no kaibō" (Analysis of the Tokyo young men's associations). *Chūō kōron* (June 1930), pp. 128–33.

Ozawa, Martha N. "Child Welfare Programs in Japan." *Social Service Review* 65.1 (March 1991): 1–21.

Pak Kyong-sik. *Chōsenjin kyosei renko no kiroku.* Miraisho, 1965.

Patrick, Hugh T. "The Economic Muddle of the 1920's." In *Dilemmas of Growth in Prewar Japan,* edited by James W. Morley. Princeton: Princeton University Press, 1971.

Pearson, Alice Lewis. "Women's Christian Temperance Union." *Christian Movement in Japan, Korea, and Formosa* (1924), pp. 311–14.

Pempel, T. J. "Prerequisites for Democracy: Political and Social Institutions." In *Democracy in Japan,* edited by Takeshi Ishida and Ellis S. Krauss. Pittsburgh: University of Pittsburgh Press, 1989.

Pettee, J. H. "Social Work: Eleemosynary Enterprises." *The Christian Movement in Japan* 4 (1906).

Pyle, Kenneth B. "The Technology of Japanese Nationalism: The Local Improvement Movement, 1900–1918." *Journal of Asian Studies* 33.1 (November 1973): 51–65.

————. "Advantages of Followership: German Economics and Japanese Bureaucrats, 1890–1925." *Journal of Japanese Studies* 1 (1974): 127–64.

————. *The Making of Modern Japan.* Lexington, Mass.: D. C. Heath, 1978.

Quigley, Harold S. *Japanese Government and Politics: An Introductory Study.* New York: Century, 1932.

Reischauer, Edwin O. "What Went Wrong?" In *Dilemmas of Growth in Prewar Japan,* edited by James W. Morley. Princeton: Princeton University Press, 1971.

Richardson, Bradley M. *The Political Culture of Japan.* Berkeley and Los Angeles: University of California Press, 1974.

Rōdō (Labor). 1918–1921.

Rōdō oyobi sangyō (Labor and industry). 1916–1919.

Sakauye, K. O. "Social Movements in Tokyo." *Japan Magazine* 12 (1922): 111–14.

Sawada Ken and Ogimoto Seizo. *Fuji bōseki kabushiki kaisha gojūnenshi* (Fifty years of the Fuji Spinning Company). Fuji bōseki kabushiki gaisha, 1947.

Scalapino, Robert A. *Democracy and the Party Movement in Prewar Japan: The Failure of the First Attempt.* Berkeley and Los Angeles: University of California Press, 1953.

————. "Elections and Political Modernization in Prewar Japan." In *Political Development in Modern Japan,* edited by Robert E. Ward. Princeton: Princeton University Press, 1968.

————. *The Early Japanese Labor Movement: Labor and Politics in a Developing Society.* Berkeley: Institute of East Asian Studies, 1983.

Schmitter, Philippe C. "Still the Century of Corporatism?" In *The New Corporatism: Social Political Structuers in the Iberian World,* edited by Frederick B. Pike and Thomas Stritch. Notre Dame: University of Notre Dame Press, 1970.

Seidensticker, Edward. *Kafū the Scribbler: The Life and Writings of Nagai Kafū, 1879–1959.* Stanford: Stanford University Press, 1965.
———. *Low City, High City: Tokyo from Edo to the Earthquake.* New York: Alfred A. Knopf, 1983.
———. *Tokyo Rising: The City Since the Great Earthquake.* New York: Alfred A. Knopf, 1990.
Shakai rōdō kyōkai. *Rōdō jinji meikan* (Labor directory), 1960.
Shakai seisaku jihō (SSJ) (Journal of social policy). 1921–1924.
Shakaikyoku rōdōbu. *Rōdō undō nenpō* (annual report on the labor movement). 1926, 1928.
Shigetō Sunao. *Tōkyō chōmei enkaku shi.* Yoshikawa kōbunkan, 1967.
Shillony, Ben-ami. *Revolt in Japan: The Young Officers and the February 26, 1936, Incident.* Princeton: Princeton University Press, 1973.
Shiota Shōbei. *Nihon rōdō undō no rekishi* (History of the Japanese labor movement). Rōdō junpōsha, 1964.
Silberman, Bernard S. "The Bureaucratic State in Japan: The Problem of Authority and Legitimacy." In *Conflict in Modern Japanese History: The Neglected Tradition,* edited by Tetsuo Najita and J. Victor Koschmann. Princeton: Princeton University Press, 1982.
Sims, R. L. "National Elections and Electioneering in Akita Ken, 1930–1942." In *Modern Japan: Aspects of History, Literature, and Society,* edited by W. G. Beasley. Berkeley and Los Angeles: University of California Press, 1977.
Skocpol, Theda. "Bringing the State Back In: Strategies of Analysis in Current Research." In *Bringing the State Back In,* edited by Peter B. Evans, Dietrich Rueschemeyer, and Theda Skocpol. Cambridge: Cambridge University Press, 1985.
Smethurst, Richard J. "The Military Reserve Association and the Minobe Crisis of 1935." In *Crisis Politics in Prewar Japan: Institutional and Ideological Problems of the 1930s,* edited by George M. Wilson. Tokyo: Sophia University, 1970.
———. "The Creation of the Imperial Military Reserve Association in Japan." *Journal of Asian Studies* 30 (1971): 45–78.
———. *A Social Basis for Prewar Japanese Militarism: The Army and the Rural Community.* Berkeley and Los Angeles: University of California Press, 1974.
———. *Agricultural Development and Tenancy Disputes in Japan, 1870–1940.* Princeton: Princeton University Press, 1986.
Smith, Henry DeWitt, II. *Japan's First Student Radicals.* Cambridge: Harvard University Press, 1972.
———. "Tokyo as an Idea: An Exploration of Japanese Urban Thought Until 1945." *Journal of Japanese Studies* 4 (Winter 1978): 45–78.
———. "Tokyo and London: Comparative Conceptions of the City." In *Japan: A Comparative View,* edited by Albert M. Craig. Princeton: Princeton University Press, 1979.

Smith, P. A. " 'The Island' and Its Prophet." *The Spirit of Missions* 88 (1923): 611–16.

Soma Masao. "Senkyo shukusei undō no shisō to yakuwari." *Toshi mondai* 50.8 (August 1959): 59–69.

Spaulding, Robert M., Jr. "The Bureaucracy as a Political Force, 1920–45." In *Dilemmas of Growth in Prewar Japan,* edited by James W. Morley. Princeton: Princeton University Press, 1971.

Steffens, Lincoln. *The Shame of the Cities.* New York: McClure, Phillips, 1904; Hill and Wang, 1957.

Stepan, Alfred. *The State and Society: Peru in Comparative Perspective.* Princeton: Princeton University Press, 1978.

Sugihara Kaoru and Tamai Kingo. *Taishō Osaka suramu: Mō hitotsu no Nihon kindaishi.* Shin hyōron, 1986.

Sugiura, Yoshimichi. "A Japanese Pastor's Plea for His People." *The Spirit of Missions* 73 (1908): 521–25.

————. "The Submerged Tenth in Japan." *The Spirit of Missions* 73 (1908): 105–8.

————. "The Beginnings of St. Paul's School." *The Spirit of Missions* 74 (1909): 770–72.

————. "A Tokyo Rescue Mission." *The Spirit of Missions* 76 (1911): 663–67.

————. "Relief Work for Tokyo's Unfortunates." *The Spirit of Missions* 88 (1923): 322–25.

————. "Sending Him Off to Heaven." *The Spirit of Missions* 91 (1926): 751–52.

Suzaki Shin'ichi, "Senkyo shukusei undō no tenkai to sono yakuwari," *Rekishi hyōron* 310.2 (February 1976): 43–56.

Suzuki Norihisa, "Christianity." In *Japanese Religion,* edited by Agency for Cultural Affairs. Tokyo: Kodansha, 1972.

Tai, Masakazu. "Thirty Years in the Sei Ko Kwai." *The Spirit of Missions* 74 (1909): 772–73.

Taikakai. *Naimushō shi* (History of the Home Ministry). 4 vols. Chihō zaimu kyōkai, 1971.

Taira, Koji. "Public Assistance in Japan: Development and Trends." *Journal of Asian Studies* 27 (November 1967): 95–109.

Taishō jinmei jiten (Taishō biographical dictionary). Tōyō shinpōsha, 1918.

Taishū jinji roku. Teikoku himitsu tanteisha, 1934.

Takeda Kiyoko. *Tennōsei shisō to kyōiku* (Education and imperial ideology). Meiji toshō shuppan, 1964.

Takenaka, Masao. "Relation of Protestantism to Social Problems in Japan, 1900–1941." Ph.D. diss., Yale University, 1954.

————. *Reconciliation and Renewal in Japan.* New York: Student Volunteer Movement for Christian Missions and Friendship Press, 1957.

Tanizaki, Junichirō. *Childhood Years: A Memoir,* translated by Paul McCarthy. Tokyo: Kodansha, 1988.

Tashiro Fujio, Editor. *Shakai fukushi to shakai hendō* (Social welfare and social change). Seishin shobō, 1971.

Tashiro Kunijirō. "Nihon shakai jigyō no tokushitsu" (The special characteristics of Japanese social work). In *Shakai fukushi to shakai hendō* (Social welfare and social change), edited by Tashiro Fujio. Seishin shobō, 1971.

Tazawa Yoshiharu. *Sōhen.* Tazawa Yoshiharu kinenkai, 1954.

Tazawa Yoshiharu kinenkai. *Tazawa Yoshiharu.* 1954.

Teaford, Jon C. *The Twentieth-Century American City: Problem, Promise, and Reality.* Baltimore: Johns Hopkins University Press, 1986.

Tiedemann, Arthur E. "The Hamaguchi Cabinet: First Phase July 1929–February 1930: A Study in Japanese Parliamentary Government." Ph.D. diss., Columbia University, 1959.

Tipton, Elise K. *The Japanese Police State: The Tokkō in Interwar Japan.* Honolulu: University of Hawaii Press, 1990.

Tocqueville, Alexis de. *Democracy in America.* 2 vols. New York: Vintage Books, 1945.

Tokkō geppō (Monthly report of the higher police).

Tōkyō asahi shinbun (TAS). 1901, 1909, 1915, 1917, 1920, 1922, 1923, 1925, 1930, 1933, 1934, 1936.

Tōkyō-fu. *Tōkyō-fu tōkei sho.* 1919, 1931, 1936.

———. *Tōkyō-fu shi: Gyōsei hen* (History of Tokyo prefecture: Administration). 6 vols. 1935–1936.

Tōkyō-fu senkyo shukusei jikkō bu. *Shūgiin giin sōsenkyo ni kansuru shirabe (SGSS)* (Investigation of the Diet elections). 1936.

Tōkyō hyakunen shi henshū iinkai. *Tōkyō hyakunen shi (THS)* (Hundred-year history of Tokyo). 6 vols. Tōkyō-to, 1972–1973.

Tokyo Municipal Office. *Annual Statistics of the City of Tokyo.* 1920.

———. *The City of Tokyo: Municipal Administration and Government.* 1931.

———. *Tokyo.* 1937.

Tōkyō-shi. *Tōkyō shi tōkei nenpyō* (Tokyo statistical yearbook). 1916–1936.

———. *Tōkyō shinsai roku* (A record of Tokyo in the great earthquake). 5 vols. 1927.

Tōkyō-shi Akasaka kuyakusho. *Akasaka-ku shi* (Akasaka Ward history).

Tōkyō-shi Asakusa kuyakusho. *Asakusa-ku shi* (A record of Asakusa Ward). 1914; reprinted 1967.

Tōkyō-shi Azabu kuyakusho. *Azabu-ku shi* (Azabu Ward history). 1941.

Tōkyō-shi Hongō kuyakusho. *Hongō-ku shi* (Hongō Ward history). 1937.

Tōkyō-shi Honjo kuyakusho. *Honjo kusei yōran* (Outline of Honjo Ward government). 1926, 1931.

———. *Honjo-ku shi* (Honjo Ward history). 1931.

Tōkyō shikai jimukyoku. *Tōkyō shikai shi* (History of the Tokyo City Assembly). 7 vols. 1932–1938.

Tōkyō-shi kikakukyoku. *Tōkyō-shi chōmei enkaku shi* (History of the development of *chō* names in Tokyo city). 1938; reprinted Meiji bunken, 1974.

Tōkyō-shi Kōjimachi kuyakusho. *Kōjimachi-ku shi* (Kōjimachi Ward history). 1938.

Tōkyō-shi Kyōbashi kuyakusho. *Kyōbashi-ku shi* (Kyōbashi Ward history). 2 vols. 1937–1942.

Tōkyō-shi Nihonbashi kuyakusho. *Nihonbashi-ku shi* (Nihonbashi Ward history). 2 vols. 1937.

Tōkyō shisei chōsakai. *Tōkyō-shi chōnaikai ni kansuru chōsa* (An investigation of the neighborhood associations of Tokyo city). 1927.

Tōkyō-shi Shiba kuyakusho. *Shiba-ku shi* (Shiba Ward history). 1938.

Tōkyō-shi Shitaya kuyakusho. *Shitaya-ku shi* (Shitaya Ward history). 1935.

Tōkyō-shi tōkeika. *Dai ikkai rōdō tōkei jitchi chōsa* (First investigation of labor statistics). 1926.

―――. *Tōkyō-shi no jōkyō: Shikai giin senkyo gaikyō* (Tokyo report: An outline of the election of representatives to the city assembly). 1933.

―――. *Dai yonkai Tōkyō-shi rōdō tōkei jitchi chōsa* (Fourth investigation of labor statistics in Tokyo). 1935.

Tōkyō-shi Ushigome kuyakusho. *Ushigome-ku shi* (Ushigome Ward history). 1930.

Tōkyō shiyakusho. *Tōkyō shisei gaiyō* (An outline of Tokyo city administration). 1925, 1929.

―――. *Tōkyō-shi kōjō yōran* (Outline of Tokyo city factories). 1926, 1929.

―――. *Toshi gyōsei soshiki* (Organization of urban administration). Daitoshi gyōsei hikaku chōsa hōkoku, no. 1. 1927.

―――. *Toshi shakai gyōsei* (Urban social administration). Daitoshi gyōsei hikaku chōsa hōkoku, no. 5. 1927.

―――. *Tōkyō-shi chōkai jigyō gaiyō* (Outline of the work of the Tokyo city neighborhood associations). 1928.

―――. *Shōwa gotairei hōshuku shi* (A history of the celebration of the enthronement of the Shōwa Emperor). 1930.

―――. *Tōkyō-shi chōnaikai no chōsa* (An investigation of the neighborhood associations of Tokyo city). 1934.

―――. *Tōkyō-shi chōkai yōran* (Survey of Tokyo city neighborhood associations). 1935.

―――. *Fukai giin sōsenkyo ni kansuru chōsa* (Investigation of the elections for the prefectural assembly). 1936.

Tōkyō-to Kōtō kuyakusho. *Kōtō-ku shi* (Kōtō Ward history). 1957.

Tōkyō-to Sumida-ku. *Sumida-ku shi* (Sumida Ward history). 1959.

Tomeoka Kōsuke. "Saikin jizen jigyō no shinpō." In *Tomeoka Kōsuke chosaku shū*, edited by Dōshisha daigaku jinbun kagaku Kenkyūjo. Dōmeisha: 1978–1980.

Totten, George Oakley, III. *The Social Democratic Movement in Prewar Japan*. New Haven: Yale University Press, 1966.

————. "Collective Bargaining and Works Councils as Innovations in Industrial Relations in Japan During the 1920s." In *Aspects of Social Change in Modern Japan*, edited by R. P. Dore. Princeton: Princeton University Press, 1967.

Toyama Shigeki and Adachi Yoshiko. *Kindai Nihon seijishi hikkei* (Political statistics of modern Japan). Iwanami, 1961.

Trimberger, Ellen Kay. *Revolution from Above: Military Bureaucrats and Development in Japan, Turkey, Egypt, and Peru*. New Brunswick, N.J.: Transaction Books, 1978.

Tsuboe Senji. *Chōsenjin minzoku dokuritsu undō hishi* (An unofficial history of the Korean independence movement). Gannando, 1961.

Tsuji, Zennosuke. *Social Welfare Work by the Imperial Household of Japan*. Tokyo: Japan Red Cross Society, 1934.

Tsukamoto Shiuko. "Yoshimi Shizue." In *Shakai jigyō ni ikita joseitachi: Sono shōgai to shigoto* (Women in social work: Their lives and work), edited by Gomi Yuriko. Domesu, 1973.

Tsunoda, Ryusaku, Wm. Theodore de Bary, and Donald Keene. *Sources of Japanese Tradition*. 2 vols. New York: Columbia University Press, 1964.

Tyrrell, Ian. "American Exceptionalism in an Age of International History." *American Historical Review* 96 (1991): 1031–55.

Varner, Richard E. "The Organized Peasant: The *Wakamonogumi* in the Edo Period." *Monumenta Nipponica* 32 (1977): 459–83.

Vogel, Ezra F. "Kinship Structure, Migration to the City, and Modernization." In *Aspects of Social Change in Modern Japan*, edited by R. P. Dore. Princeton: Princeton University Press, 1967.

Wada, S. K. *Japan's Industries and Who's Who*. Osaka: Industrial Japan, 1910.

Wagner, Edward W. *The Korean Minority in Japan, 1904–1950*. New York: Institute of Pacific Affairs, 1951.

Wakabayashi, Bob Tadashi. "Aizawa Seishisai's *Shinron* and Western Learning, 1782–1825." Ph.D. diss., Princeton University, 1982.

Walser, Gladys D. "The Door of Hope." *Japan Evangelist* 30 (March 1923): 92–93.

Waswo, Ann. "In Search of Equity: Japanese Tenant Unions in the 1920s." In *Conflict in Modern Japanese History: The Neglected Tradition*, edited by Tetsuo Najita and J. Victor Koschmann. Princeton: Princeton University Press, 1982.

Waters, Neil L. "The Second Transition: Early to Mid-Meiji in Kanagawa Prefecture." *Journal of Asian Studies* 49 (1990): 305–22.

Weber, Max. *The City*. Translated and edited by Don Martindale and Gertrud Neuwirth. New York: Free Press, 1958.

Weiner, Michael. *The Origins of the Korean Community in Japan, 1910–1923*. Atlantic Highlands, N.J.: Humanities Press International, 1989.

Weiner, Susan Beth. "Bureaucracy and Politics in the 1930's: The Career of Gotō Fumio." Ph.D. diss., Harvard University, 1984.

Westney, D. Eleanor. "The Emulation of Western Organizations in Meiji Japan: The Case of the Paris Prefecture of Police and the Keishi-cho." *Journal of Japanese Studies* 8 (1982): 307–41.

White, James W. "Internal Migration in Prewar Japan." *Journal of Japanese Studies* 4.1 (1978): 81–123.

Who's Who in Japan. Keiseisha. 1938.

Yamamuro, Colonel. "Tokyo Paupers." *Japan Magazine* 5.5 (1914): 287.

Yamamuro Buhei. *Jindō no senshi Yamamuro Gunpei* (Yamamuro Gunpei, a fighter for humanity). Tamagawa daigaku shuppanbu, 1965.

Yasui Seiichirō-shi kinenzo kensetsu. *Yasui Seiichirō den* (Biography of Yasui Seiichirō). Nihon jihōsha, 1967.

Yazaki, Takeo. *Social Change and the City in Japan from Earliest Times Through the Industrial Revolution*. Translated by David L. Swain. Tokyo: Japan Publications, 1968.

Yokoyama Gennosuke. *Nihon no kasō shakai* (The lower classes of Japan). 1899. Reprinted Iwanami shoten, 1949.

Yokoyama Haruichi. *Kagawa Toyohiko den* (Biography of Kagawa Toyohiko). Kirisuto shinbunsha, 1952.

Yoshida Kyūichi. *Nihon kindai bukkyō shakai shi kenkyū* (Research on the social history of modern Buddhism). Yoshikawa kobunkan, 1960.

————. *Nihon shakai jigyō no rekishi* (History of social work in Japan). Keiso shobō, 1960.

————. *Shōwa shakai jigyōshi* (History of social work in the Shōwa era). Kyoto: Minerva shobō, 1971.

————. *Shakai jigyō riron no rekishi* (History of the theory of social work). Hitotsubusha, 1974.

Yoshida Kyūichi and Ichibangase Yasuko, editors. *Shōwa shakai jigyōshi e no shōgen* (Eyewitness accounts of the history of Shōwa social work). Domesu, 1982.

Yoshida Kyūichi et al. *Jinbutsu de tsuzuru kindai shakai jigyō no ayumi* (Modern Japanese social workers). Zenkoku shakai fukushi kyōgikai, 1971.

Index

Pitt Series in
POLICY AND INSTITUTIONAL STUDIES

Bert A. Rockman, Editor

Pesticides and Politics: The Life Cycle of a Public Issue
Christopher J. Bosso

Policy Analysis by Design
Davis B. Bobrow and John S. Dryzek

The Political Failure of Employment Policy, 1945–1982
Gary Mucciaroni

Political Leadership: A Source Book
Barbara Kellerman, Editor

Political Leadership in an Age of Constraint: The Australian Experience
Colin Campbell, S.J., and John Halligan

The Political Psychology of the Gulf War: Leaders, Publics, and the Process of Conflict
Stanely A. Renshon, Editor

The Politics of Expert Advice: Creating, Using, and Manipulating Scientific Knowledge for Public Policy
Anthony Barker and B. Guy Peters, Editors

The Politics of the U.S. Cabinet: Representation in the Executive Branch, 1789–1984
Jeffrey E. Cohen

Politics Within the State: Elite Bureaucrats and Industrial Policy in Authoritarian Brazil
Ben Ross Schneider

Post-Passage Politics: Bicameral Resolution in Congress
Stephen D. Van Beek

The Presidency and Public Policy Making
George C. Edwards III, Steven A. Shull, and Norman C. Thomas, Editors

Pressure, Power, and Policy: Policy Networks and State Autonomy in Britain and the United States
Martin J. Smith

Private Markets and Public Intervention: A Primer for Policy Designers
Harvey Averch

The Promise and Paradox of Civil Service Reform
Patricia W. Ingraham and David H. Rosenbloom, Editors

Public Policy in Latin America: A Comparative Survey
John W. Sloan

Regulation in the Reagan-Bush Era: The Eruption of Presidential Influence
Barry D. Friedman

Reluctant Partners: Implementing Federal Policy
Robert P. Stoker

Researching the Presidency: Vital Questions, New Approaches
George C. Edwards III, John H. Kessel, and Bert A. Rockman, Editors

Roads to Reason: Transportation, Administration, and Rationality in Colombia
Richard E. Hartwig

Scrambling for Protection: The New Media and the First Amendment
Patrick Garry

The SEC and Capital Market Regulation: The Politics of Expertise
Ann M. Khademian

Site Unseen: The Politics of Siting a Nuclear Waste Repository
Gerald Jacob

The Social Democratic State: Bureaucracy and Social Reforms in Swedish Labor Market and School Policy
Bo Rothstein

The Speaker and the Budget: Leadership in the Post-Reform House of Representatives
Daniel J. Palazzolo

The State Roots of National Politics: Congress and the Tax Agenda, 1978–1986
Michael B. Berkman

The Struggle for Social Security, 1900–1935
Roy Lubove

Tage Erlander: Serving the Welfare State, 1946–1969
Olof Ruin

Thatcher, Reagan, Mulroney: In Search of a New Bureaucracy
Donald Savoie

Traffic Safety Reform in the United States and Great Britain
Jerome S. Legge, Jr.

Urban Alternatives: Public and Private Markets in the Provision of Local Services
Robert M. Stein

The U.S. Experiment in Social Medicine: The Community Health
Center Program, 1965–1986
Alice Sardell